With best wishes,

Diana May

MISCELLENNIUM

A commonplace book
for the Millennium

DIANA MAY

WILTON 65

Published 1998

by

WILTON 65
Flat Top House, Bishop Wilton, York. YO42 1RY
England

Copyright © Diana May

ISBN 0 947828 59 1

All rights reserved. No part of this publication may be reproduced, stored in a retrieval system, or transmitted, in any form or by any means, electronic, mechanical, photocopying, recording or otherwise, without the prior permission in writing of the Copyright owner.

Typeset by the Author
Printed in England

CHAPTER HEADINGS

Pages

1. The Double Chiliad — 1 - 19

2. People Will Be Talking Of Nothing Else — 20 - 54

3. The Phoenix Also Rises — 55 - 72

4. New Millennium's Eve — 73 - 95

5. Time and Nature — 96 - 117

6. Whose Birthday? A Spiritual Perspective — 118 - 140

7. How Green is My Planet? — 141 - 163

8. Millennium Commission — 164 - 180

9. Millennium Projects — 181 - 195

10. Greenwich and London — 196 - 215

11. Other Countries' Celebrations — 216 - 236

12. The Future: Utopia or Dystopia? — 237 - 267

THE PHOENIX & THE SUNFLOWER

From Arabia came that fabled bird,
Whose fire precautions clearly were absurd;
The Phoenix, bird of circumstance unique,
Was in Nature something of a freak.
Though its fame has always been perennial,
Her actual life is only half-millennial.
After years five hundred, followed immolation;
Sad, but not a cause for total desolation
As out its ashes rose a phoenix new
And took its place, with never fuss undue.
This bird of hope and infinite renewal
In Time's crown certainly's the jewel.
Amazing bird; a cause for celebration
Whence we learn about regeneration.
Out of the ashes of the old we see
A new phoenix that is yet to be -
A fresh phase starts, the situation we review.
Observe our bird; sign of a century new
And millennium third; our hopes arouse
That we will have good reason to carouse.
The 1890's flower of its times
With our *fin-de-siècle feeling chimes.*
And thus we have two symbols of the age,
The bird, the sunflower, united on this page.

CHAPTER 1 : THE DOUBLE CHILIAD

Once in a hundred lifetimes ..... well, certainly not in the lifetime of anyone living in the last forty generations, has anything as exciting happened to the calendar as when the great triple zero comes! There will be a tide in the affairs of man, firstly lapping gently at our consciousness, then overwhelming us all recklessly in a tide of millennial fever. In a sense it is an artificial achievement, because a date is an abstract that you cannot see or feel; but of course it is universally recognised throughout the world, and not merely in the countries (accounting for about two billion of the world's six billion people) which are part of the Western Judaeo-Christian tradition. For once, it is an unequivocally joyous event which can bring the world together: it is not politics, it is not war or conquest, it is not even a sugared drink. It celebrates the birth of a baby, an event that delights and unites everyone. It is both a pinnacle of human progress, and a time for reflection as to where we as a species are heading. It is a new benchmark against which to compare things to take the place of *the greatest (something) since the War*. It is a chance for the whole world to turn over a new leaf; 'Newsweek' called it *the hoopla of all hooplas*. Like the double-headed Roman Janus, who gave his name to the month of January with his ability to look both back over the past and forward in to the future, it is a time both of reflection and anticipation. It cannot nor should not be ignored; the whole millennium has rightly been described as *everybody's birthday*, and to some extent it will thrill us all.

Here is a commonplace book for the Millennium. It is a collection of offerings to mark the 'Big M', which has been five years in the making in one sense, and two thousand in another. It encompasses facts about the occasion, interleaved with poetic expression and photographs and drawings, most topical and relevant, but some chosen just because of their intrinsic interest. Of course the book can only be up-to-date at the time of writing, and things are changing so fast that one or two things might have been nudged on by events.

The commonplace book originally gained its name as a translation of the Latin 'locus communis' or the Greek 'koinos topos', general place, that is, an everyday saying but still one that is worth recording, a notable passage; but sadly 'commonplace' is one of those words that has come down in the world, a word that is a bit frayed round the edges, and now has come to mean simply something you take for granted, and therefore *un*worthy of attention. (Similarly, the millennium will seem strange to us before becoming familiar and comfortable; but let's hope it does not lose all its magic.) The Anglo-Irish satirist Dean Swift wrote in 1704 in' The Tale of the Tub' in the chapter 'A Digression on Digressions':

What though his head be empty, if his commonplace book be full?
The commonplace book is a worthy successor to the 'pillow books' of medieval Japan; or of journals, which are diaries free of the printed format that only allows a few inches a day, and so allows the writer to ramble along curious paths, and to include other people's *aperçus*. Notable producers of journals were such fascinating writers as Samuel Pepys, John Evelyn, Fanny Burney, Francis Kilvert, William Cobbett, George Eliot, Gilbert White, Virginia Woolf, Katherine Mansfield, and Chips Channon. All start better than my aunt, Hettie Sophia Annie, whose journal in the 1920's misguidedly stated on January 1st that 'Today I have resolved to keep a dairy'. Too many published diaries or journals today are nothing but politicians trying retrospectively to justify their actions; but it is fun to read the fictionalised diaries of Adrian Mole or Helen Jones, or to read the whole genre (especially the eighteenth century variety) satirised by Peter Simple. We are lucky too to have had published in 1981 the Notebooks of Geoffrey Madan; and the yearly 'Christmas Crackers' or commonplace books of John Julius Norwich, with once-a-decade collections (he has promised us *I certainly hope to publish another in 2000.*)

The contemporaries of the French writer George Sand wrote the following description of her, which I would like to think could also function as a description of this book itself :

She has a brilliant well-stocked mind and a warm heart; she has courage, energy, vitality, generosity, responsibility, good humour, and charm; she has aristocratic distinction combined

> *with bohemian informality; she is wise, passionate, a down-to-earth human being, and disappointingly sane.*

A commonplace book is a resting place for old favourites and nostalgia; and from the familiar we can move on to the challenge of the new. This essentially is the journey we are all about to make from the previous millennium to a fresh one.

People may mark the advent of the Millennium in their own way, privately with partners, families and friends, or spiritually in the quiet of their own souls; but no one will be able to ignore the countrywide, indeed world-wide, upsurge of *joie de vivre* as new projects emerge, buildings, bridges and exhibitions are assembled, and some very special events take place. Many a town will be saddled with a 'Millennium Restaurant' (often mis-spelt with one 'n') or 'Year 2000 Café', which will all too soon begin to show its age. Some worthy projects, begun with all hopes and a fistful of Lottery cash, will never see completion because the search for matching funding was in vain. The newspapers will be so full of it, that it will be like election coverage for a whole year ..... but no one will be so blasé, no one so jaded, that it will not raise at least a flicker of interest, even if vituperative. As a later chapter says, people will be talking of nothing else.

Purists will want us to wait until December 31st, 2000, when they say the previous millennium - like the figure ten which finishes off a decade - properly ends. But emotionally the last day of 1999 will feel like the turning point, as at midnight we roll in to January 1st, 2000 ('the round thousand'), and officially most celebrations will start then. This also has the wonderful effect of allowing us to go on making whoopee all that year and having a second bonanza New Year's Eve on December 31st 2000, when the purists can join in, too. Though, as Russell Forgham said, *I reckon most of us will be too tired to do it all over again!* So, what are we going to call the years after the big shot? Collectively as 'The Noughties', maybe; and 'two thousand and ..... ', or 'zero, zero .....' or 'twenty-oh-oh', 'twenty-oh-one', etc. Common practice will emerge, and in no time at all we will wonder why we ever thought it strange.

The word *millennium* literally means, of course, a period of a thousand years, but it also has enormous religious significance; in addition, as the dictionary notes, it figuratively expresses a period of good government, great prosperity and happiness. (A double millennium could be called a bimillennium.) The equivalent Greek word was chiliad, with a hard 'c' like 'chorus', hence the title of this chapter; a chiliast is therefore someone who believes in millennial doctrine. Other peoples do not count by our system: the Egyptians had a calendar five millennia before Christ, the Chinese about three; the Jewish people are now in their year 5760; the Buddhists mark dates as from the death of Buddha 2543 years ago; but Muslims are only in the Annus Hegirae 1420. They will be unable to join us in celebrating at the end of 1999, as it will be the middle of Ramadan, but can do so at the end of the year 2000.The Julian calendar refined earlier Roman calendars by introducing leap years, in 46 B.C (this in its turn was superseded by the Gregorian one dating back to 1582, though England took nearly two centuries to get around to it.) Centuries are leap years if the century is divisible by 4, so 2000 is also a special leap year!

The significance of the double millennia we are celebrating being dated from the birth of Jesus Christ will be debated in a later chapter, and another chapter will discuss the whole notion of time as an abstract concept. What may be interesting now is to look at what happened in the millennia stretching back before the first year Anno Domini (Year of our Lord, or as politically correct language would have it, *Common Era.*) When did our species emerge from the sea, the jungle or the plains? When did recorded history begin? Has mankind always had the atavistic longing to return to some pre-lapsarian paradise without sin? The Mikado of Japan, according to W.S. Gilbert, was born sneering, because

I can trace my ancestry back to a protoplasmal atomic globule.
Consequently, my family pride is something in-conceivable.

But of course we can all pride ourselves that we go back to the same ancestors. Who might they have been, and where did they come from?

It is generally agreed that our universe came in to being - maybe from raw material no bigger than a mustard seed - in what is known as the Big Bang 15 billion years ago, which suffused all space with neutrinos and electrons. About ten billion years ago, the galaxies and the Milky Way formed, and five billion years later the sun and its planets (including Earth) were formed. As time passed, something happened, of which the story of Creation in Genesis is an eleogical myth, which meant that about four billion years ago there was the right combination of water, gases and organic material (and who knows what divine spark?) to encourage microbes and primitive invertebrates to grow in the seas, and life had begun. Great global crises did not extinguish it completely. Life somehow survived the great continental drift when Pangaea split into Laurasia (North America, Europe and Asia) and Gondwanaland (Australia, South America, Africa and India); and despite, as magnetic traces in rocks confirm, the Earth rotating 90° on its axis. Life weathered the five great extinctions (possibly the result of comet or asteroid collisions), which may have extinguished 90% of existing species; and the great changes in climate known as the ice ages. Somehow, something survived, dragged itself out of the seas, diversified amazingly (as Darwin noted) and over a period of thousands of generations started to evolve and improve.

The amphibious dinosaurs or terrible lizards emerged about 230 million years ago, but then disappeared, probably taken off by the last of the great extinctions. Life continued. Twenty-five million years ago, a range of early primates began to appear (ancestors of orang-utans, chimpanzees, and gorillas); twenty million years ago the first humanoids began to appear, maybe evolving from the pig-like lystrosaur, an early warm-blooded mammal. By six million years B.C. 'homo habilis' was to be found in the 'Garden of Eden' of East Africa, from whom two million years ago evolved 'homo erectus', who migrated northwards in to Asia, Europe and maybe over the land bridge from Siberia to Alaska to America about 40,000 years ago. The Neanderthal strain, who co-existed for 200,00 years with the woolly mammoth and the sabre-tooted tiger in a swathe from Western Europe to central Asia, was upstaged by a later wave from the African continent via the near East.

This 'homo sapiens' or wise man, according to new evidence, had evolved there by about 100,000 B.C., and may have come to Europe between then and 40,000B.C. In Europe he is known as Cro-Magnon man, named after a site in the Dordogne where five skeletons were found, and he was truly our ancestor. He was quite tall, with a straight forehead, prominent cheekbones and a marked chin. His brain was practically equivalent to ours; indeed, recent research confirms that our brains are their optimum size (any larger, and we would fall over) and within 20% of their maximum information processing capacity.

Mankind continued to evolve, and gained the distinction of becoming homo sapiens sapiens - doubly wise. They began to use tools and weapons more effectively, buried their dead, used and hoarded fire, invented the wheel, painted on cave walls, made music with bone flutes, worked out the yearly rhythms to produce calendars, developed medicine, organised religious practices, started the early signs for writing, and philosophers began to think. Pre-history dawns in to history, and we are up to the time of the great civilisations; Aztec, Inca, Mughal, China, Mesopotamia, Egypt, Greece, Rome, European, American ..... and who knows where the historical spotlight will shine next?

Jesus Christ, the reason for our millennium, was born in a country ruled by the Roman civilisation, and the marvel of Christianity is that it finally triumphed over Roman society *from within*. Thereafter, Western civilisation has been carried around the world, with more sureness in the second millennium and even more so since the Reformation half a millennium ago. Was this because of any innate superiority of European genes? Or our continuous acquaintance with the great animal-borne diseases, so that we were effectively inoculated against total devastation by them? Theories have been put forward for the advance of European civilisation as diverse as plumbing, Protestantism and its respect for the individual, dentistry, cotton underwear, an independent judiciary, the hardiness of our cereal crops, spectacles to lengthen a craftsman's working life, female emancipation, superior fire-power, press freedom, the mechanical clock, contraception, improved transport, and the near-separation of state and religion. Other major reasons, of course, have been the great 'Revolutions', the Agricultural, the Industrial and the Transport. These have been then followed by the amazing Information Revolution, of which we are only just seeing the beginning. It enables you to trace your nearer ancestors by genealogical Internet; another interesting example is a website called the Tree of Life on which we can see back to our ancestral roots. The Times said (*It) is designed to contain and show information about the phylogenetic - that is, evolutionary - relationships and characteristics of all organisms, to illustrate the diversity and the unity of all life on earth.* A sort of electronic Noah's Ark, and a wonderful way of uniting the present and the past …..

What has added precision and interest to archaeological investigation of fossils, bones and artefacts from the past, is the new tool of DNA testing. This is a useful device to compare the ancestry of different people, and track their ancestral wanderings. (This also requires the already-mentioned tool, the computer, to help us analyse all that DNA and also archaeological finds.) DNA testing meant a Somerset man is told he shares genes with a 9,000 year old skeleton from Cheddar Gorge; villagers from the self-contained Oxfordshire hamlet of Otmoor are told they have genes that came from Asia even older than African 'homo sapiens' genes; and DNA also reveals that one ancestor, of a type similar to the Bushmen of the Kalahari, passed on the Y human chromosome to every man who has come afterwards, and that there was a corresponding 'Genetic Eve' who carried the DNA potential of modern woman. As Shylock cries in a desperation over the anti-Semitism of his fellow-countrymen,

> *Hath a Jew not eyes? Hath not a Jew hands, organs, dimensions, senses, affections, passions? Fed with the same food, hurt with the same weapons, subject to the same diseases, healed by the same means, warmed and cooled by the same sun as a Christian is? If you prick us, do we not bleed? If you tickle us, do we not laugh? If you poison us, do we not die?*

How vitally important a reminder it is to us all as we enter the new millennium that we truly are all brothers. Civilisations ebb and flow; we may have been born by chance in to a comfortable life, but our lot could change. In truth, each of us has more in common with every other human being (the great fundamentals of birth, relationships and death, and the hierarchy of needs for shelter, warmth, food and occupation) than we have differences. We should concentrating on the common humanity we share both with those who went before - the dead are said to outnumber the living by a factor of 20 to one - and with those alive but under very different circumstances (including tribes who have had no contact with the rest of humanity, in the Andaman Islands, the Paraguyana Chaco, the Andean foothills of Bolivia, and the Amazon basin.) Thus we will recall our essential human-ness, and think of other people not as representatives of another species but as long-lost siblings.

TO HIS BOOK

Before the press scarce one could see
A little peeping-part of thee;
But since th'art printed, thou dost call
To show thy nakedness to all.
My care for thee is now the less,
Having resigned thy shamefastness;
Go with thy faults and fates; yet stay
And take this sentence, then away:
Whom one beloved will not suffice,
She'll run to all adulteries.

Robert Herrick (1591-1674)

Seventeen centuries before, the Roman poet Catullus launched his 'libellus' or little book thus, translated by Sir James Cobban:

Plus uno maneat perenne saeclo.
May it outlive this generation and still be around.

SONNET FOR **THIS MILLENNIUM**

Thousands of years have all too swiftly passed,
High pile the ruins, banked up are the dunes,
In many lands, pollution, war, typhoons .....
So, let us think, how man's Fate is cast?
Medicine cures ills, herbs and drugs do soothe;
In countries bless'd, democracy holds sway;
Lucky are we who work, and rest, and play.
Life can be pleasant, wealth one's path may smoothe,
Equality is here, so most can choose
Not only whom to meet, but what to do.
Now is the time for seizing openings new .....
It's up to us, our chances well to use.
Use grace, compassion; aim to make all free,
Mankind must celebrate humanity.

THE EMPTY HOUSE by Maurice Hewlett © 1920

The gate is padlockt, and the blinds
Close-drawn, the chimney's task is o'er;
Pity the traveller who finds
His journey's ending at this door.

How still, how watchful! Like a grave,
It keeps a secret in its hold;
The very tree-tops fear to wave,
The very shadows are a-cold.

Come in the garden. Cabbage stalks
Withered and bleacht in sorry rows;
But arabis aligns the walks,
And still the golden wallflower blows;

And tangled o'er the apple-stump
A budding Gloire or Maiden Blush;
And there's a thriving lily-clump,
And ribës still a burning bush.

Tread lightly, for this place is haunted;
Who knows what guarded eyes might peer
Between those curtain-folds enchanted?
The ghost of Love inhabits here.

Those curtains, poor and yet discreet,
I know not how they hold the air
Of hearts which must have loved and beat,
And drawn each other up the stair.

Pass lightly, lest the dead should waken;
Ask no more questions, lest the dumb
Should tell of love foresworn, forsaken:
Respect this house of shadows - come.

from THE RUBÁIYÁT OF OMAR KHAYYÁM

Into this Universe and 'Why' not knowing,
Nor 'Whence', like water willy-nilly flowing:
And out of it, like wind along the waste,
I know not 'Whither', willy-nilly blowing.

Translated by Edward Fitzgerald (1809-83)

BYGONE DAYS VERSUS THE FUTURE

Aromatherapy, hypnotherapy, reflexology,
Political correctness, citizen's charter, plea bargaining,
Zits, AIDS, transplants, in vitro fertilisation,
Digital watches, Walkmans, midi-systems,
Videos, auto focus, zoom lens,
Aerobics, mountain bikes, trainers.

Where has 'thee' and 'thou' gone ?
Quarter sessions, I am Sir your obedient servant,
I crave your indulgence, gaslights,
Spinning tops, five-stones, stool-ball,
Sheaves of corn, packets of soda, blue-bags,
Aspro, 'In Town Tonight', bodices ?

Surplus to requirements, old hat!

Change, change, change, change,
Rolls relentlessly on through life
As the earth revolves around the sun,
Onward, onward, onward, onward.
But where are we rushing towards?

A land of robots, plastic people,
Living until we are 1,000, neither male nor female,
You don't possess your own organs, do you?
Unable to communicate directly - technology can do that!

Surplus to requirements, old hat!

Betty Peake ©

13

WHAT IS OUR LIFE?

What is our life? A play of passion;
Our mirth the music of division;
Our mother's wombs the tiring-houses be
Where we are dressed for this short comedy;
Heaven the judicious sharp spectator is
That sits and marks still who doth act amiss;
Our graves that hide us from the searching sun
Are like drawn curtains when the play is done.
Thus march we playing to our latest rest,
Only we die in earnest, that's no jest.

Sir Walter Raleigh (1552?–1618)

THE 'DREAM' SEQUENCE

Direction
    Relationships
        Energy
            Agenda
                Monitoring

Gael Lindenfeld ©

The Year 2000

Calligraphy by Kaneyoshi

Reading downwards, the characters show *Sei - reki ni sen nen,* meaning *2000 years in the Western Calendar.*

Below is the ideograph of the calligrapher.

西歴二千年

包義

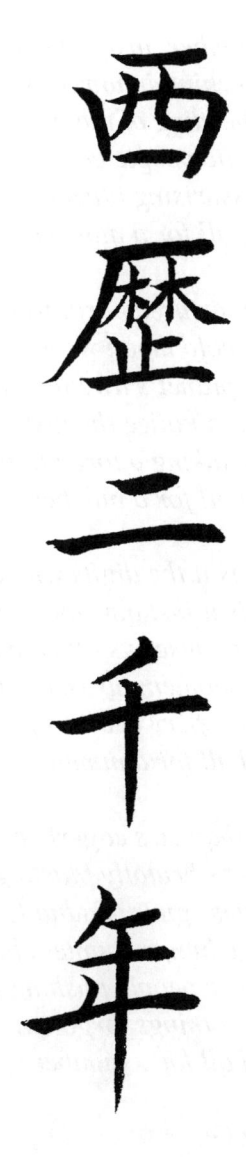

THE MILLENNIUM

A number, insignificant in itself,
Drowning in unrealistic ecstatic hopes.
Unheeding of the poverty and war that stand ahead,
Plastic people continue to live plastic lives.
Pressurising others to follow their foolish example:
And all for a number.

The tortured earth trembles in fear of another era,
The cold moon weeps icy crescents in despair.
The planet's dwellers, distracted by their own greediness,
Fail to notice the distinct signs that prompt their inevitable fate
Like taking a torch to the sun:
And all for a number.

But is it the digits who are to blame?
Or is it just our gormless stupidity,
That causes us all conveniently to overlook
The momentous issues that lie in wait for us, in vain
Like a fiery deathtrap earnestly pleading for a hose:
And all for a number.

Earthquakes eagerly erupting everywhere,
Bombs brutally blasting our brains;
Gutless guns gradually grinding us,
Huge hungry hunters heaving helpless creatures,
Plastic people pushing pointless politics.
These things forgotten .....
And all for a number.

Roz Gater ©

THE UNTHINKABLE CARRIER

>John o'Groats,
>South Atlantic,
>13th November 2000

Strange to think, as one sits under the palm trees gazing at the dolphins in the calm blue waters, how nonsensical that dateline would have seemed in 1960. Strange, also, to realise, amid the happy laughter of our children as the world looks forward eagerly to this most wonderful of centuries, that less than forty years ago the world was wracked by the fear of war. Although the British still knew in their hearts that they were the only people with any common sense (except for that curious aberration at Suez), not many of us said so out loud, feeling that we had lost our nineteenth century power of imposing this common sense on the world through the Pax Britannica.

Economically, Britain stood hesitating between a Commonwealth with dwindling Imperial Preference and a Common Market run by foreigners with peculiar ideas on the Congo, America, the Polish frontier. An election was fought on the issue of 'a telly in every garage', while America and Russia made bigger and bigger missiles. There seemed to be no leadership, and .....

..... all the time we were working secretly on this superb plan which has brought the world its ardently desired peace.

The scientific committee set up in the last days of the Churchill Government to investigate the possibilities of making Britain float began with three great advantages.

1. *So much of the work had been done already.* The task of cutting Britain loose from the solid earth was a logical follow-up of our advantage in a long history of mining, from the Phoneicians in Cornwall to all that modern coal-and-iron getting at which we, as pioneers of the Industrial Revolution, had worked longer than any other country. Mining, as Lewis Mumford points out, is, in German *Abbau* or unbuilding; and the committee found that what with the Cheddar caves, the Yorkshire and Derbyshire potholes, and all theses mines, there were already enough 'un-built' parts of Britain for it to be feasible to join them all up and fit them with buoyancy tanks.

2. *Britain's early lead in atomic know-how.* It was widely thought at the time that this, dating from Rutherford's Cambridge experiments, had been lost to Russia and America. But the world learnt otherwise on that extraordinary day in June 1966 when Britain, propelled by the giant atomic engines strategically mounted round her coastline, moved majestically towards the South Atlantic. The essential secrecy was greatly helped by

3. *The absence of a 'middle-class' in scientific knowledge.* Science in Britain has always been sharply divided into geniuses and an uncaring general public. The former were all 'in the know'. The latter were easily lulled by all kinds of explanations of such preparations as could not be hidden. They were perfectly ready to believe that the engines were 'atomic power stations', even though there was plenty of power already and the huge gaunt buildings were all on marshy desolate coasts far from any possible demand for power.

The vast establishment at Harwell was explained away by ingenious stories of 'peaceful application of H-power', complete with hand-outs about temperatures much hotter than the sun obtained for millionths of a second (!) in little glass things. There were even photographs of a circular wooden fantasy (made by a Harwell carpenter) mysteriously called Zeta.

The increasingly frequent window-rattling explosions as the unbuilding was hurried forward with atomic blasting were explained as 'aircraft breaking the sound-barrier'; the public were easily convinced that sound travels at over 700 miles an hour, whereas anyone who has observed, say, the time between flash and report of a gun on a quite small sports field may have guessed that in fact it travels very slowly (15.27 miles an hour, in fact). Even the littering of the country with huge machines plainly marked EARTH MOVER only suggested road making.

Now Britain enjoys this scientific extension of her traditional balance-of-power policy, and the world's peace is no longer at the mercy of a few cross-looking American admirals or Russian generals. The world knows that any missile, instantly detected by British radar, would automatically set off the Ultimate Weapon - a 'full speed ahead' order to our mighty atomic engines, causing the country to leap forward at 800 knots and make a tidal wave that only we should survive. Much more than in the nineteenth century, Britain *is* now the British Fleet.

The fears of the Isle of Wight that the tow-chain might break, or the island simply used to carry the baggage, have long since disappeared (and how happy Ireland, in this Jubilee Year of her President, Dame Siobhan McKenna, now feels as the only island off Europe!) By careful course-plotting we are able to have three crop-growing seasons a year, and we have become a net exporter of food.

The off-shore coal and iron mining rights we have maintained in the old sea area we occupied for so long bring in huge revenues. Our own output, now that the industrial strife of the past, attributed by psychologists to the 'Old Climate', is just a memory, flourishes in the clean air of our healthy sub-tropical climate, which has also made the wonderful sandy beaches of the Northumberland Riviera one of the world's great tourist centres. Our currency is the hardest in the world .....

But we should not be too complacent. Our agreement with Japan, whereby she, under licence, keeps the Pacific peace as we keep the Atlantic, has worked splendidly. But we may not always keep this technical lead. There are rumours of an imminent German-inspired break-off of Spain from Europe, and China is known to be experimenting with Korea. A world in which every country was a giant marine nuclear dodgem would be a horrifying thought, reviving the worst fears of the sixties. No doubt, however, Britain would come up with a solution. She usually does.

from ODDLY ENOUGH by Paul Jennings,
by permission of The Bodley Head.

CHAPTER 2 : PEOPLE WILL BE TALKING OF NOTHING ELSE

The chance to think about language, about words - about words as symbols, words as message-bearers, words as names, words as the necessary organisation not just of language but of thought processes - is useful to consider early in this book. Indeed, you may think that words (no, the Word) came ahead of everything, as one can tell from the fourth Gospel, written by John, son of Zebedee.

John begins in his majestic way by saying that Jesus was the eternal word of God, who became incarnate (as the Gospel goes on to show) as a real living person. John uses the metaphor of the word applied to Jesus; and shows how men long to aspire to worship a higher being, but also crave empathy with their fellow human beings. Worship of God may be nameless (the Jews were unable to bring themselves to pronounce the name of Yahweh or Jehovah); but to express their feelings for Jesus, God made man, we must think of Him by name, as a way of focusing our thoughts. What does this tell us about language? We can observe that words are both a means of communication and of interpretation (as of course Jesus interpreted God for us), but also in an important sense, are important in their own right. Some charismatic Christian churches encourage *glossolalia* or speaking in tongues, where the expression of feeling predominates over sense.

Words are what they stand for but also, as Lewis Carroll reminded us, take on a life of their own :
> *'When I use a word,' Humpty Dumpty said, in a rather scornful tone, 'It means just what I choose it to mean - no more, no less.'*
> *'The question is,' said Alice 'Whether you can make words so many different things?'*
> *'The question is,' said Humpty Dumpty, 'Which is to be master, that's all.'*

What are words? Are they unique to us? Although the animal kingdom can communicate with each other by various means, from the alarum call of a startled bird to the subsonic *musique concrète* of whales, man alone can pass on complex thoughts in structured grammatical forms. There have been recent experiments with chimpanzees, who are closest to us in evolutionary terms (Darwin said that language in hominids had emerged from the cognition of our common ape ancestor); the famous Washoe and her son learned to use dozens of American Sign Language gestures meaningfully, and even used it between themselves and others in their group when they thought they were unobserved. Real speech allied to language, though, is part of our human-ness, and is part of what separates man from the beasts. Speech development in the growing child develops in parallel with mental development, and the shaping of thought is to a certain extent dependent on language. However, American psychologists did some experiments with children of three to five years old, deaf from birth, who had not formally been taught sign language, and they found that they could communicate using gestures and actions for single words, and also for sentences. The syntax that evolved was not dissimilar in both American and Chinese children. From this, the researchers concluded that sentence construction is inbuilt, in their words 'hard-wired from birth': deaf children may find it more difficult to express themselves on abstract things in language that we understand, but they have both inherent skills, and skills that develop. Throughout history, our use of language, the variety of our personal vocabulary, is so amazing that one controversial idea is that our language is as unique as our fingerprints, and that the technique of so-called 'Cumulative Sum Analysis' can prove authorship of documents.

When did language evolve? Did this depend on the size of the caveman's brain; as part of general historical advancement; or when there was sufficient development of his laryngeal anatomy, perhaps through tree-climbing or similar activities which developed the muscles of the lungs and throat, to be able to form words? The latest research on skulls suggests Neanderthal man 'spoke' 400,000 years ago; but when did his grunts become sufficiently separate and articulate (that is, strung together) to become words as part of a meaningful and recognisable language? The part of the brain that is responsible for understanding and generating language, whether in speech or visual form, is the area just above the left ear called the planum temporale. A stroke of the right side of the body usually takes away speech, which a left-side stroke does not, as the right side is controlled by the left brain, and vice-versa; a partial stroke may have the rare effect of 'foreign accent syndrome', when for instance one victim started speaking in a French accent although he had never left America, and recently a Scotswoman started speaking in a South African accent.

Speech is truly, as someone once said, a mouthful of air. Sounds are formed when we deliberately expel air over the vocal chords, two parallel folds of muscular tissue at the top of the larynx or windpipe, which then vibrate. The vibration is carried forward into the mouth and throat, which act as a loudhailer to increase the volume of sound; helped by resonance in the sinuses, which are hollow bones over and behind the eyes. Sound is then shaped by the soft palate, which blocks air to the nose (when this is affected by a cold, our voices sound curious); and shaped by the tongue, the jaw and the lips. After the recent pioneering transplant of vocal chords, the patient had acquired the donor's deep voice, but retained his own accent. Speech is common to all mankind, but there is still a difference in the speech abilities of different nations. You have to have been exercising your tongue in a certain way since childhood to form the English 'thorne' sound (th) or Welsh 'll'. Brewer tells us that *Croakumshire (is) a name given to the county of Northumberland because the natives were supposed to speak with a peculiar croak. It was supposed to be especially observable in Newcastle and Morpeth, where the people were said to be born with a burr in their throats preventing their giving effect to the letter 'r'.* Ethnic groups with long top lips use the 'p' sound more often than those with short top lips, who use 'k' and 'f' more frequently. English people have trouble reproducing the French nasal vowels (all four being represented in the phrase *Un bon vin blanc*), and the guttural sounds in Gaelic, German or Spanish; is all too easy to deride what you cannot manage! There is a distinct whistling dialect in Cuskoy, a village in eastern Turkey cut in half by a steep ravine; the Gaunches, the original tall, fair inhabitants of the Canaries, used a similar device from hill top to hill top, under circumstances when the Swiss would be yodelling.

'Clicks' are used in the Xhosa group of languages in southern Africa, the Bushmen having four, the Zulus three. The sound is pronounced simultaneously with other sounds, a feat only learnt in childhood, and when used in song by Miriam Makeba or Yvonne Chukachuka are most impressive. When Japanese children are being taught the 'katakana' alphabet, they learn a verse (quite poetical in its own right) called the 'I-ro-ha' which in the original Japanese language gives practice in each syllable they might need to learn. In the Book of Judges in the Old Testament, the Ephraimites were distinguished by their enemies the Gileadites because they *could not frame to pronounce* the 'sh' sound in the word 'shibboleth', and thus were slain.

It has been estimated that recognisable human speech patterns evolved perhaps about 50,000 years ago. Just as homo sapiens may have evolved from common ancestors on the African continent, so languages may have developed from a common ur-language. In the vivid language of the Bible, we are told that the eight post-diluvian survivors from the Ark spoke as one: *The whole earth was of one language, and of one speech.* However, Noah's descendants started to flout God's laws and to show off, by building a big tower or ziggurat at Babel (possibly based on the real city of Babylon), *whose top may reach unto the heavens.* God showed his disapproval and thwarted their vaingloriousness thus :

> *Let us go down and confound their language, that they may not understand one another's speech.*
> *So the Lord scattered them abroad from thence upon the face of all the earth; and they left off to build the city.*
> *Therefore is the name of it called Babel; because the Lord did there confound the language of all the earth; and from thence did the Lord scatter them abroad upon the face of all the earth.*
>
> Genesis, Chapter 11.

The word may have come from the Aramaic 'Bab-ilu' (meaning Gateway of God), but it has entered our language as 'babble', with similar versions in many other languages. Babylon was also the scene of the 'writing on the wall', when the prophet Daniel interpreted for King Belshazzar (otherwise known as Nebuchadnezzar) the vision he had seen while feasting, of a disembodied hand writing these words in Aramaic on the wall behind him: *Mene, Mene, Tekel, Upharsin.* Daniel said they meant *numbered, numbered, weighed and divided*, and correctly foretold that the King would be slain that night.

How do languages differ from each other? What is their scope? In English, there are five written vowels (Welsh has 'y' in addition), but twelve vowel sounds; with another nine dipthongs or double vowels like 'boys', 'tour' or 'aeon'. The *schwa* or neutral sound is an unstressed vowel such as the 'e' in 'the', the 'o' in 'cannon' or the 'a' in 'about'. There are twenty-six consonant sounds in spoken English, and some letters like 'g' or 'c' can be hard or soft. The 'th' may be voiced as in 'this', or voiceless as in 'think'. Combinations of letters such as 'sh' and 'ar', are known as phonemes. In a so-called perfect alphabet (like Welsh) there is only one phoneme per letter, and only one letter per phoneme; but English with twenty-six letters in our alphabet (having added j, u and w to Latin's twenty-three) has forty-seven speech sounds. Consider the word 'thought', which has seven letters but only three phonemes. The projection of the language depends on accent (regional, class), intonation, emphasis, timbre, and the accompanying non-vocal communication, also known as body language, including eye contact.

So, how many words do you think you know? And what does one mean by know: is it a question of recognising a word in context, understanding it when someone else uses it, or using it unhesitatingly oneself not just on the page but in speech? Most educated people are pleasantly surprised that they recognise and can explain about twenty to twenty-five thousand, that is, half the words in a common-sized dictionary; but a full quarter of that number will be from a short list of a hundred that we use for three quarters of the time, so-called 'key words' which do all the dirty work for us. A child starts school at five with about two thousand words; the average office worker needs about 18,000; that sum is what is also necessary for the reading of even a tabloid newspaper (a broadsheet nearly twice as much.) The size of our vocabulary is not necessarily the sign of a fine mind - it might be a parrot-like ability unallied to strengths of reasoning - but it is useful for dazzling the slower-tongued, and usually taken as one of the signs of intelligence; what does that say about the eighteenth century Bishop Berkeley, who said that he found words were an obstacle to his thought? It is interesting that John Milton's published vocabulary was only 8,000 words, while his predecessor Shakespeare (who was amazingly free even with the spelling of his own name) with his incredible word-play and neologisms used over 20,000; who is to say which is the 'better' writer?

It would be interesting to know how many words there are in English. Systematic collection and collation only came about gradually. Remember James Murray in the 1860s in a leaking shed collecting laundry-baskets full of slips about words and their first printed mention, to produce the first Oxford dictionary ....? The job is now done electronically on a database called the British National Corpus maintained by a consortium of publishers and academics, which contains 100 million words. Many will be variations on a head-word, that is, plurals, combination words and so on; but it is a huge number, and increasing every year by 200,000, of which only a thousand may actually be considered for inclusion in published dictionaries. From America, you can check the University of Chicago's Wordsmyth Dictionary on the Internet web on *http://www.lightlink.com/bobp/wedt*.

There are said to be 10,000 living languages (6,000 of any size) in the world, with 65 different alphabets. Languages are divided in to over 200 'families', that is, a group of related languages; a family takes about 6,000 years to develop and be distinguished. Apparently similar languages may have little relationship between them; Japanese, for instance, though it shares a script with Chinese and Korean, is not related to any other language. The actual speakers of two languages that are related may, curiously, not have any other characteristic in common, either racial or cultural. A dialect is subordinate version of a recognised language which may have non-standard grammatical forms, accent, idioms and vocabulary (what fun English philologists have had mapping, for instance, where words for left-handedness change from 'cack-handed' to 'southpaw', and regional variations in names for icicles and making tea!) but is still recognisably allied to the original; the exception to this is Chinese, where varieties occur that are called 'dialects' which cannot be orally understood, but use the same orthography. The definition of a 'patois' overlaps with this but was essentially an unwritten regional dialect, especially of French origin, regarded rather negatively. Pidgin differs in that it was not originally the mother tongue of any of the speakers, but a spontaneously-developed highly simplified lingua franca or language of convenience used along the trade routes of the West and East Indies, the Americas, Africa and the Pacific, based on a mixture of English, Spanish, Portugese or French as appropriate. When a pidgin became more complex and did become the mother-tongue of a group, taking on a life of its own (as in Jamaica, and Tok Pisin in New Guinea), it technically becomes a 'creole'.

Most European languages are either related to the Germanic languages of northern Europe, or the latinate Romance languages of the south. Some exceptions are the extinct language Etruscan; modern Hungarian, Finnish, Estonian and Basque, whose positions as 'isolates' was first pointed out by the German von Humboldt; the dialect known as Beurla Reagaird spoken by those who fish for wild pearls from freshwater mussels in Scottish rivers; and the Rom of travelling Romanies.

Linguists carefully study the morphology, or the several parts of a word, looking at the morphemes (the smallest indivisible units of meaning) within it. These will be roots, prefixes, suffixes and compound-words, and the linguist will then try to establish the rules governing the way words are formed. There is a distinction between agglutinative languages such as Turkish, Swahili and Japanese, where words are made up of a sequence of elements; and fusional or inflexive languages in which there may be little correspondence between the string of elements and the total meaning of the word. Words are then strung together by slowly-evolving rules of syntax and grammar to form language as we know it. Nothing can be taken for granted in languages: some so-called primitive ones may have enormous vocabularies (the

Inuits' thirty-plus words for snow) and complex grammars (some of the 123 Amerindian languages, or Chukchee spoken in Siberia, or the Zulu language, or Bantu which has twenty classes of noun), some like Samoan very little. On the other hand, languages of more developed cultures may have little grammar (English, for instance) or much (modern Greek.) What is certain is that it may well tell us a lot about a people's history and culture: American English as well as embracing some Native American words (woodchuck, raccoon, tomahawk, pow-wow) still uses some Elizabethan words like 'gotten' that have shrunk in our everyday speech but remain as they were when the Pilgrim Fathers took them out there. The gentle Bushmen of the Kalahari, who may well be of the race from whom we are all descended, have a complex and fascinating language that has no word at all for 'murder', because the concept is unknown to them. British English has many words from the old Empire: banana, voodo and banjo from Africa; bungalow, char for tea, catamaran from India; bamboo, gong and batik from the Malay; typhoon, silk, soya from Hong Kong and China; budgerigar, kiwi and tattoo from Australasia; as well as words from the Celtic languages of Wales (flannel, coracle, corgi), Ireland (galore, blarney, smithereens) and Scotland (plaid, slogan, loch.)

It is sad when a language dies, because with it withers a little bit of people's history. Dolly Pentreath, the last exclusively-Cornish-speaking person, died in the late eighteenth century; although it, like Manx, lingers on rather artificially as a learned language in the South West, and in dialect form on the Island of Tangier in Chesapeake Bay off the coast of Virginia. In Nigeria, the last surviving speaker of the Bikya language has just died; in the Middle East the language Aramaic which was probably the mother tongue of Jesus two millennia ago, has now dwindled to use only in a few small villages in Samaria. The non-European 'isolates', and the Ainu language in Japan, and Tarasca in Mexico, are likely to disappear. Of the native South American languages, which may have numbered nearly two thousand, only about 600 remain, some only perilously (in 1995, for instance, an old couple were found in the Brazilian rainforest who had no ethnic links with other groups, and whose language was unique.) The Papal declaration in the late fifteenth century to divide the continent between Portugal and Spain, ensured that those then became respectively the major languages of Brazil and the rest of the land mass.

Language is more than just words, it is part of tribal continuity and a way of ensuring group identity. The world is becoming a global village, but conversely there has been a growth in linguistic nationalism and pride. People may speak a major language, but are rather ambivalent about its dominance; they long for the maternal comfort of their original tongue, which they do not want to lose, and resent being told that their language is inferior (supporting the so-called 'hypothesis of linguistic equality.') It may be a secret defence against a dominant and maybe threatening linguistic imperialism. As expert Dr David Dalby says, *Monolingualism is as bad as illiteracy ..... it defies diversity*, and it is that diversity that brings interest to life. The Welsh say
Cenedl heb raith; cenedl heb galon
A nation without a language is a nation without a heart

However, the spread in the major world languages seems inexorable. Some with over a hundred million speakers at the moment - Hindu/Urdu, Russian, Bengali, Portugese, Bahasa from Malaysia & Indonesia, French, Japanese and German - may well decrease, while the four largest languages (English, Chinese, Spanish and Arabic) will increase. Mandarin Chinese is the language of two thirds of China already, and Taiwan and Singapore; the Cantonese speakers of Hong Kong are now learning it too. The Spanish winner of the Nobel Prize for Literature, Camilo Jose Cela, predicted in 1997 that when another two millennia have passed, *The world's population will use only (those) four languages; while others will survive as regional dialects or in the form of love poetry.*

English is a curious winner in the world language stakes. Originally the obscure dialect of the East Midlands, when the average uneducated person may only have had a vocabulary of five hundred words, it has by its hybrid vigour and by historical good fortune (the early use of printing in this country in the fifteenth century, then the spread of the British Empire in the eighteenth and nineteenth centuries, and the trade attendant on it) become world class. This is despite the fact that its spelling is illogical, its pronunciation irregular, and some of its sounds are crucially too similar (imagine an air traffic controller trying to say 'eighty' not 'eighteen'); and it has a dual system for many verbs, one informal prepositional verb such as 'to put up with', the other being formal like 'to endure'. Idioms are curious, and metaphorical language frequent. Thank goodness I have never had to learn it! The spoken language has great drawbacks; in 'Pygmalion', Professor Higgins says *The moment an Englishman speaks, he makes every other Englishman despise him.* It is a language which adult learners can seldom speak without an accent or intonation. Accents in English make a fascinating field of study, as we are branded by the tongue in to stereotypes whether we like it or not. It may be generational; youngsters seem to have picked up the rising-voice at the end of a sentence, for instance, or 'questo-babble' as it has been called, which was originally Antipodean. Recent research put the Birmingham Brummie accent at the bottom of the list of favoured regional accents (the kind of thing about which telesales advertising makes great play), and yet in times past it would have been the accent of Chaucer, Shakespeare and Dr Johnson. Research at the University of Leeds has shown that soap operas may after all be helping to preserve the regional patterns of British speech, which had been becoming more uniform.

However, thanks to its mongrel beginnings, English glories in many synonyms (often one latinate, one Anglo-Saxon), making the language infinitely varied and subtle; it is relatively succinct, for example when text is translated into French or German it takes up a third more space; and it has an alphabet of only 26 letters unlike the 74 in Khmer, 85 in Cherokee, and the basic 2,000 characters that any educated Chinese or Japanese must learn. Additionally, as already said, it has a fairly simple grammar - no genders, nor agreement of adjectives, for instance - and much is conveyed by word order. An American linguist noted that it has *A range of varieties, and is a flexible medium for literary and other types of creativity.* Although difficult to speak really well, it is easy enough to string together in simple form: a senior

European diplomat once said *Using English means we don't talk too much, because none of us knows its nuances.* Years ago the German statesman Bismarck noted wistfully that there was great significance in two of the great states of the world speaking the same language, Britain and the United States: it gave them, he said, *A great advantage over other countries.* Certainly in earlier times of mass immigration by fragmented groups of language speakers, the American ideal of aiming at English proficiency was a unifying force that empowered the newly-arrived adult immigrants and gave them a stake in their new country, in a way that today's politically correct respect for Hispanicism or Ebonics (Black language patterns) may not, and indeed is now beginning to be seen as a mistake. Luckily, most children go their own sweet way, having the ability to cope with one language or dialect at home and one outside.

Recently, of course, English has increasingly become the 'lingua franca' of the world (how curious that we have to use a Latin phrase for that; it originally meant a mixture of Italian with Spanish, Arabic, French and Greek that was used as a means of communication in Levantine countries, but now is taken to mean any language serving as a medium between different countries whose languages are different.) It is understood by a billion and a half people (throughout Europe, more than 40% of people can use it), and is used internationally for air traffic control, academic conferences, music lyrics, business, and computers, on which it is reckoned that 80% of material is in English. For already three decades, the Swedish ball-bearing company SKF have used it in their offices, followed more recently by ABB, Electrolux, Astra, Ericsson, Skandinaviska Banken's merchant banking division and the truckmakers Scania. In Germany Siemens, Hoechst, Deutsche Telekom and Commerzbank are using it too. Even the French attitude to it has recently changed, as the French Minister for Education is now M Claude Allègre, a fluent English speaker, who has decreed that all children should learn English from the age of eight: *The fight against English is a fight that cannot be won ..... it is clear that the younger one starts learning, the better,* he said. Worldwide, requests for written material from libraries are nine times more likely to be in English than any of the other languages put together. The then-poor Indian state of Kerala decreed in the 1960s that English be compulsory in schools, which empowerment has led to good business, as international work (like computing on the Internet) floods in, and also leaves the Keralans well-fitted for working overseas.

There are obvious benefits in having a universally understood language. In classical times, for instance, partly due to the conquests of Alexander three centuries before Christ, Greek spanned the whole eastern Mediterranean. The epistles of Paul were written in it, and could be immediately understood by Christian converts from Ephesus in what is now Turkey to Corinth in Greece itself. Later, Latin took precedence, as Roman civilisation was spread over Europe from Scotland to the Carpathians, from the Rhine to North Africa, by twin funnels of communication, that is, good roads and a common language. After the Reformation, the use of classical Latin declined in to a learned language or became evolved in to modern Italian or Spanish; but it still, for instance, had to be the common language for the Elector of Hanover who became our King George I, who had no English, and his Prime Minister Sir Robert Walpole, who spoke no German. The Vatican still has an official Latinist, Monsignor Carlo Egger, who recently brought out the 'Lexicon Recentis Latinitatis' and is keen to keep up spoken Latin; and launched a Latin website: *www.unigre.urbe.it/vallejo/breviter.htm*

There have been hundreds of projects for an artificial universal language dating back many centuries. Leibnitz, inventor of the infinitesimal calculus, Descartes and Bomenius are just three of the famous philosophers who have expressed their opinions about the principles that should be followed; in the seventeenth century, a Scotsman Sir Thomas Urquhart was the first to create a complete language, but his manuscripts were destroyed by Cromwell's soldiers. Many curious forms of 'language' have been offered, including musical notes, colours of the spectrum, numbers, strange symbols and codes. Some were modifications of national languages (e.g. Latino sine flexione, Novangla). The first practical language was Volapük (vol = world, pük = speak) published by a German cleric in 1878. It was based on an English vocabulary but the grammar was too hard for most people. Probably the best known is Esperanto (= 'one who hopes'), created in 1887 by the Pole Ludwig Lazarus Zamenhof, which now has well over 100,000 speakers in 110 countries, a body of original literature, a World President who is from China, and its own web site. Church services in London have been held in it every month for 85 years. With an original core of 700 roots, it is an agglutinative language like Hungarian, Japanese and Swahili; derived primarily from Western languages, its syntax and morphology show strong Slav influence. Here is a message wishing us well for the Millennium (in Esperanto, 'jarmilo'):

La universala lingvo Esperanto estas simpla kaj interesa. Granda nombra da studentoj kapablas lerni la lingvon rapide, kaj konversacias post mallonga tempo. En la jaro 2000 la komenco de la nova jarmilo la uzo de unu komuna lingcvo por la popoloj de la mondo estos tre tre necesa. La facila metodo de komunikado helpus al komprenado sen miskompreno. Ordinara homo deziros kontakti amikojn en multaj landoj. La nova jarmilo estos granda oportuno por iniciato de uzo de internacia lingvo. Nun la lingvo rapide kreskas per la Internethttp://www.cs.chalmers.se/martinw/esperanto/veb/. Esperantistoj sendas bondezirojn por la sukceso de MISCELLENNIUM kaj ni salutas unu la alian tra la mondo je la komenco de la nova jarmilo.

There have been another six hundred or so attempts, but none with any great success, such as BASIC English (British American Scientific International Commercial), which promised to be a simple introduction to English, and more extraordinary ones like Solresol, Ido, Glosa, and Novial. They are all known by the generic term 'interlinguas'. Even Klingon, the so-called language of Star Trek, is sometimes seen as an attempt at a universal tongue.

Rather than a completely new language, what about reforming our idiosyncratic spelling? It was George Bernard Shaw who said tongue-in-cheek that the word 'fish' should be spelled 'ghoti' : gh as in rough, o as in women, and ti as in station. He himself was very keen on spelling reform, and left money in his will for its reform by devising a completely new English alphabet on phonetic principles, which came to be known as Shavian. Other solutions contented themselves with trying to simplify and make more logical our present alphabet, creating standardised systems in which the existing alphabet is used in a way that more consistently reflects the correspondence between sound and symbol. One such was the now-lapsed initial teaching alphabet (i.t.a.), invented by James Pitman in 1959, a lower-case system of 44 symbols in which each symbol represented a phoneme, giving a closer correlation between symbol and sound than traditional English orthography. Although it was intended to precede and supplement, not (like Shavian) replace traditional English, it suffered like all artificial languages from the fact that the student usually has at some stage to unlearn something learned; and after all, what one sees all about on hoardings, notices, television, in books, magazines and so on, is the original language.

There have been great efforts over the last four hundred years to study how language has evolved. This has of course been made more difficult by the lack of written evidence in the past, and even more so by the lack of recorded speech; the so-called 'Great Vowel Shift' of the late fourteenth century in England has had to be deduced from the spelling, which is less prone to change, and tends to preserve the values of an earlier period of pronunciation. The study was very much tied in with theories of evolution on the one hand, and with the art of lexicography (that is, collecting words and their etymology) on the other. In the 1750s came the famous Dictionary of Dr Samuel Johnson; the Scottish Lord Monboddo wrote six volumes of 'The Origins and Progress of Language' between 1773-1792; around that time the Berlin Academy of Sciences, noticing the amount of scholarly interest in philology, offered an academic prize for the best study of it. Some fifty years later the brothers Grimm (known mostly to us as collectors of folk tales) wrote their 'Deutsches Wörterbuch' and produced the so-called Grimm's Law of sound changes. Significant advances were made in the late nineteenth century by the afore-mentioned James Murray (brought up bi-lingually in English and Lowland Gaelic, and whose fascinating biography was told by his granddaughter in 'Caught in the Web of

Words'.) It was agreed with the publishers in 1879 that the book was to be not more than 7,000 pages, but grew to 15,487 pages, and it came to establish the Oxford dictionary tradition; the famous slips are still in use at the Oxford University Press.

The French have not always been allowed to be so enquiring; Rousseau had trouble with some of his studies of language, and in 1866 the Linguistic Society of Paris forbade enquiry in to language origins. For three and a half centuries, the Academie Française (current average age of academicians, 81 years old, with three women out of 320) has tried to maintain a rearguard action about English words in their tongue, blaming slackness and snobbery for the invasion. The Germans are also fighting a rearguard action against indiscriminate use of trendy English phrases in advertising. The Russians, led by President Boris Yeltsin, have tried to ban foreign words from advertisements and encourage Russian alternatives to English technical terms; though some observers feel that it would be more important to clean the language of 'mat', the rich vocabulary of expletives in Russian, which even the draconian measures of Article 209 of the Soviet Criminal Code in the communist era could not remove. It is interesting to remember that when the Warsaw Pact was drawn up at the end of the Soviet era, it was couched in English.

Overseas, much useful work was also done by European missionaries in the field of native languages from the eighteenth century onwards, usually in order to translate the Scriptures. In the wake of the garrison and the trading post, came the mission. Thus Bartolomaus Zeigenbalg translated the Bible in to Tamil, Henry Martyn in to Persian, William Carey in to Bengali, and Robert Morrison in to Chinese. In 1804 the British & Foreign Bible Society was formed, and in its first century distributed over 180 million copies of Scripture. The Bible Society, as it is now, is part of the United Bible Societies who spend over £35 million a year in translation, production and distribution (nearly twenty million complete Bibles every year and three times as many part-Bibles). Their efforts have translated the Bible in to 2,167 languages. Although of course many speakers of minority languages are bi-lingual, the Bible Society points out :

> *People can only fully appreciate God's Word when it is in their mother tongue. When a Bible has been translated into a language, people are overjoyed, and one comment often made is 'Now God speaks our language.'*

What is sad is that only about a third of the world is said to be functionally literate. Imagine not being able to read or write; how left behind you must feel not being able to read road signs, sign forms, use a computer, read a newspaper, and how vulnerable you are to the manipulations of people of ill-intent who misuse your ignorance. Even in this country, the Basic Skills Agency found that in some urban areas, a quarter of all adults are poor readers (and nearly half had trouble with sums.) John Keats said two centuries ago: *I have good reason to be content, for thank God I can read.* It is a skill which, once mastered, is taken for granted, but how lucky we are to have had the education to lift us out of illiteracy, to be 'people of letters'. As we enter the third millennium, there are many worthwhile moves both governmental and charitable to ensure that no one is denied the empowerment that being able to read brings with it.

There have been problems in translation from time immemorial. Some languages have been as impenetrable as codes (indeed, during World War II, the American Navy sometimes used the complex Hopi Indian language for transmission of top-secret documents.) Bible translators have had cross-cultural problems like trying to find an equivalent for 'white as snow' for the Tongans who have never seen it (they elected for 'white as a flock of egrets'), or even 'Lamb of God' for sheepless lands. Such posers, along with the perils of translating idioms, dog the search for translating machines: remember the machine that translated 'out of sight, out of mind' as 'invisible, insane'? The Bible Society makes use of Machine Assisted Translation providing computer-based tools for linguists, but at the moment that is all that they can be, tools, not the definitive answer. A solution to the so-called 'knowledge representation problem' starts with the assumptions like those of the American linguist Naom Chomsky, who views language as being the result of innate cognitive structures which are 'wired up' instinctively to grasp grammar, especially verbs, nouns and adjectives. Computer translating machines, like those of Lernout and Hauspie in Belgium and at the Rank Xerox laboratory in Grenoble, are translating with up to 97% accuracy, and improving all the time. With greater accuracy, this will enable simultaneous translation at the conference table, on radio travel and weather reports, on the Internet, for news-gathering, and for academic and business submissions. If this is thereafter allied to improved speech recognition systems, currently being developed (partly by the Ministry of Defence) and refined both for artificial voice boxes such as used by Stephen Hawking to replace vocal chords, and for control of machines such as computers and dictating machines, then these will be incredibly powerful communications tools. Some dentists are already using them.

One way speech-recognition computers could be used, for instance, would be in the compilation of the National Life Story Collection, based on the National Sound Archives, which has received substantial millennial funding, or the equivalent Hamari Kahani (Our Story) which has gathered together orally the life stories of immigrants from the Indian sub-continent. Both projects aim to gather people's life stories, both to dignify the memories of the elderly and also for historians of the future.

Swear words, though all too frequent, still have power to shock. A Broadcasting Standards Commission report in early 1998 showed that, above all, people were keen to keep such sounds from children, and corralled beyond the nine-o'clock watershed. Sadly, blasphemy seems to have regained its use (as it did in the Middle Ages, using most explicit imagery), along with certain short sharp words of Anglo-Saxon origin that because of their plosive power can be spat out explicitly and aggressively. Sensible are those who use them infrequently, because when used they have the benefit of surprise, and listeners may believe you truly mean it.

Naming of things is another powerful process. Objects, people and their nick-names, ships (complaints have recently been made about the Royal Navy no longer using aggressive names like 'HMS Invincible', but anodyne names like flowers instead), boats, houses, roads ..... Some years ago, house-purchasers in a pretty Essex town picked up their six-bedroom house for a song, because the road name was 'Scrub Rise'. Was a new development in South London called 'Pinkerton Place' after the hero of the opera 'Madam Butterfly', the detective agency, or after a local worthy? Roadnames have to be notified under the Public Health Act of 1925, and have council approval; but many oddities are historical, which 'just growed', and usually far more interesting than those made-up names given (too often without thought to local history) on new estates. The Halifax Building Society did a survey of ten million homes, and found that if houses had names, they were strictly 'traditional and timeless': the first two were simply 'The Cottage' and 'The Bungalow', but thereafter were names such as 'Ivy Cottage', 'The White House', 'Three Pines' and 'Hill View'. Different names, more often chosen by older couples, tend to the whimsical. Rural and urban pub names, about which books could and indeed have been written, were originally symbolic of local events or characters; but now too often changed to ludicrous combinations of salad vegetables and creepy-crawlies.

When it comes to commercial brand names, such care has to be taken that fees of up to half a million pounds are paid to consultancies by companies wanting a powerful and positive name, especially one that works in other countries. The Vauxhall Nova was renamed the Corsa, because in Spain 'no va' means 'no go'; Rolls-Royce had to reject the name 'Silver Mist' because 'mist' means 'dung' in German. Even the translation of the film 'King Kong' into Danish had to reversed years ago, as 'kong' means king in Danish.

The power that resides (as we learn in the case of Yahweh) in names is very powerful; and as a child, the bitterest taunt is calling somebody names. The worst rejection that you can have is to be 'ignominious', that is, not deserving a name. Even though our own given names come from our parents originally, most of us like our names and are quite bonded to them - sometimes hard for women if they change their surnames on marriage. How blessed we are if our name does not become infamous through association with a notorious public figure, margarine, catfood, or a cartoon character ..... Sometimes, other people have expectations of us because of association of our name with someone they didn't like in the past, or because of a general stereotyping of names (why is 'Susan' said to be a sexy name? Why are Sharons meant to be loud-mouthed? Why do English people dislike Australian names which end in the '-ene' sound?) How refreshing an American friend is, who once remarked that she never picked up the snobbery implicit in English people's names. Frequent analyses are printed of the names of 'top people's babies' - in 1997, they were James and Olivia - but what is also interesting is analysis of GP patients' lists, in other words, looking at the names of people of all ages. Some good old-fashioned Christian names just go on and on, like John (whose diminutive Jack has been the most popular British name in recent years, and which with its variants worldwide is probably the world's most popular name too.) In 1998 these lists showed the population had 823,652 separate names, 562,030 being one-offs; the majority of us do have common first names, because more than 37 million people have names shared by 100,000 others!

Lucky we are not to be Chinese, for they only have about three thousand surnames to share between 1.2 billion people, with the most-used five covering one third of the population (and 87 million of them being of the Li family.) Jewish surnames have a fascinating history. In earlier centuries, surnames as such were not used. A last name might be given to describe someone's birthplace or hometown, a nickname describing a physical characteristic, their occupation; or only patronymics, similar to the use of prefixes like Mac (Scotland), or O' (Ireland), or suffixes like -son or -s (England), -ov (Russia), or -er (Germany), all meaning son or daughter of their father, as still used in Iceland today. The female equivalent, deriving your name from your mother's, is called metronymic. In 1787, the Austro-Hungarian Empire issued a decree requiring that all Jewish people must have surnames, when its Jews were given a restricted list to choose from; many, that linguists today categorise as 'Ornamental', were names incorporating minerals, mountains, animals, trees and flowers like 'Goldberg', 'Blumenthal' or 'Nüssbaum' (others were not so flattering.) The Prussian government quickly followed suit, and in July, 1808, Napoleon decreed the same in France; these governments felt that surnames were necessary with so many men were being conscripted in to their armies. Later, with a further diaspora of Jews in to America, they all had to go through the bureaucracy of getting official papers, when surnames were formalised, and sometimes anglicised.

Words of course change all the time, sometimes almost by chance (just as in the past 'a norange' became an orange, and 'a nuncle' became an uncle.) Also, new words come in to being. Recently, the lexicogaphers Collins requested help in selecting the one neologism that summed up the century just slipping away; and the winner by a long way was 'television'. It is a hybrid word, with all the vigour that implies, coined in 1904 from the Greek word 'tele' = faraway, and 'vision' from the Latin 'video', I see. This object can surely stand as a symbol for our times. It is the technology of our times at the end of the second millennium, about which even now there are further developments going on which will sweep us surely in to the third millennium, like flat screens that fill up a wall, interactive television, all-pervasive television screens used with computers, 'feely-tv', who knows what? Yet what is interesting is that the whole concept is named by two languages that were common in the time of Jesus Christ two thousand years ago, from which our own time is measured and whose millennium we are celebrating at this time.

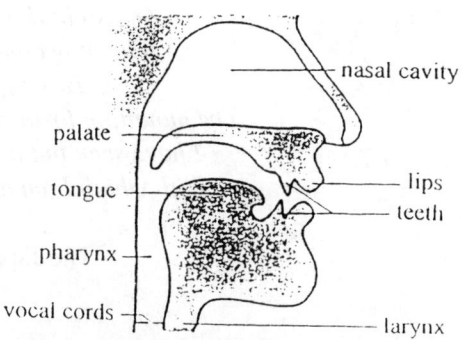

THE VOCAL ORGANS

*In the beginning was the Word, and the Word
was with God, and the Word was God,
The same was in the beginning with God. All things were made by Him;
and without Him was not anything made that was made.
In Him was life ; and the life was the light of men.
And the light shineth in darkness;and the darkness comprehended it not.*

St John's Gospel, I, 1-5

THE FATE OF THE BLOSSOM

*Though their hues are gay,
The blossoms flutter down.
And so in this world of ours,
Who may continue for ever?
Having today crossed
The mountain fastness of existence,
I have seen but a fleeting dream
With which I am not intoxicated.*

The Japanese 'I-ro-ha'

ODE

We are the music makers,
And we are the dreamers of dreams,
Wandering by lone sea-breakers,
And sitting by desolate streams; -
World-losers and world-forsakers,
On whom the pale moon gleams:
Yet we are the movers and shakers
Of the world for ever, it seems.

With wonderful deathless ditties
We build up the world's great cities,
And out of a fabulous story
We fashion an empire's glory:
One man with a dream, at pleasure,
Shall go forth and conquer a crown;
And three with a new song's measure
Can trample a kingdom down.

We, in the ages lying
In the buried past of the earth,
Built Nineveh with our sighing,
And Babel itself in our mirth;
And o'erthrew them with prophesying
To the old of the new world's worth;
For each age is a dream that is dying,
Or one that is coming to birth.

Arthur O'Shaughnessy (1844-1881)

THE FLOWER

Who would have thought my shrivelled heart
Could have recovered greeness? It was gone
Quite underground, as flowers depart
To feed their mother root when they have blown,
Where they together
All the hard weather,
Dead to the world keep house unknown.

These are thy wonders, Lord of Power,
Killing and quickening, bringing down to hell
And up to heaven in an hour;
Making a chiming of a passing bell.
And now in age I bud again,
After so many deaths I live and write;
I once more smell the dew and rain,
And relish versing: O, my only Light .....!

George Herbert (1593-1633)

WORDS, WORDS, WORDS

*What do I care what a word might mean
When the sound of it is mellifluous?
Give me a, piccolo, chough,
Or jackanape, brougham, oleaginous.*

*I relish the bosky, the crank and the eulogy
And other words polysyllabic
Heliotrope, catnap, hazel and pinch
Are sounds that are truly terrific.*

*Keep talking of magpies, of ponderous, whack,
Of dyspepsia, corkscrew, voluminous;
Genuflect, albatross, aquiline, crisp,
Give pleasure that is instantaneous.*

*Proper names linger, like Vlad the Impaler,
Blue Vinney, and Sharp's, Gridley Miskin
And Harley Davidson, Cockfosters, Hodge,
Paternoster, Vim, Katchaturian.*

*Lubricant, mountebank, doggerel, weft,
Happenstance, clang, serendipity -
Some people so dull they refuse to be charmed
By names (more's the pity.)*

*Tell me of belwether, chimpanzee, frump,
Huckaback, cockroach, funereal,
It's the pleasure of euphony, delighting in sound
Uniting the aural and ethereal.*

from RASSELAS

(The poet) must write as interpreter of nature, and the legislator of mankind, and consider himself as presiding over the thoughts and manners of future generations; as a being superior to time and place.

Dr Samuel Johnson (1709 – 1784)

WRITING TIPS FROM SUSAN HOWATCH, WRITER ON CHRISTIAN THEMES

- *Never give up.*
- *Keep writing even if it is only a little bit a day.*
- *When you have something on paper you can work on it.*
- *Do not get bogged down with research.*
- *Do not get diverted by other things.*
- *Do not take characters from real life unless they are dead*

QUATRAIN: POET

To clothe the fiery thought
In simple words succeeds,
For still the craft of genius is
To mask a king in weeds.

Ralph Waldo Emerson (1803 – 1882)

SONNET 106

When in the chronicle of wasted time
I see descriptions of the fairest wights,
And beauty making beautiful old rhyme
In praise of ladies dead, and lovely knights;
Then in the blazon of sweet beauty's best
Of hand, of foot, of lip, of eye, of brow,
I see their antique pen would have exprest
Ev'n such as beauty as you master now.
So all their praises are but prophecies
Of this our time, all, you prefiguring;
And for they look'd but with divining eyes,
They had not skill enough your worth to sing:
    For we, which now behold these present days,
    Have eyes to wonder, but lack tongues to praises.

William Shakespeare (1564 – 1616)

17TH CENTURY NUN'S PRAYER

Lord, Thou knowest better than I know myself that I am growing older and will someday be old. Keep me from the fatal habit of thinking I must say something on every subject and on every occasion. Release me from craving to straighten out everybody's affairs. Make me thoughtful but not moody: helpful but not bossy. With my vast store of wisdom, it seems a pity not to use it all, but Thou knowest Lord that I want a few friends at the end.

Keep my mind free from the recital of endless details; give me wings to get to the point.

Seal my lips on my aches and pains. They are increasing, and love of rehearsing them is becoming sweeter as the years go by. I dare not ask for grace enough to enjoy the tales of other's pains, but help me to endure them with patience.

I dare not ask for improved memory, but for a growing humility and a lessening cocksureness when my memory seems to clash with the memories of others. Teach me the glorious lesson that occasionally I may be mistaken.

Keep me reasonably sweet ; I do not want to be a Saint – some of them are so hard to live with – but a sour old person is one of the crowning works of the devil. Give me the ability to see good things in unexpected places, and talents in unexpected people. And, give me, O Lord, the grace to tell them so.

Amen.

The title of this prayer is traditional, the source is unknown.

NUNS DO NOT FRET

Nuns fret not at their convent's narrow room;
And hermits are contented with their cells;
And students with their pensive citadels;
Maids at the wheel, the weaver at his loom,
Sit blithe and happy; bees that soar for bloom,
High as the highest Peak of Furness-fells,
Will murmur by the hour in foxglove bells:
In truth the prison, unto which we doom
Ourselves, no prison is: and hence for me,
In sundry moods, 'twas pastime to be bound
Within the Sonnet's scanty plot of ground;
Pleased if some Souls (for such there needs must be)
Who have felt the weight of too much liberty,
Should find brief solace there, as I have found.

William Wordsworth (1770-1850)

RONDO A LA TURQUOISE

Thoughts flash jewel-like as kingfishers over stream,
Here - just seen - soon gone;
Did I see them? They gave no notice they would come,
No sooner seen than gone.

YOUR DAD DID WHAT?

Where they have been, if they have been away
or what they've done at home, if they have not,
you make them write about the holiday.
One writes 'My Dad did.' What? Your Dad did what?

That's not a sentence. Never mind the bell.
We stay behind until the work is done.
You count their words (you who can count and spell);
all the assignments are complete bar one

and, though this boy seems bright, that one is his.
He says he's finished, doesn't want to add
anything, hands it in just as it is.
No change: 'My Dad did.' What? What did his Dad?

You find the 'E' you gave him as you sort
through reams of what this girl did, what that lad did,
and read the line again, just one 'e' short:
'This holiday was horrible. My Dad did.'

Sophie Hannah ©

THE ROSE'S NAME

What's in a name? That which we call a rose
By any other name would smell as sweet ......

William Shakespeare, 'Romeo and Juliet', II,ii,43

THE QUEST FOR THE WORD, Elizabeth Drummond©

Whilst scribbling at some poetry
I saw the Perfect Word.
It brushed me for an instant, then
Flew from me like a bird.

I dropped my pen and hunted through
The by-ways of my mind,
A net all ready to ensnare
The beauty of my find.

It lurked in disused sheds and hid
To throw me off its trail.
I tripped on ancient memories
And missed its sparkling tail.

It flew in to my stately hall,
A chamber high and grand.
Amongst assembled conscious thoughts
It quickly slipped my hand.

It smashed a precious, fine idea
And made escape that way.
I asked them all where it would go,
But none of them could say.

I saw it fly through trailing clouds
Of varied visions bright,
Unwilling to give up my dreams
Of catching it that night.

I left the search; I could not trap
That shadow of a thought.
So I returned, and had forgot
The meaning I had sought.

from THE DESERTED VILLAGE

Beside yon straggling fence that skirts the way,
With blossom'd furze unprofitably gay,
There, in his noisy mansion, skill'd to rule,
The village master taught his little school;
A man severe he was, and stern to view;
I knew him well, and every truant knew;
Well had the boding tremblers learn'd to trace
The day's disasters in his morning face;
Full well they laugh'd, with counterfeited glee,
At all his jokes, for many a joke had he;
Full well the busy whisper, circling round,
Convey'd the dismal tidings when he frown'd;
Yet he was kind; or if severe in aught,
The love he bore to learning was in fault;
The village all declared how much he knew;
'Twas certain he could write, and cypher too;
Lands he could measure, terms and tides presage,
And even the story ran that he could gauge.
In arguing too, the parson own'd his skill,
For e'en though vanquish'd, he could argue still;
With words of learned length and thundering sound
Amaz'd the gazing rustics rang'd around,
And still they gaz'd, and still the wonder grew,
That one small head could carry all he knew.

Oliver Goldsmith (1730?-74)

MIDDLE AGE

Middle Age has balance, it can sort out dross from gold,
It does not rush to catch things new and cast aside the old,
It is like a sun-washed harbour where ships of every size
Bring home from life's rough sailing, good bales of enterprise.

Middle age is crowded with multi-coloured things,
Though it means a little folding of youth's bright, strident wings
It means deep understanding which moulds instead of breaks
And helps to bind up ugly wounds of other folks' mistakes.

Middle age is gracious, it's steady and it's kind,
It has learned through hard experience to be a trifle blind
When youth shouts out its challenge and brandishes its torch
For one day youth will also come to rest within its porch.

Anonymous

Shakespeare's SONNET 16

But wherefore do you not a mightier way
Make war upon this bloody tyrant, Time?
And fortify yourself in your decay
With means more blessed than my barren rhyme ?
Now stand you on the top of happy hours;
And many maiden gardens, yet unset,
With virtuous wish would bear your living flowers,
Much liker than your painted counterfeit:
So should the lines of life that life repair,
Which this, Time's pencil, or my pupil pen,
Neither in inward worth, nor outward fair,
Can make you live yourself in eyes of men.
To give away yourself keeps yourself still;
And you must live, drawn by your own sweet skill.

from ELEGY WRITTEN IN A COUNTRY CHURCHYARD

The Curfew tolls the knell of parting day,
The lowing herd winds slowly o'er the lea,
The plowman homeward plods his weary way,
And leaves the world to darkness and to me.

Let not ambition mock their useful toil,
Their homely joys, and destiny obscure;
Nor Grandeur hear with a disdainful smile
The short and simple annals of the poor.

Knowledge to their eyes her ample page
Rich with the spoils of time did ne'er unroll;
Chill penury repress'd their noble rage,
And froze the genial current of their soul.

Full many a gem of purest ray serene
The dark unfathom'd caves of ocean bear :
Full many a flower is born to blush unseen
And waste its sweetness on the desert air.

Some village Hampden that with dauntless breast
The little tyrant of his fields withstood,
Some mute inglorious Milton here may rest,
Some Cromwell guiltless of his country's blood.

Far from the madding crowd's ignoble strife
Their sober wishes never learned to stray;
Along the cool sequester'd vale of life
There kept the noiceless tenor of their way.

Thomas Gray (1716-1771)

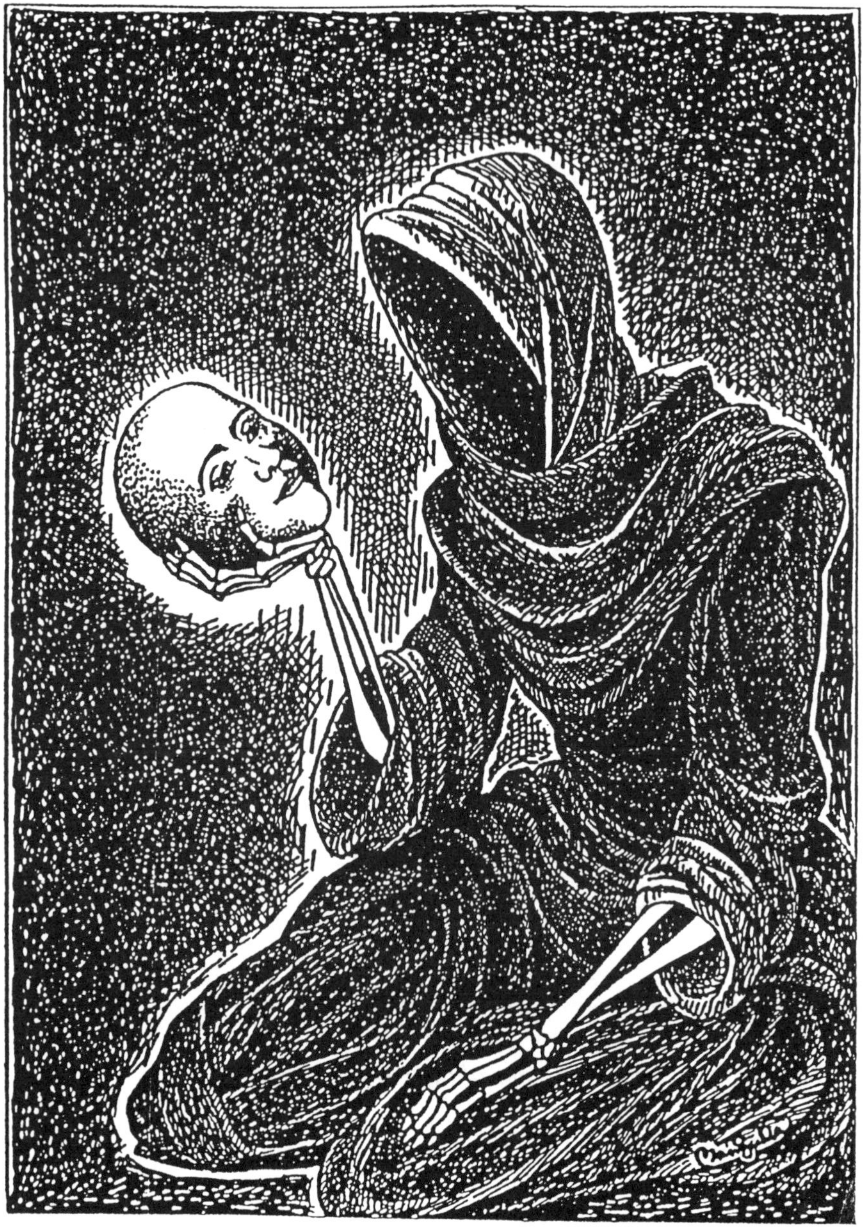

CHAPTER 3 : THE PHOENIX ALSO RISES

We assume that we plop into this world, fulfil our allotted span, and then shuffle off to infinity leaving behind only the memory of ourselves in the minds of those who loved us, and our genetic inheritance to our blood descendants. What is so bewitching about the mythical bird the phoenix is that it is here today, gone tomorrow, but back again the next day ..... Naturally its fabled powers of regeneration and self-renewal are unbelievable; but wouldn't we secretly like to believe that it truly is capable of hermaphroditic reproduction, endlessly cloning itself back in to youth again, and continuing for ever? Maybe we can think of it, like certain butterflies whose life-cycle relies on the burning of Wessex heathland, being reliant on the carbonisation of fire; or more likely needing the purifying atonement of white heat. We can see this as a particularly suitable icon for the millennium, partly because its lifetime is sometimes said to be half that time; but mainly because of its death-wish symbolising the millennial fin de siècle feeling, and its perpetual restoration indicating universal hope for the future.

The fables about it differ in detail, but all feature perpetual life through a cycle of self-immolation followed by reconstitution as before. What is interesting is that it is an eleological myth, that is one that attempts to explain the vagaries of the universe, and one that features in many cultures. In some countries, such as Egypt, it was more to do with the daily loss of the sun as night comes and its return next morning, like the Greek Apollo and Phaeton myth. Legend has it that its endless capacity for renewal was the reward for resisting certain temptations offered by Eve in the Garden of Eden, which has made it a symbol of steadfastness and loyalty. Best-known is the Arabian bird, truly unique and surpassingly beautiful, which lived for half a millennium on nothing but air, in a sacred wood; after which it would make a nest of spicy twigs, flap its wings to fan the flames, sing a melodious dirge, be reduced to a pile of ashes, and then experience re-birth not as an egg but as a worm that became the bird. Sometimes it is described as a huge bird, half-eagle, half-pheasant; the word 'phoenix' comes from the Greek word 'phoinos' meaning blood red or purpley-red (the sea-faring

Phoenicians were 'red Syrians'), and many early descriptions say that it is reddish purple in colour with a golden ruff around its neck. In alchemy, the phoenix corresponded to the colour red, and the mark of successful completion of a process, steadfast to the end; and because of the connection, it was sometimes adopted as a sign over chemists' shops.

The Greek historian Herodotus mentioned the bird in 459 B.C. after visiting Egypt. While confessing that he had never seen it and did not believe it, he did go in to some detail. He said that the locals believed that when it died in its Arabian homeland, the newly-fledged bird carried the dead parent in a ball of myrrh to the temple of the Sun in Egypt. The British Museum has a wonderful papyrus roll of a 'Book of the Dead' showing a phoenix with a heron, which was found in the tomb of Nakht, a Royal courtier of the 18th Dynasty (approximately 1300 years before Christ.) It was mentioned by two Roman historians a century or so after Christ, Pliny (who thought it lived for a thousand years), and Tacitus, who in his famous *Annals* mentioned it appearing four times in Egypt. In medieval times, it featured in many 'bestiaries', which were books with stories and illustrations which depicted real and mythical animals, such as the dragon, the unicorn, and the phoenix, which often provided a moral, sometimes specifically Christian. The beasts were taken from a fascinating collection of such stories assembled in second-century Greece called the Physiologus, which in the middle ages was being translated in to French, Italian and English. The Swiss physician Paracelsus mentioned it in the sixteenth century. In 1593 an anthology appeared in England entitled *The Phoenix Nest*, opening with three eulogies for the poet Sir Philip Sidney, the 'phoenix' of the title; Shakespeare wrote his poem *The Phoenix and the Turtle* at this time, the turtle being a turtle dove.

The phoenix appears in many cultures. It is found in Central America; in Turkey where it is called the 'Kerkes'; in the area then known as Persia lived its near-cousin the 'Senmurv' (a cross between a bird and a dog); Egypt, as well as the visiting Arabian bird, had its own version in the heron-like 'Bennu' or 'Bird of the Sun'; in India and other parts of the East they had their own versions. In China, there was the Fêng Hwang or vermilion bird (also known in Japan as the Ho-o bird), which came in two varieties, but only because the Fêng was 'yang', masculine and fiery, the Hwang was 'yin', feminine and gentle; only one was seen at a time. Its appearance was always a sign of peace and humanitarian rule. Whatever the country, whatever the lifespan (and commentators have suggested between 250 and 7,000 years), the common factors were a bird of fable which at that place and moment was totally unique, which was gorgeously-arrayed, and which departed life through fire only to rise again.

There are obvious echoes in its story of the divine Second Coming of the Messiah and of Jesus' sacrifice and resurrection. From Old Testament times, fire is seen as atoning and cathartic, leading on to renewal. In Isaiah, a live coal is applied to the prophet's lips by a seraph, who declares :
> *Behold, this has touched your lips; your iniquity is taken away, and your sin purged.*

In Ezekiel, God appeared to the prophet Moses through the burning bush, which was not itself consumed by the fire. In St Luke's Gospel, John the Baptist says : *One mightier than I is coming ..... He will baptise you with the Holy Spirit and with fire;* and subsequently, in the Second Letter of Peter, when the end of the world is being discussed, the author says:
> *..... the coming of the day of God, because of which the heavens will be dissolved being on fire, and the elements will melt with fervent heat ..... look for new heavens and a new earth.*

With this emphasis on fire being a necessary evil, a 'sine qua non' without which the new order cannot come, Christianity was able to embrace - as it did with many ideas from earlier religions - the phoenix as a suitable symbol for Christ's death and return, and thereby our hopes for resurrection too. From St Clement of Rome in his letters to the new churches, and Tertullian (in *De Res Carnis*) onwards, Christian writers have frequently regarded it as an image of the Resurrection. It has appeared in the art of Christianity from Constantinian times, for instance in Roman churches dedicated to St Cosmas Damian, Praxedes and St Cecilia, and the famous floor mosaic of the Christian Phoenix at Daphne, in Greece. In the fourth century A.D. a descriptive poem by a Christian apologist called Lactantius entitled *Carmen de ave phoenice* appeared, which went in to some detail about the religious significance of the phoenix, and enjoyed wide popularity (Lactantius was tutor to the son of Constantine, the Emperor who ensured that the Roman world embraced Christianity.) That poem may well have influenced a tenth-century Anglo-Saxon 'beast allegory' of 677 lines called *The Phoenix* contained in the Exeter Book, at one time attributed to Cynewulf, which uses vivid imagery to moral effect.

The phoenix might mark the replacement of something removed by fire; but surely it is tempting Fate, and may yet become a self-fulfilling prophecy? That, sadly, is what happened in January 1996 to the great opera house in Venice called La Fenice, Italian for phoenix. It was given that name in 1792 when Antonio Selvas built it as a replacement for an earlier building on the site; then another fire gutted it in 1836, when it was re-built by Tranquillo Orsi. Plans are well afoot for it to re-open in glory in November 1999 constructed 'com'era e dov'era', as and where it was.

Thus we come to the end of our curriculum vitae of the phoenix, who departs with a blaze of glory only to rise triumphant from the ashes. What could be a better symbol of our transition from one millennium to another? In the frontispiece poem I have given it the supporting logo of a sunflower. That was a flower beloved by the fin de siècle dandies of the 1890s; and reproductions of the jug-full of them painted at that time by Van Gogh are still seen in many a modern house, while the real thing often sprouts cheerfully in suburban gardens. It is a large, confident flower, which though it dies in the Autumn, renews itself every year; it is yellow, it is bold, it seems to worship the sun as it follows it across the heavens. It produces healthy salad oil, its seeds are crunchy and delicious in bread, it is useful but it is fun, and it is a very *modern* flower. With the phoenix and the sunflower, we have twin symbols for the millennium.

SUNFLOWER

The sunflower moves with time,
elegantly following the sun,
with its broad yellow face
stalking it from east to west.

From the beginning of its life
to its life's end, the sunflower
always stays with the sun:
never going ahead of it, never falling behind.

You could never separate
the sunflower from the sun,
for they are like Siamese twins;
but if you did, it would die.

It wakes in the morning
tall and proud; and at sunset
when the sky turns black,
the sunflower stoops to the ground.

Ben Carne ©

from VANITY FAIR

There are garden-ornaments, as big
as brass warming pans, that are fit
to stare the sun itself out of countenance.
Miss Amelia Sedley was not
of the sunflower sort.

William Makepeace Thackeray (1811-1863)

The normal phoenix legend is fairly well known. However, among the Al Maruf Saar, a rather bad-tempered tribe of Bedouin who live in the upper Hadramaut, there is a story that on occasion after the normal immolation and resurrection TWO Phoenix, twins, rose from the flames. One was a normal magical and pretty tough chap, but the other was a complete poltroon and took off at high speed in a south westerly direction with his tail feathers on fire and yelling 'Miskeen, Miskeen', which can be translated as 'Cor - I am sore afflicted!' He disappeared in to the Empty Quarter; but is believed to be the ancestor of the 'Murgi', which is the inevitable offering at all travellers' bungalows and caravan sarais in the Near and Middle East. It has muscles like wire, and is always overcooked.

David Barry-Jackson

PHANTASUS

Rote Rosen
winden sich und meine düstre Lanze.
Durch weisse Lilienwälder
scnaubt mein Hengst.

Aus grünen Seen.
Schilf im Haar,
tauchen schlanke, schleierlose Jungfraun.

Ich reite wie aus Erz.

Immer,
dicht vor mir,
fliegt der Vogel Phönix
und singt.

Red roses
are winding around my gloomy lance.
My stallion is breathing through
woods of white lilies.

From green lakes,
slender virgins with reeds in their hair
emerge unveiled.

I ride as if I were bronze.

As always,
the Phoenix bird
is flying right in front of me
and singing.

Arno Holz (1899)
 translated by Friederike Eggers

This female bird, larger than an eagle,
Part of an ancient myth of Greece,
Lived exactly five hundred years,
And then to the fire returned.
A new Phoenix rose from the one that had died,
Its beauty renewed by the dancing flames.
Feathers coloured by the flames,
It flew to its mythical home.
The bird had huge red talons,
The head was raised in pride,
The eyes all-seeing, sharp as a knife,
The body sleekly-dolphin smooth.
This bird was believed to represent the sun,
By the Christians and by Greeks.
Now, after a couple of thousand years,
Renowned as bird resurrecting from fire.

Sagar Kothari ©

The Christian Phoenix, from a floor mosaic at Daphne in Greece.

SUNFLOWER

The seed landed on the rich fertile ground,
The stem rose out of the soil,
The sunflower grew higher until its head stretched out.
It swayed from East to West, catching the most light possible,
Lifting its head to wake up and lowering it to sleep.
Other flowers grew and flourished,
So that after about a year there was a huge field,
Each one lifting up in the morning and lowering in the evening.
Though in winter, these sunflowers die of cold;
Yet in other times, the seeds of these sunflowers will grow again.

John Carter ©

A CREATURE OF LEGEND

Of what am I writing? It is not a pixie,
Nor hobgoblin, gryphon, nor elf -
It's known to us all on the earth as the phoenix; she
Lays but one egg on a shelf.
This surely's a talent exceptionally tricksy,
This creature gives birth to herself.

THE SHULAMITE TO HER BELOVED

Set me as a seal upon your heart, as a seal upon your arm;
For love is as strong as death, jealousy as cruel as the grave;
Its flames are flames of fire, a most vehement flame.
Many waters cannot quench love, nor can the floods drown it.

from The Song of Solomon.

Phoenix's our spirit, our life-force, our soul,
    It rewrites us with love, it makes us feel whole;
For, when we're in misery, dark, desolation,
    A Divine Hand, whom you may have forsaken
(Ruler of Death, and of Life and Creation)
    Will despatch the phoenix to be your salvation.
From ashes it rises, new life from the womb,
    Re-incarnated, like Jesus escaping the tomb.

Phoenix supreme, almighty, forever,
    Your soul and hers are bonded together.
Its shadow so fiery, its power so great,
    That out in the galaxy, phoenix will wait,
She will await you until your last breath.
    Imbued with the aura of life after death.,
Our end will come down (whatever you've heard)
    Down to the phoenix, to th'immortal bird.

Terence O'Sullivan ©

A mythical, mystical and magical bird of fire, from the dire
Arabian desert dunes; which no creature is said to survive -
except for the mythical, mystical and magical bird of fire.
It lives for hundreds of years, then burns upon a funeral pyre, and rises
from its ashes. Living again, the cycle continues, repeating, repeating -
O mythical, mystical and magical bird of fire.

Mark Stent ©

KING HENRY VIII'S BLESSING ON HIS DAUGHTER
ELIZABETH, AND HER SUCCESSOR.

Nor shall this peace sleep with her; but as when
The bird of wonder dies, the maiden phoenix,
Her ashes new create another heir
As great admiration as herself,
So shall she leave her blessedness to one -
When heaven shall call her from this cloud of darkness -
Who from the sacred ashes of her honour
Shall star-like rise, as great in fame as she was,
And so stand fix'd. Peace, plenty, love, truth , terror,
That were servants to this chosen infant,
Shall then be his.

William Shakespeare, 'The Famous
History Of The Life Of
King Henry VIII', Act V, Sc. v.

THE LIFE-CYCLE OF THE PHOENIX BIRD

The innocent, golden egg lay there in peace.
This small life form had no fear,
It was there, in its shelled house, for many millennia,
Unconscious of terrible wars,
And victorious moments of history.

The egg began to move.
It then rolled frantically around,
The life form trying to free itself from its natural prison.
It then came to rest upon its base,
And a small crack seemed to creep upwards,
Which preceded a flash
Of blinding white light.
A column of flame rose into the air,
Brighter than light itself.
Cutting away from the egg,
The sides became jagged
And feathery,
And the phoenix formed.

When it had cooled,
The phoenix cried and flew around,
To show its full magical abilities.
Wherever the phoenix flew,
It was followed by golden glitter from the heavens.
As the phoenix came to rest,
An era of peace started.

The hands of time passed through
Centuries of the phoenix's influence;
So while evil danced in shadow,
The good of mankind prevailed to the end.

Alex Morley ©

from THE CANONIZATION

Call us what you will, wee are made such by love;
Call her one, mee another flye,
We are Tapers too, and at our owne cost die,
And we in us finde the Eagle and the Dove.
The Phoenix ridle hath more wit
By us, we two being one, are it.
So, to one neutrall thing both sexes fit,
We dye and rise the same, and prove
Mysterious by this love.

John Donne (1572–1631)
(The final five lines of this were inscribed on a cigarette
 case given by Lord Alfred Douglas to Oscar Wilde.)

> *The phoenix is a blazing bird,*
> *A fire ball wrapped in feathers.*
> *It is a reincarnated soul*
> *We see glide through the ether.*
>
> *With scaly skin like dragon,*
> *Its claws as rough as bark;*
> *Its eyes are glowing rubies,*
> *Its feathers smooth as ice.*
>
> *The phoenix is a blazing bird,*
> *With wings that glint and sparkle,*
> *It thunders through the calm of night*
> *With tail a-trailing fire.*

Tejus Patel ©

SONG OF LIFE

I am the waking caress of feathered song,
Heralding new life returned in the fresh of today,
I am granite torn from the crucifix of earth's womb,
Rent from the silence of a million years,
I am the healing energies of ancient oaks,
Grown for me, and earthed for you.
I am the magpie's last goodbye ..... Invisible tears saluting
Feather and blood consumed by asphalt's speeding war,
I am the akashic record of the minutiae of life and death,
Holy weave within the turn of life's rebirth.

I am dull, I am dazzling, I am young, I am old,
I am every love kissed, and every heart scorned,
I am pain transmuted into love, into joy,
Layered through life into dimensions unseen,
I am heaven, I am hell, carried in you, carried in me,
The arc of my wings encompassing more than this turn.
I am a message beyond bible, church or creed,
Beyond now, will be, was, and ever is,
Beyond group soul's observations inside out,
Hand forged in eternity's revolving circle of joy.

I am the pendulum of life,
Uncentred, yet centred in the still of deep gold,
Eternity's clock, running in, running out,
Virgin and open in the third of each heart,
Beyond the song of that chamber or its verse.

I am earth, wind, moon, distant fire in the stars,
I am the death of everything that grows,
And the birth of everything that repeatedly dies

Ivan Sanders ©

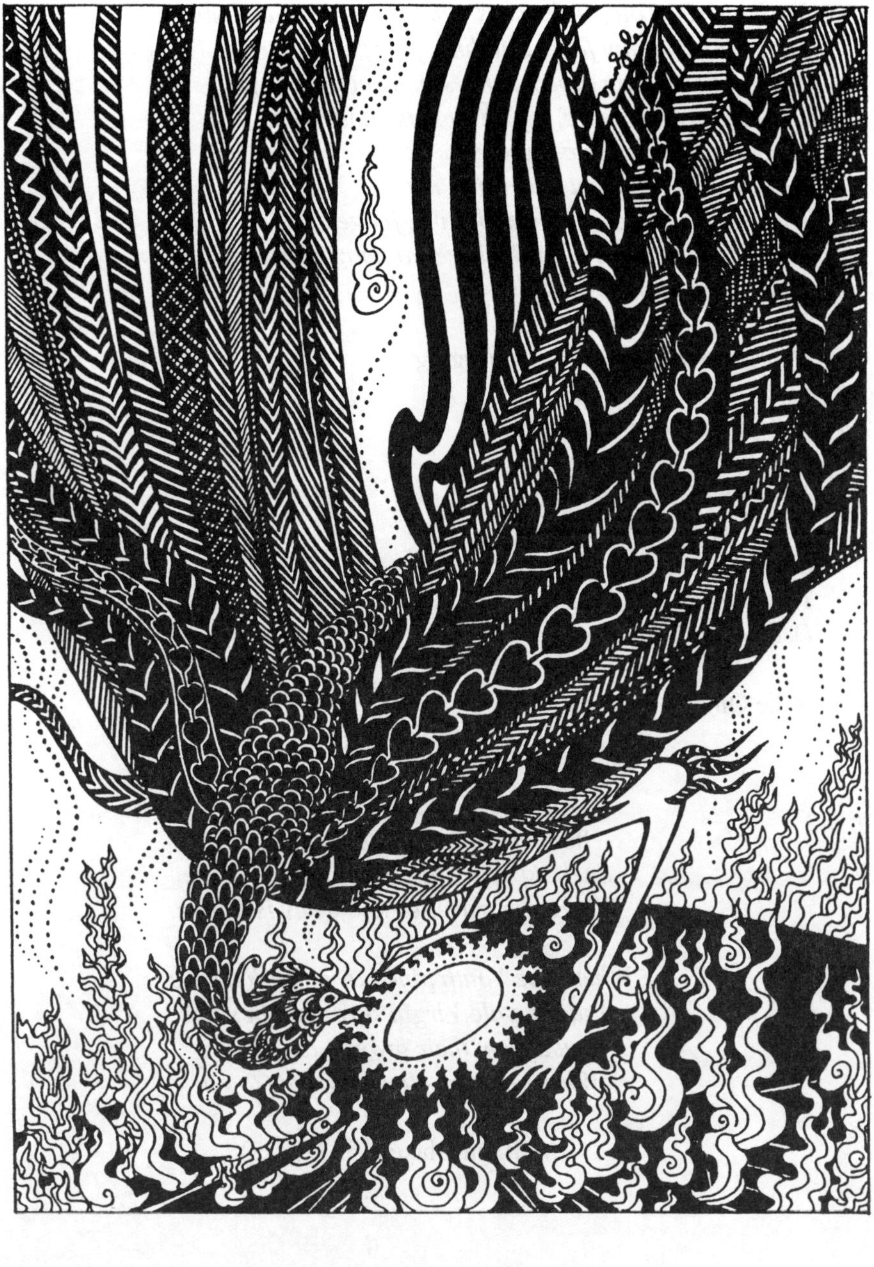

THE PHOENIX

My body rises out of the seas and mists that claimed me,
Light shines in my face, blinding, pain;
A blur of swishing blood dances in front of my eyes,
They close once more, my chest sinks and stills.
Shadows flurry round my shell.
Darkness fades, light envelopes me.
The Phoenix faces me, watches me, judges me,
The cold eyes burn in to the tattered images of my soul.
Time stops, worlds cease.
Me and the Phoenix, together
Hearts no longer beating, merging,
I step forward, feel no fear.
The wings close over me.
Joy shoots across the sky,
I'm with the Phoenix ,she and I.
People cry, people mourn,
Earth is a waiting ground.
The real joy is to come.....
Death is still unfound.

Jodie Omega Portugal ©

Ah, Sun-flower! Weary of time,
Who countest the steps of the Sun,
Seeking after that sweet golden clime
Where the traveller's journey is done :

Where the Youth pined away with desire,
And the pale Virgin shrouded in snow
Arise from their graves, and aspire
Where my Sun-flower wishes to go.

William Blake (1757-1827)

THE PHOENIX AND TURTLE

Let the bird of loudest lay,
On the sole Arabian tree,
Herald sad and trumpet be,
To whose sound chaste wings obey.

But thou shrieking harbinger,
Foul precursor of the fiend,
Augur of the fever's end,
To this troop come thou not near!

From this session interdict
Every fowl of tyrant wing,
Save the eagle, feather'd king;
Keep the obsequy so strict.

Let the priest in surplice white,
That defunctive music can,
Be the death-defying swan,
Lest the requiem lack his right.

And thou treble-dated crow,
That the sable gender makest
With the breath thou givest and takest,
'Mongst our mourners shalt go.

Here th'anthem doth commence
Love and constancy is dead;
Phoenix and the turtle fled
In a mutual flame from hence.

So they loved, as love in twain
Had the essence but in one;
Two distincts, division none:
Number there in love was slain.

Hearts remote, yet not asunder;
Distance, and no space was seen
'Twixt the turtle and his queen:
But in them it were a wonder.

So between them love did shine,
That the turtle saw his right
Flaming in the phoenix's sight;
Either was the other's mine.

Property was thus appalled
That the self was not the same;
Single nature's double name
Neither two nor one was called.

Reason, in itself confounded,
Saw division grow together,
To themselves yet either neither,
Simple were well compounded;

That it cried, How true a twain
Seemeth this concordant one!
Love hath reason, reason none,
If what parts can so remain.

Whereupon it made this threne
To the phoenix and the dove,
Co-supremes and stars of love,
As chorus to their tragic scene.

THRENOS

Beauty, truth, and rarity,
Grace in all simplicity,
Here enclosed in cinders lie.

Death is now the phoenix' nest;
And the turtle's loyal breast
To eternity doth rest,

Leaving no posterity:
'Twas not their infirmity,
It was married chastity.

Truth may seem, but cannot be;
Beauty brag, but 'tis not she;
Truth and beauty buried be.

To this urn let those repair
That are either true or fair;
For these dead birds sigh a prayer.

William Shakespeare (1564-1616)

CHAPTER 4 : NEW MILLENNIUM'S EVE

So, after a thousand years of waiting, a hundred years of speculation, a decade of planning, a year of mounting excitement, we reach the last day of 1999, and prepare to enter the new millennium. The arguments about whether this *is* the right date seem futile, we have agreed that it is fairly arbitrary in terms of chronological accuracy and we unite to celebrate, come what may. Indeed, if it crosses the mind, it is only to encourage continued revelry up to and beyond the next new year; now it is time, with the incurable optimism of humanity, to make whoopee and rejoice. Even followers of pagan ritual, who will have already celebrated their new year called Samhain on October 31st, may join their fellow humans. Amid the stresses and strains of the quotidian, we all need excuses to be frivolous and enjoy ourselves. Surely the satisfactory nature of the rounded 2000, which will come round as we celebrate this particular night, seems a symmetrical and comfortable start to the freshly minted century?

Maybe your idea of marking the new year most years, as it apparently is for eighty per cent of the population, is sharing a quiet evening with family and friends, or a cosy tête-à-tête with your partner, finishing off the Christmas mince pies and ginger wine and watching pseudo-Scottish dancing on television, as the minutes count down. But surely this is the year to let your hair down, your champagne corks shoot up, and bonhomie flow? This really is the Big One, the New Year's Eve to tell your grandchildren about, and to do something specially memorable. This is the rite of passage of the old millennium in to the new; and, as with each new year, it brings the renewal of hope, and the hope of renewal. It is goodbye, old millennium, and hello to the tomorrow of the new. Let your first resolution be - to enjoy!

So how will the New Year be celebrated? Your idea of bliss might be the most crowded disco, the most elegant of soirées, the most garish of fireworks, laser lights, neon flashes, electric colours or the most daring of entertainments. You could be in a hideously expensive but riotously successful outfit which everyone admires, fresh and relaxed.

What special foods could there be: a great steak, the latest in ethnic foods, the lushest of imported vegetables, the lightest of airy desserts? To accompany it must surely be the champagne you laid down some time ago for this unique occasion, a golden wisp of bubbles and excitement - and despite some earlier hype, there will be enough champagne to go round. Music to fire the heart or curdle the brain; and an unidentifiable savour of excitement. Above all, the ideal way to celebrate will be with the companions you have chosen: it is the fellow-revellers who will reinforce and increase your own enjoyment. Too often on New Year's Eves in the past, the best parties have always been elsewhere: but this time, wherever you are, is the place to be! As Horace urges in his famous Ode :

Carpe diem, quam minimum credula postero.
Grasp with both hands what today has to offer,
and give no thought to the morrow.

It is a Friday night, a four-day weekend with both Friday and Monday being declared Bank Holidays, so there's no need to worry about the office in the morning: indeed, you can carry on celebrating all weekend, as long as the fizzy stomach remedies last ..... That means you can celebrate with the light of your life; with the office gang; with the old schoolfriends; *and* with the family. (Don't forget to get out lots of cash in advance for all the drinks-buying, of course; the cash dispensers may be affected by the millennium bug.)That weekend you might choose, as a group of children in Harmondsworth long ago vowed, to turn the television off (also recommended by the politician John Butcher, who suggested that television and radio be switched off for five days, one for each thousand of the 5,000 known years of civilisation in Britain); or you might weaken and see the specially-taped edition of 'Only Fools and Horses'. You might be inspired by the church bells, mentioned in a later chapter, to go to church again; or to try a sortie on a newly-restored walk way, cycle path or canal. You could be involved in lighting, viewing and cheering a series of beacons throughout the countryside. You might make this a time of bumper New Year's Resolutions, and try to ensure that this year they really will last longer than January 5th: indeed, you might resolve really to change your life for the better, prioritising your life and setting some achievable goals to better the situation of yourself, your partner, your family, your friends and your fellow-men.

Many people will have decided to celebrate with a visit to somewhere really different, or a place loved before but which is putting on a special show this date. Others will splash their savings on what will truly be a trip of a lifetime to somewhere exotic. Let's look at a few of the options now.

You could be at the Grand Launch party of the Millennial Festival and at the Millennium Dome Plaza in Greenwich, which we will visit in more detail in a later chapter. You could be a short distance south at the National Maritime Museum, home of time, at the Greenwich 2000 Party in Greenwich Park for 50,000 guests including some very famous ones such as Brian Cobby, voice of the Speaking Clock, who will provide the countdown (also to be transmitted by the BBC from there.) It will also beam a laser round the world to end up back at the Dome nearby. There will be a sit-down dinner for 18,000 people, organised by the London Millennium Party Company, at Woolwich Royal Arsenal Barracks. The traditional London site of Trafalgar Square will be open as usual, heavily policed; and there will be a street party with fireworks at the Pool of London, stretching from Tower Bridge to London Bridge. It is still unsure whether the novelist Jeffrey Archer will be hosting his traditional shepherd's-pie and champagne party. Many hotels will have been booked for years: the Savoy chose its lucky guests by ballot; outside the Dorchester there will be the four giant numbers '2000' sculpted in ice. The Ritz sold out of Millennium overnighters at £2,000 a head some while ago.

Special parties will also be going on at famous London Clubs like Naval and Military (the 'In and Out', recently moved from Piccadilly to St James's Square), whose party is being hosted by John Stanley. The Royal Albert Hall, recipient of £40 million from the Lottery, has been booked out for a quarter of a century; there will then be a week of the best productions selected from village halls across the country. Wembley and Tower Bridge are two more likely venues. On Uxbridge Common in West London, the residents are planning a party in a marquee. There will be parties in major cities, such as at Bristol Docks or in Birmingham's

Centenary Square; with Manchester's being graced by the arrival home on cue of Robert Garside after his jog around the world. The Tower Ballroom at Blackpool is hosting a great extravaganza. Some pubs especially in metropolitan areas will be open for 24 hours a day from Christmas 1999 until New Year's Day 2000.

Many country house hotels will be laying on special events: the Redworth Hall Hotel in Co. Durham has set its price at (surprise, surprise) £999.99. Join 400 people at the Elizabeth Castle on a peninsula of St Helier, Jersey; the tide will have come and surrounded it by midnight. You could have hired some of the more exotic Landmark Trust properties (follies, lighthouses, Lundy Island); or Hatton Castle in Aberdeenshire, Scotland, which would cost you £55,000. The Lamb family from London have hired the fourteenth century Duns Castle in the Borders, a marvellous place usually only for hire from the Hay family who have lived there for three hundred years, for film shoots like 'Mrs Brown' or for exclusive weddings.

One suggestion for entertainment to celebrate this new year of all new years, could be by taking part in or watching the olden-time mummers' plays, with which our ancestors celebrated mid-winter festivals. Locals with masks or blackened faces, exotic costumes and wooden swords would turn up at the manor-house or farm-house and act out traditional scenes, passed on by word of mouth over generations. It would often be preceded by a prologue and some sword-dancing; and be concluded by the throwing of dice to decide on the distribution of small gifts. Later, by the eighteenth century, the format became more formalised and pegged to Christmas by the introduction of carols, but retaining the champion (often St George or Robin Hood) who might be slain but then brought to life again by the doctor figure. Other characters would be a vaguely Middle Eastern villain, relic of the Crusades, and sometimes male and female clowns called Tommy and Bessy. Having echoes of pagan rituals, the miracle plays, even *commedia dell'arte*, nonetheless it was essentially a pageant of the working people of the countryside, and had interesting regional variations. The climax of the sword-dance was apparently the locking of swords in a complex pattern (as still seen in some morris dancing displays) to celebrate the death of the old year; after which, the swords' withdrawal was said to symbolise the coming of a new year.

Rather than such a very English entertainment, you could be in Edinburgh, maybe approaching and leaving the city on the newly-restored 'Flying Scot' steam train, which will be re-tracing its forty years of journeys to connect the two capitals. The Scottish capital has a marvellous annual bash, already said to be the biggest in the world with over 300,000 people each year, and it will expand to flow through the whole city centre; a high point could well be the lift-off of sponsor Richard Branson in his airship 'Millennia' from Edinburgh Castle before it then cruises around the world to the Sydney Olympics, that is, if he has not retired with his family to their Caribbean island of Necker for that period. Glasgow is also having a big party; and is also the home of the YES 2000 (Youth and Environmental Support for the Year 2000) project, part supported by UNESCO, which is organising televised fund-raising parties. Many Scots people, who for historical reasons celebrate New Year more than Christmas, will be welcoming in Hogmanay (a Scottish word similar in meaning to the Old French word 'aguillanneuf') as they do every year, giving gifts of cake to children, and welcoming a dark man across the threshold, a 'first footer', bearing a lump of coal. This coal was to hope that you never ran out of fuel in the year to come - but often now the action is carried out by someone who is well-fuelled in another sense. What is also traditional is the singing in a circle, with arms crossed to grip your similarly knotted-up neighbours, of Rabbie Burns' 'For Auld Lang Syne', as a remembrance of times gone by.

In Wales, the singing of carols in times past was not associated with Christmas as in England, but more with New Year. During New Year's Eve, men would go round the villages singing 'nòs Galan', and people would throw money down to them from their windows, and maybe give refreshment; on New Year's Day (but only until midday) children would go out warbling and be rewarded with 'calennig', that is, some small change. This special new year, there will be the Rugby World Cup Round Off Extravaganza in Cardiff. In Ireland, the lubricating of the nation's throats (worn out by all that blarneying) with their liquid black velvet has always been a national tradition to welcome the new year; maybe going out in the streets as midnight comes to embrace fellow revellers. In Belfast, there will be the Odyssey Complex to admire; later in the year a thousand youngsters are going to be raising a monolith quarried in the Mourne Mountains, the Strangford Stone, in County Down. In Eire on New Year's Day, they used to sing a song entitled 'The King of the Wrens'; Dublin's Liffey Millennium Countdown Clock did not last long, as it got obscured by mud and algae, but the river will have a new pedestrian bridge and lighting. Preparations will be being made for March 17th, when people of Irish descent from all over the world will trek along Pilgrim Paths around the country.

Later, we will be looking at how people will be celebrating overseas, and especially how some jetsetters will be 'chasing the sun' to be the first to catch the sunrise of the millennium. However, purists will tell you that the same Meridian Conference decreed that the day does not start world-wide until it was the dark hour of midnight at Greenwich. When it turns midnight at Greenwich on January 1st, the Pacific will actually have already reached noon; so where will the rising of the sun be at that very moment? Apparently, at the time of 12 midnight here, the sun will be coming over the horizon of the hardly inhabited Nicobar Islands.

A few hours later, you could be chasing the sunrise in Britain. Great disappointment was evinced by the East Anglian town of Lowestoft, which had been marketing itself as the most easterly town in England and were arranging lots of New Millennium revelry, when it was discovered that actually, because of the tilt of the earth in winter, first dawn would break at 7.58 a.m. at South Foreland, east of Dover; then a minute later in Dover, Ramsgate, Folkestone and Dungeness. Not until 8.04 will the sun (weather permitting) rise in Lowestoft.

There is one big drawback to many of the planned New Year's Eve events, and that is that they involve some element of service from other people; and yet those people themselves have a right to celebrate at the party of all parties with their families. If you are in a hotel, there will be reception staff, waiters, chefs, chambermaids; if you are flying off, there will be technicians working behind scene, ticket office staff, air stewardesses, and captains; if you are in Trafalgar Square, there will be traffic wardens, hot-dog vendors and first aid staff. Already by early 1998, police in forces like the Metropolitan, and the Devon and Cornwall, were warned of the need to be on duty. The Kent police called it 'the Millennium Emergency'; the Derbyshire police said 'It will be a stressful time, not just because of the extensive partying but because of all the other potential problems such as computer breakdowns. We are anticipating potential chaos, with traffic lights and street lights going wrong, so we need to be sure we have enough people to cope.' Many supermarkets, e.g. Waitrose with its 100-plus stores, are to be closed on Saturday, January 1st, 2000.

Godfrey Smith, in his Sunday Times column in early 1998, declared that he would like television to broadcast this night 'an all-night programme of films that together encapsulate best the terrible and marvellous century we shall have just bid adieu. It should celebrate each of those titanic breakthroughs that were the twentieth century's curse and blessing: the coming of the car, radio and records, penicillin and the pill, jazz and jets, computers and cassettes, television and the film.' He also said that he doubted whether he would be going to all the hyped-up events that had been talked of : *I'll keep my junketing money in my pocket; and so, I suspect, will you.*

Some more exotic Millennium Party choices can be found on *www.jepa.co.uk/shopping/party*; but there will also be those like my Jamaican friend Jennifer Williams who said: *I love having a moment to myself just before the New Year to pray and give God thanks for every thing, and to say a special prayer for the New Year.*

Probably those amongst you who are enjoying yourselves most, are those who planned ahead about *where* you want to celebrate, *how* you want to do it, and above all *with whom*. Thereafter, just go with the flow!

DARE WE CELEBRATE?

*Another year has come
And the last has passed us by;
Twelve months seemed an awful long time,
But somehow they just flew by.*

*Last year was bad in part,
But it can't get any worse.
The New Year brings joy and happiness for most -
But to others, at what cost?*

*Turn our minds to the positive,
Concentrate on the good to come;
So people sing and dance with joy
As the New Year comes.*

Misba Khan ©

A TRADITIONAL JEWISH NEW YEAR PRAYER.

At the beginning of a new year, O God, I want to open my innermost self to those deeper thoughts and feelings which I often shut off from my mind and heart, in my preoccupation with worldly pursuits. Grant me real responsiveness to your spirit, so that I may consecrate my mood of the moment by sentiments which outlast the moment.

Now let me learn lessons from the past, before the old year is gone. Help me put past experiences in their true perspective. Let me see how more numerous were my blessings than my privations, how my losses, trials and sorrows contained the seeds of higher good, how needlessly I fretted over things which at the time seemed all-important, and now seem small and insignificant. Let no self-deception hide my sins and shortcomings from me, the neglected opportunities, misspent time, gifts and abilities perverted to lower purposes against my own better judgement. Grant that like Jacob, wrestling with an adversary in the dark, I may not let the departing year go, until I have wrested blessing from its trials.

And now, by your grace, may I turn into blessings the endless possibilities of the new year which stretches out before me in solemn mystery. Let its message of time and eternity remind me of the uncertainty of human life and the passing of all earthly things. But let me not live in fear of death. You will be with me wherever I go. Relying on your wisdom and loving generosity, let me face the future with courage and hope.

We are strangers to the year ahead. We need your light to lead us. Guide us in the safe way. Bless our home, and our relationships, keep and protect our affections, strengthen our loyalties, and increase our powers of helpfulness. Inscribe me, I pray, in the Book of Life, help me to understand that life is measured more in terms of character and service than in length of days.

May the beauty of the Lord rest upon us. Establish the work of our hands - the work of our hands, establish it, Lord. Amen.

from BY THE CENTURY'S DEATHBED

I leant upon a coppice gate
When Frost was spectre-grey,
And Winter's dregs made desolate
The weakening eye of day.
The land's sharp features seemed to be
The Century's corpse outleant,
His crypt the cloudy canopy,
The wind his death-lament.
The ancient pulse of germ and birth
Was shrunken hard and dry,
And every spirit upon earth
Seemed fervourless as I.

At once a voice arose among
The bleak twigs overhead
In a full-hearted evensong
Of joy illimited;
An aged thrush, frail, gaunt, and small,
In blast-beruffled plume,
Had chosen thus to fling his soul
Upon the growing gloom.
I could think there trembled through
His happy good-night air
Some blessed Hope, whereof he knew
And I was unaware.

Thomas Hardy (1840-1928)
Hardy dated this December 31st, 1900; it is
sometimes known as **THE DARKLING THRUSH**.

HATS OFF FOR THE MILLENNIUM

The Millennium, a time to mark and treasure,
A time to celebrate and laugh and sing;
So, wear your titfer for this grand occasion
And - go on - throw your hat in to the ring.

Your choice of hats is wide and quite inspiring,
Your flat-cap, derby, pork-pie, topper posh ;
There's bowler, trilby, montera and snood,
Homburg, stetson, boater, bonnet, cloche.

(The cloche should surely be your choice that day
In French it means no more than 'bell-like':
So why not wear one, flaunt one, throw one,
When New Year's bells do then assault your shell-like?)

These further thousand years have passed away
Celebration is now where it's at ;
So, pass around the hat (don't eat it)
The twentieth century is now old-hat.

They say that some time back in history
The merchants got their headgear from Milan:
Thus came their name, the quaintish name of 'milliner'
For hat-sellers of fashion and élan.

So dictionaries acknowledge no connection
'Twixt 'milliner' and assonant 'millennium'.
Don't worry! Think 'hats', think 'a thousand years',
And flout the lexicographical tedium.

Two thousand years of history may be marked
By jangling bells and cap of merry jester,

By fancy dress, and silly party hats;
By fêtes, by follies, fireworks and fiesta.

The Mexicans will dance upon their hats,
And baseball players fling their caps and roar;
The wedding ushers toss their hats for joy,
The milkmaids wave their rustic hats of straw.

The Millennium is time to mark and treasure,
A time to celebrate and laugh and sing;
So, if you want to maximise your pleasure
To wear a hat is really quite the thing!

"So I wanted a change of image, okay?"

THE KING'S PRAYER FOR THE NEW YEAR

A new year is at hand. We cannot tell what it will bring. If it brings peace, how thankful we shall all be. If it brings us continued struggle we shall remain undaunted. In the meantime, I feel that we may all find a message of encouragement in the lines which, in my closing words, I would like to say to you:

> *I said to the man who stood at the Gate of the Year, 'Give me a light that I tread safely into the unknown'. And he replied, Go out into the darkness, and put your hand into the Hand of God. That shall be to you better than light, and safer than a known way'.*

King George VI's Christmas Message in 1937

ALONE AT NEW YEAR

She threw out red roses
which nobody saw;
tore up the party hats
nobody wore;
finished the wine,
put the records away,
blew out the candle
that was melting away;
looked at his picture,
whispered his name;
the mistletoe beckoned,
but he never came.

Margareta Lee ©

NEW YEAR'S EVE

Every man hath two birth-days; two days, at least, in every year, which set him revolving upon the lapse of time as it affects his mortal duration. The one is that which in an especial manner he termeth his.

The birth of a new year is of an interest too wide to be pretermitted by king or cobbler. No one ever regarded the First of January with indifference. It is that from which all date their time, and count upon what is left. It is the nativity of our common Adam. Of all sound of all bells (bells, the music nighest bordering upon heaven) - most solemn and touching is the peal which rings out the Old Year. I never hear it without a gathering-up of my mind to a concentration of all the images that have been diffused over the past twelvemonth; all I have done or suffered, performed or neglected, in that regretted time. It was not poetical flight in a contemporary, when he exclaimed:
'I saw the skirts of the departing Year.'
It is no more that what in sober sadness every one of us seems to be conscious of, in that awful leave-taking. Some of my companions affect rather to manifest an exhilaration at the birth of the coming year, than any very tender regrets for the decease of its predecessor. But I am none of those who 'Welcome the coming, speed the parting guest.'

Not childhood alone, but the young man till thirty, never feels practically that he is mortal. He knows it indeed, and, if need were, he could preach a homily on the fragility of life; but he brings it not home to himself, any more than in a hot June we can appropriate to our imagination the freezing days of December. Every dead man must take upon himself to be lecturing me with his odious truism, that 'Such as he now is, I must shortly be.' Not so shortly, friend, perhaps, as thou imaginest: I am alive! The New Year's Days are past. I survive, a jolly candidate for 1821. Another cup of wine - and let that turn-coat bell, that just now mournfully chanted the obsequies of 1820 departed, with changed notes lustily rings in a successor.

Charles Lamb (1775-1834) in his ESSAYS OF ELIA

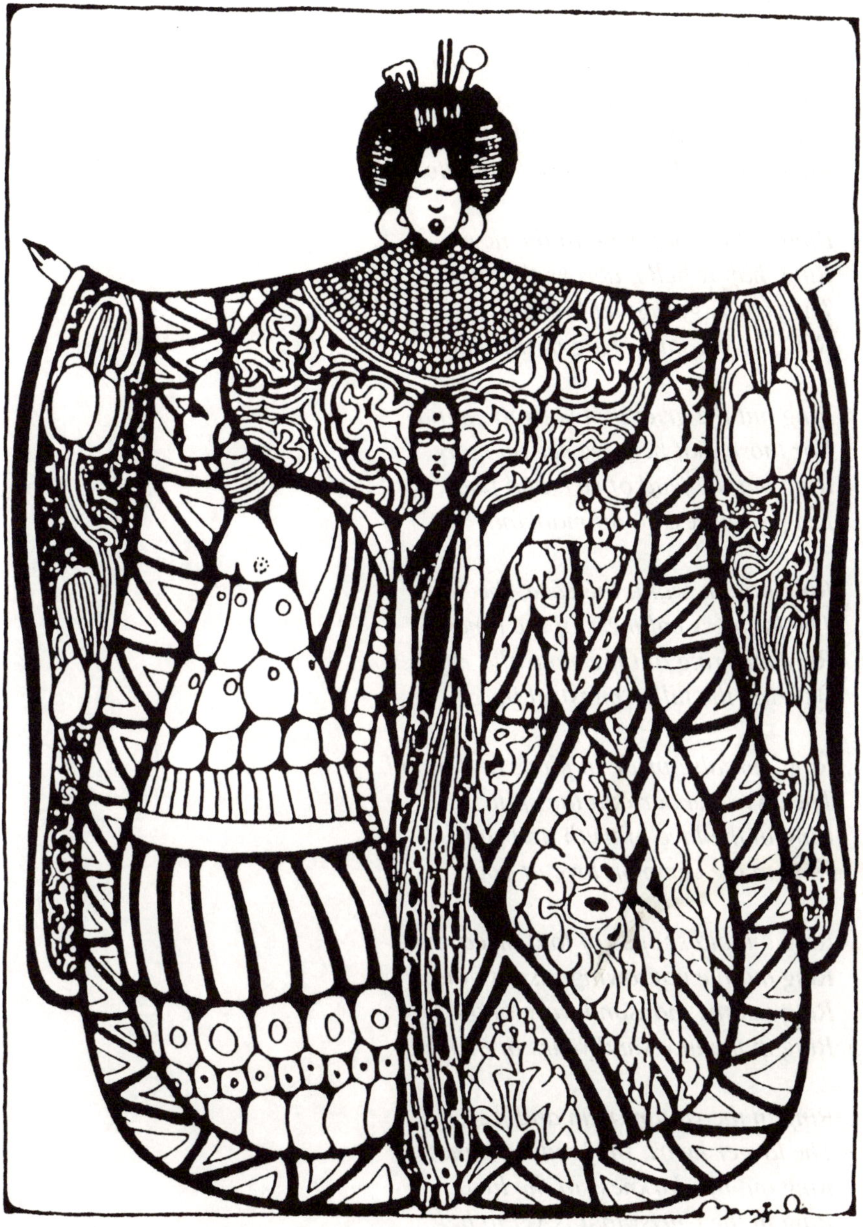

from IN MEMORIAM by Alfred, Lord Tennyson (1809-1892)

Ring out, wild bells, to the wild sky,
The flying cloud, the frosty light;
The year is dying in the night;
Ring out, wild bells, and let him die.

Ring out the old, ring in the new,
Ring, happy bells, across the snow,
The year is going, let him go;
Ring out the false, ring in the true.

Ring out the grief that saps the mind,
For those that here we see no more;
Ring out the feud of rich and poor,
Ring in redress to all mankind.

Ring out the want, the care, the sin,
The faithless coldness of the times;
Ring out, ring out my mournful rhymes,
But ring the fuller minstrel in.

Ring out false pride in place and blood,
The civic slander and the spite;
Ring in the love of truth and right,
Ring in the common love of good.

Ring out old shapes of foul disease;
Ring out the narrowing lust of gold;
Ring out the thousand wars of old,
Ring in the thousand years of peace.

Ring in the valiant man and free,
The larger heart, the kindlier hand;
Ring out the darkness of the land,
Ring in the Christ that is yet to be.

MILLENNIUM NEW YEAR: A GHOST STORY

It had been a bad year, 1999. Why was she so restless, why did everything seem so pointless? Surely she was too young to be dogged by insomnia, curse of middle age and the old? Yet night after night, after her busy day at work, she would doze off only to re-emerge in to a different world of dreams. Most nights it was the same scenario, unthreatening, but inexorable and remorseless.

She would find herself moving along a moonlit road, all shades of indigo and silver. On her left would be a glinting lake, then came a bend, and a stand of inky-black trees on the right. Ahead was a Queen Anne-style country house, dimly-profiled against the moon-splattered sky. She was impelled to walk up the drive, gravel grumbling underfoot, and lift the knocker in desperation.

At this point she always jerked awake, sweating and disorientated. Why always this dream? Why so often?

But it would be a good day today. It was New Year's Eve, the last day of the old year, and celebrations everywhere would be thrusting people in to the new Millennium. A lunchtime bash at the office, then off through the extra-Friday traffic to some friends' new family home in the Cotswolds. Thus it was, as the day waned crepuscular and dim, that she was driving westwards to a strange destination. Rob and Josephine had sent a vague map of how to get to Coxcomb-in-the-Wold, but she had learnt by long experience not to trust their cartographic skills.

The motorway became a road, the road faded in to a lane, the lane merged in to a track, when suddenly her stomach lurched, as the car came to a halt. *This was it!* Getting out of the car as though under hypnosis, she stumbled forward. The daylight had quite faded by now, but by the light of an icy moon she noted the lake - *the* lake - on her left; then the bend; then the stand of trees on her right ..... every detail of her dream landscape unfolded on cue. Scudding clouds behind it highlighted the dark outline of the box-like house. As if possessed, she floated up the drive, and clasped the knocker with its old familiarity. This time though she heard its clangour resonate through the house.

The door swung open to reveal a strange pleasant couple, who smiled a welcome as she stood irresolutely before them.

'Welcome, my dear,' said the man calmly, 'You must come in and help us toast the future. You see, you are the ghost who has haunted our house all year.'

This new year's eve's so special,
It has about it the fresh excitement
Of a precious new-born babe;
Uniting everyone in human-ness,
Bringing warmth, a smile to our lips.
Janus, the god of faces twain,
Urges us to look back down
The generations that begat us,
Bore us, nourished, succoured us -
*But also to look **forward** to re-birth.*

Bring the new year gifts of welcome;
Crack a party popper in its honour,
Take a photo, snapshot, video,
Read the papers hail its advent,
Dance and sing and praise the Lord,
Let off fireworks galore,
Light the celebratory candle,
Wet its head with fine champagne.
Promise fulfilment of its wishes;
Gather it a bouquet of dreams.

THE PRESENT FUTURE

There were massive parties, people going wild,
On that crisp winter's evening, sunny and mild,
But not many people actually thought back
To when Christ was born in that little shack.

Flying cars and outer space,
Sweets that never lose their taste!
Communications with alien life,
The No-Blade user-friendly knife.
Virtual Reality no longer a dream,
Buying your groceries off the T.V. screen.
Cloning now a common issue,
Factories making human tissue.
Robot vicars giving out pardons,
Time machines in your back gardens.
Children no longer attending school,
The Internet is now the rule.

There were massive parties, people going wild,
On that crisp winter's evening, sunny and mild,
But not many people actually thought back
To when Christ was born in that little shack.

Cara Cummings ©

THE NEW YEAR

Hark, the cock crows, and yon bright star
Tells us, the day himself's not far;
With him old Janus doth appear,
Peeping into the future year,
With such a look as seems to say,
The prospect is not good that way.
But stay! but stay! methinks my sight,
Better inform'd by clearer light,
Discerns sereneness in that brow,
That all contracted seem'd but now.
That which this way looks is clear,
And smiles upon the New-born Year.
Why should we then suspect or fear
The influences of a year,
So smiles upon us the first morn,
And speaks us good so soon as born?
Plague on't, the last was ill enough,
This cannot but make better proof;
Or, at the worst, as we brush'd through
The last, why so we may this too;
And then the next in reason should
Be superexcellently good:
For the worst ills (we daily see)
Have no more perpetuity,
And who has one good year in three,
And yet repines at destiny,
Appears ungrateful in the case,
And merits not the good he has.
Then let us welcome the New Guest
With lusty brimmers of the best;
Mirth always should Good Fortune meet,
And render e'en Disaster sweet:

Charles Cotton (1689)

A NEW YEAR CAROL

Here we bring new water
from the well so clear;
For to worship God with
this happy New Year.

Sing levy dew, sing levy dew,
the water and the wine;
The seven bright gold wires
and the bugles that do shine.

Sing reign of Fair Maid,
with gold upon her toe;
Open you the West Door,
and turn the Old Year go.

Sing reign of Fair Maid
with gold upon her chin;
Open you the East Door,
and let the New Year in.

Sing levy dew, sing levy dew,
the water and the wine;
The seven bright gold wires
and the bugles that do shine.

English traditional.

HERACLITUS

They told me, Heraclitus, they told me you were dead,
They brought me bitter news to hear and bitter tears to shed.
I wept as I remembered how often you and I
Had tired the sun with talking and sent him down the sky.

And now thou art lying, my dear old Carian guest,
A handful of grey ashes, long, long at rest,
Still are thy pleasant voices, thy nightingales, awake;
For Death, he taketh all away, but them he cannot take.

William Cory (1823 – 1892), also author of the Eton Boating Song

AULD LANG SYNE

Should auld acquaintance be forgot,
And never brought to mind?
Should auld acquaintance be forgot
And auld lang syne?

For auld lang syne, my dear,
For auld lang syne,
We'll take a cup o' kindness yet,
For auld lang syne.

We twa hae run about the braes,
And pu'd the gowans fine;
But we've wander'd mony a weary foot
Sin' auld lang syne.

We twa hae paidled i' the burn,
From morning sun till dine;
But seas between us braid hae roar'd
Sin' auld lang syne.

And there's a hand, my trusty fiere,
And gie's a hand o' thine;
And we'll tak a right guid-willie waught,
For auld lang syne.

And surely ye'll be your pint-stowp,
And surely I'll be mine;
And we'll tak a cup of kindness yet
For auld lang syne.

Robert Burns (1759-1796), published
in the year of his death.

Although originally written as verse of greeting *Auld Lang Syne* is usually used at parting; now, by tradition, on New Year's Eve.

auld lang syne = time long since
braes = hills
pu'd the gowans = plucked the daisies
braid = broad
fiere = companion
guid-willie = hearty, with good will
waught = drink
pint-stowp = pint-drinker

CHAPTER 5 : TIME & NATURE , THE NATURE OF TIME

As the cycle of time rolls on, as the clocks roll over at midnight, it is a good moment to think about the nature of time itself. What is Time? Why does nature gives us Mother Earth, but we are ruled by Father Time? Someone once said that time is nature's way of preventing everything from happening at once. Its underlying beat guides our lives by our circadian rhythms, that is, the way our body clock speeds up and slows down over the day, of which jet-lag is an extreme misalignment; all living things above primitive bacteria have this clock. New medical research suggests that medicine is more effective if administered at the right moment of our daily cycle. Caveman felt a real need to measure the length of days, and obviously decided that light was more important to him than heat, as he decreed midwinter to be when it started to get lighter again, even though most of the cold weather was yet to come. It has been measured by sundials, marked candles, water clocks, tumbling sculptures, carriage clocks, anti-clockwise clocks, grandfather clocks ..... not all of them going like clockwork. How does the ordinary person see Time? How does the poet see it? How does the physicist see it? What is its relationship with matter, with space, and with energy? Are we likely to know more about the nature of time as the next millennium passes?

Time is involved with everything under the sun. Most things are not static, finite 'things', but processes; they blossom, flower and wither. Pythagoras described it as the soul of the world. Like the tides, time waits for no man; yet it has the seeming elasticity to drag when we are miserable but to flash by when we are happy (there is no time like the pleasant.) Shakespeare said in 'As You Like It':

Time travels in divers paces with divers persons. I'll tell you who Time ambles withal, who Time trots withal, who Time gallops withal, and who he stands still withal.

Whether or not we had a happy childhood, we learnt so much that was new each day that it crept by so slowly then; but dashes by, almost leaving us behind in its wake, as we grow old. Even in society as a whole, changes that used to take centuries to effect, now happen in a matter of decades. As we saw in the first chapter; what used to take a year to change, is now done in a few weeks; what happened in minutes is now done in nano-seconds, that is, one-thousandth-milllionth of a second.

      Time is the fourth dimension, but - as yet - the mysterious one-way trip. Why should that be, when you go backwards in the other three spatial dimensions? It is all to do with Einstein's theory of relativity (replacing the Newtonian idea of time as absolute) and with entropy, the theory of the order and disorder of the universe that is one of the laws of thermodynamics (ice replaced in the freezer will only get colder again, as it reverts to the ambient temperature.) In particle physics you can observe time dilation, when moving unstable particles appear to decay more slowly than identical stationary particles. Stephen Hawking has decided that what came before the Big Bang that created our cosmos 12 billion years ago was a small object like a pea suspended in a timeless void, which inflated and led to the explosion that shook our universe (still infinitely expanding) in to being. Maybe, after all, it really had no beginning and will have no ending? A dictionary-type definition of something so abstract ('giving to airy nothings a local habitation and a name') is difficult, but this is one: *That which distinguishes sequential events from simultaneous events.* This means that we can divide the panoply of events in to past, and present, and future. Only eternity, which can be understood both as the origin of time and infinite time without end, is without such categorisation; it is infinity, that is, without a finishing point. Time is like an arrow, supreme creation of God the Fletcher, which flies surely onwards, piercing the future and brushing aside with its flight-feathers all the distractions of the present, whirling them in to the past. Time is like an ever-rolling stream, which bears all its sons away; it is, as Heraclitus said half a millennium before Christ, a river in which you can never step the same more than once. Time is quite inexorable, its momentum dragging us ever forwards. The unknown future becomes the known present, and then fades in to the forgotten or repressed past. Even if we were to live it backwards, we would never know, as we would be going backwards too and so experiencing it as if it were going forwards. If the progression of time really were ever reversed, we would shed our wrinkles to become smooth-skinned babies again, and ultimately part of our parents; the mighty oak tree would regress to a shrivelled acorn; the great river would be nothing but a stream; the bird would be nothing but an egg.

Time means different things to different people. Chronometric dating of artefacts is a way for archaeologists to date new finds by reference to a fixed datescale of earlier discoveries (which may be by carbon dating, dendrochronology of trees, potassium-argon dating, archaeo-magentic dating or dating by electron spin, fission tracking or thermoluminescence.) In legal terms, time only began in 1189, because when the Statute of Westminster was drawn up in 1275 it was felt that time before then, which was the start of the reign of Richard I, was 'time immemorial', that is, out of the time limit for bringing certain types of action. Cyber-time began on January 1st, 1970 , the earliest date of an e-mail. For a sportsman in times past, the Time of Grace was the hunting period from mid-June to mid-September. In the seventeenth century, Nicholas Poussin was inspired to paint 'A Dance to the Music of Time', with the four seasons gravely pacing an outward-facing circle to music played on a lyre by grey-bearded old Father Time. For yet another Frenchman, Marcel Proust, it was strictly something to remember in the past. For Parkinson, it was not elastic, but the activities within an allotted span expanded or contracted according to the span available. Idlers pass it daily. Prisoners 'do' it, not for killing time but for killing a fellow-creature (and how it must lag for the old lags); Voltaire said in the eighteenth century:

There's scarce a point whereon mankind agree
So well as in their boast of killing me;
I boast of nothing, but when I've a mind
I think I can be even with mankind.

Procrastination merely steals it away. For evolutionists, time is the process that allowed the fine-tuning that has produced the wonders of nature today. For horticulturists, one can only hope the time is ripe. For metalworkers, may it be a crucible. For doctors, it is the great healer; for beauticians, the great enemy. In marriage, it is the destiny that shapes the end of men, and ends the shape of women. For Shakespeare, the times of our lives were seven acts of a play. For other writers, time was a travelling gypsy; or elusive elixir :

> *Made, bitter-sweet, from fruits of life there is a wine;*
> *It quenches every human thirst - we call it Time.*

There is a story about Friar Roger Bacon (1214-1294), the pioneer of science and philosophy, inventor of the magnifying glass and many other scientific instruments. He made a talking head of brass (such heads were popularly of Eastern origin, and the tenth century Pope Sylvester II had one) which was supposed to tell fortunes. One day it spoke the phrase 'Time is'; half an hour later, it said 'Time was'; and after another half an hour it proclaimed 'Time's past', fell off the shelf, and was smashed to smithereens.

Time is often portrayed as an old man with a scythe, ready to cut the fair corn of our youth; certainly, this is how the old year is shown in New Year cards, in contrast to the new-born 'putto' of the arriving year. The figure of Death also carries a scythe; for instance, on the tarot cards he is a skeleton carrying his scythe symbolising both the severance and liberation of self from the body. The Roman God Saturn, equivalent to the Greek God of time Khronos ('the cosmic clock') is also often portrayed with a scythe; and, like time, he devoured his own children. The scythe is shaped like the sinister horned sickle moon as it wanes completely, but fortunately we know that it will lead back to a new moon, so that regeneration will surely follow annihilation, again showing the dual nature of time (and reminding us of the phoenix with its perpetual renewal.) Time unites opposites, birth to death, death to spiritual re-birth, youth to age, night to day, work to rest. We think of time in terms of cycle or circles, shape of the movement of the turning world, as opposed to static squares or rectangles; but what is at its quiescent centre?

Only occasionally, in the memorable phrase used by John Buchan, is the curtain of time drawn back and a chink of the future is revealed; like the well-known precognitions of John Godley (later Lord Kilbracken) the horse-race tipster, and frequent well-documented cases of premonitions about disasters. However, for every story in the papers of the man who refused to board a plane because he had dreamt it was to crash, or the woman with precognition about the devastating landslide, how many un-newsworthy cases were there of people who had imagined these things without them being fulfilled?

Other quirks of time are the many instances of coincidence, or synchronicity, that is, things happening at the same time. These curious and simultaneous occurrence of causally unconnected events may comfort us with the idea that they are manifestations of an all-embracing universal order. There is a perennial fascination in the idea that the space / time continuum may sometimes be ordered by an element of something that may seem to be, but may be is not, chance. Haven't we all experienced the curious feeling when the same unusual word is used several times in one day; or we are looking up something in a library when an adjacent book falls open by serendipity to reveal just what we want to know (so-called 'library angels')? Some coincidences seem so enormously strange that it feels that Fate or a sort of universal consciousness really is taking a hand; like the scarab beetle at the window of the psychoanalyst Dr. Carl Jung at the very moment a patient was talking about scarabs, or the couples who met on holiday and seem to share the same circumstances, names, families and so on.

Here is another true story: three girls had worked in the same office together for several years, getting to know each other's friends and families fairly well. They went out for lunch one day, occupying a four-seater booth in a nearby restaurant. Spilled food meant that Felicia had to accompany Ewa to the ladies' to clean up; she returned first to find the third girl Mary, in casual conversation with a diner who had arrived by herself. 'Hello, Lucinda', said Felicia in surprise, 'Mary, this is my father's secretary'. At this moment Ewa, cleaned up, returned and greeted Lucinda as a long lost old school friend ..... This double coincidence does seem to be buck the odds of mere chance; but statistically, is this so? How many other times did the girls lunch without meeting people known to them, and maybe on occasion meeting some other person whom only one of them knew? We say 'It's a small world' ..... but in a country of sixty million people we probably only mix with a very small coterie of people who may share our social background, our geographical roots, our educational establishments. Someone once said that with only six 'degrees of separation' (there was film with that title in 1993), that is, six links of connection, you could link everybody in the world; mathematicians recognise the 'small world effect' of random connection.

New research in to Extra-Sensory Perception (ESP), clairvoyance and telepathy, and the ability with computers to digest vast armies of statistics and discover correlation and periodicity, has also resulted in more investigation in to coincidence, partly through the establishment in 1985 of the Koestler Chair of Parapsychology at the University of Edinburgh. The brilliantly unstable Austrian who codified the law of seriality, Paul Kammerer, delighted in collecting examples of coincidences or 'clusters' (as did Jung); he wrote in the 1920's that seriality is *a recurrence of the same or similar things or events in time or space ..... (it is) ubiquitous and continuous in life, nature and the cosmos. It is the umbilical chord that connects thought, feeling, science and art with the womb of the universe which gave birth to them.* He believed in non-causal, non-physical forces acting in nature. Another Austrian theoretical physicist, Wolfgang Pauli, carried out important research; but is better remembered now for coincidences that happened to him himself, the so-called 'Pauli effect'. Ten per cent of adults have involuntarily experienced strong hallucinations while fully awake, many of them connected with 'time slips'. Jung believed that some so-called ghosts, some poltergeists, were as it were 'exteriorisations' of emotions felt by those who precipitated them.

To continue talking of the space/time continuum could take us ..... well, quite a long time. Where else has the actual centre of the study of time for generations been other than in Greenwich itself? How appropriate that this area which unites the elements of time, the sea and the meridian inter-twined throughout History, is going to be - as will be seen in a later chapter - the home of many millennial festivities. The National Maritime Museum down in Greenwich Park is at the heart of all time, and appropriately has been given nearly twelve million pounds from the Lottery to build a huge covered courtyard with eleven new galleries. Dr Jonathan Betts, Curator of Horology at the Museum, has explained :

The National Maritime Museum has an interest in the history of timekeeping and time telling because fundamental to its remit was Navigation., more specifically finding one's longitude at sea, which is a function of Time. The foundation of the Royal Observatory itself in 1675 was expressly to discover a method of finding longitude, and this astronomical research required the use of very accurate clocks. As it turned out, the solution to the longitude problem (found in the eighteenth century) proved to be a highly accurate portable clock, later to be termed a Marine Chronometer. Thus, the fundamental horological connection with maritime studies can be summarised as 'Precision Timekeeping'; and although a number of other horological areas are well-covered in their collections, it is this specialisation in which the National Maritime Museum is unique in this country, and in which it has the best collection worldwide.

Dr Betts' responsibilities include the major collections and related collections, their history, completeness, documentation and conservation, loans, education and care of very special outside collections like that at Belmont Park, Faversham. The Old Royal Observatory has its own Millennium Project entitled *2/0°0'0"* which starts with a great exhibition on 'The Story of Time', also including a special logo, and the Accurist Millennium Countdown Clock which has noted the last thousand days, plus a series of television documentaries to be shown here and abroad. On the night of 31st December, just a few miles south of their fellow party-goers in the Dome, there is to be an evening of entertainment in the grounds of the Maritime Museum and the Royal Parks, which will also be televised.

At the 1884 International Meridian Conference in Washington, D.C, it was decreed that the Prime Meridian of the world, that is 0° Longitude, be 'at the centre of the Transit Instrument at the Observatory at Greenwich.' The actual Meridian cuts England in two north to south from the East Coast just north of the Humber via Louth, Boston, Waltham Abbey, Greenwich of course (where a laser beam at night marks the line),

East Grinstead and Lewes to Peacehaven east of Brighton, at some parts marked by plaques, trees, and painted lines. In Epping Forest at Chingford is an obelisk marking the Bradley Meridian sixty years earlier. The 1884 delegates voted to confirm that the clock be altered around the world in 24 time zones, to compensate for the gain or loss of time (one hour per 15°) which occurs when moving around the 360° of the globe; and accept the formula of the universal day, which is 'to begin for all the world at the moment of mean midnight of the initial meridian.' This means without doubt that the Prime Meridian at Greenwich is the point from which the new Millennium will begin, not the far-flung Pacific islands to which jet-setters will jet set. Greenwich is the basis of the International Time Zone System including Greenwich Mean Time ('mean' as in equidistant from the extremes, in the middle), the standard time used by astronomers, when the sun is overhead and equidistant from the horizons at midday, twelve hours away from midnight. It is really all to do with the natural time-scale defined by the diurnal rotation of the earth on its own axis, with reference to the position of the sun and the stars. Scientists now often measure by Co-ordinated Universal Time, confirmed in 1972, because although ship's navigators seldom need to rely on clocks' accuracy as before, there are many areas of research such as astro-physics where the demand for greater accuracy increases all the time. As the Earth is cooling down, every so often (about once a year at the moment) atomic clocks have a 'leap second' to counter the slowing of the earth, so that they are in total synchronisation with Earth's rotation; and of course there are quadrennial leap years, even leap centuries, to accommodate the fact that the year is really 365.24219 days long. In this century, variations on British Summer Time have been tried, meaning we put the clocks forward in Spring and back in the autumn ('Spring forward, Fall back'.) People talk of 'daylight saving', but of course we don't actually create any more daylight, what we gain at the end of the day we lose at the beginning. What is forgotten, perhaps, is that northern Scotland is not only so much further north than England, but also more westerly, and so the sun rises even later there in winter.

Britain's chronological importance is also shown in the amazing engineering of the National Physical Laboratory Caesium-Atomic clock (part of the Global Positioning Satellite System) whose timekeeping is beamed from a BT mast in Rugby over a range of 900 miles, being accurate to plus or minus one second in a million years. The radio beam will automatically change between summer and winter time, leap years and so on. In Frankfurt, they have the Central European Time Clock whose signal transmits as far as Britain, and is able to put the clocks back and forward for clocks purchased here, even though the period of British Summer Time differs slightly from its Continental equivalent.

The best known clock in the world is Big Ben, the huge bell nine feet in diameter and weighing 13 tonnes cast in 1858, looming over the Palace of Westminster. It is looked after by Mr Mike McCann, who has the wonderful title of 'Keeper of the Great Clock'; accuracy is assured by the addition or subtraction of heavy 'bunpennies', that is, coins with the head of the young Queen Victoria. Not everyone likes the sound of clocks, of course; John Major, when Prime Minister, asked the firm A.A. Osborne, established in 1615 who now look after all Whitehall clocks, to silence all the ticking and chiming timepieces in 10, Downing Street (they have since been replaced for the present Prime Minister.) The world's largest clock is on the waterside at St Helier in Jersey, unveiled in 1997 and costing a quarter of a million pounds, being a fifty foot high replica of a nineteenth century paddle steamer. In a letter to The Times, Dr John Wall pointed out that one way to mark the millennium in a chronophilic manner would be to ensure that all existing public clocks were working, and that more be erected. He tells me that nothing officially is under way, but that many individuals have expressed support.

Let us leave our thoughts on time at this millennium with a group of school children, who wrote about Time as 'the spirit of generations of years ..... You've just come but it's time to go ..... Time stretches our destinies and our wills ..... Don't you ever sit back and wonder "What happened to my time?" ..... If you deny time, you've done a serious crime ..... If you cannot beat it, cherish it.' They follow the honourable tradition of writers from classical times, which era of course gave us the word for chronological time from the name of Khronos, the Greek god of time. In the order they were written, we hear first Euripides, who said in the fifth century B.C. that 'Time will discover everything to posterity; it is a babbler, and speaks even when no question is put.' Then Plato some decades later said:

> *Time on his back bears all things far away.*
> *Shape, fortune, name and nature all decay …...*
> *Time carries off all things; would you exchange*
> *Name, looks, nature, luck ? Just give time full range.*

Then we conclude with Seneca in 65 A.D., who said 'A man who has taken your time recognises no debt; but it is the one he can never repay.' Time is an infinitely precious and sometimes irreplaceable resource. As the year 2000 rolls us into the new millennium, it is an appropriate moment to question the nature of time; and also to hope that any millennial activities we indulge in will have been worth the investment of time, and that some permanent reminders of the events are left for the amazement and wonder of generations to come.

OZYMANDIAS

I met a traveller from an antique land
Who said: Two vast and trunkless legs of stone
Stand in the desert. Near them, on the sand,
Half sunk, a shatter'd visage lies, whose frown,
And wrinkled lip, and sneer of cold command,
Tell that its sculptor well those passions read
Which yet survive, stamp'd on these lifeless things,
The hand that mock'd them and the heart that fed:
And on the pedestal these words appear:
'My name is Ozymandias, king of kings:
Look on my works, ye Mighty, and despair!'
Nothing beside remains. Round the decay
Of that colossal wreck, boundless and bare
The lone and level sands stretch far away.

Percy Bysshe Shelley (1792-1822)

TIME FLIES AWAY

Time flies away,
That second that just went by, will never come back.
One minute you have someone beside you,
The next, the person who was so close to you,
gone forever,
Time has taken over that person.

Time has overtaken that person;
Time flies like the wind,
Incoming and going out now ;
But memories last until eternity,
Everlasting,
Something that will never die.

Anik Sodha ©

from GROWING OLD

Ambition was my idol, which was broken
Before the shrines of Sorrow, and of Pleasure;
And the two last have left me many a token
O'er which reflection may be made at leisure;
Now, like Friar Bacon's Brazen Head, I've spoken,
'Time is, Time was, Time's past': a chymic treasure
Is glittering Youth, which I have spent betimes -
My heart in passion, and my head on rhymes.

What is the end of Fame? 'tis but to fill
A certain portion of uncertain paper:
Some liken it to climbing up a hill,
Whose summit, like all hills, is lost in vapour;
For this men write, speak, preach, and heroes kill,
And bards burn what they call their 'midnight taper',
To have a wretched picture and worse bust.

What are the hopes of man? Old Egypt's King
Cheops erected the first Pyramid
And largest, thinking it was just the thing
To keep his memory whole, and mummy hid;
But somebody or other rummaging,
Burglariously broke his coffin's lid:
Let not a monument give you or me hopes,
Since not a pinch of dust remains of Cheops.

But I, being fond of true philosophy,
Say very often to myself, 'Alas!
All things that have been born were born to die,
And flesh (which Death mows down to hay) is grass;
So thank your stars that matters are no worse,
And read your Bible, sir, and mind your purse.

George Gordon, Lord Byron (1788–1824)

TIME'S PACES

When as a child I laughed and wept,
Time crept.
When as a youth I waxed more bold,
Time strolled.
When I became a full-grown man,
Time ran.
When older still I daily grew,
Time flew.
Soon I shall find, in passing on,
Time gone.
Christ! Wilt thou have saved me then?

A poem from Chester Cathedral

ECCLESIASTES

To everything there is a season, and a time
to every purpose under heaven:
    A time to be born and a time to die;
    A time to plant and a time to pluck up that which is planted;
    A time to kill and a time to heal;
    A time to weep, and a time to laugh;
    A time to mourn, and a time to dance;
    A time to cast away stones, and a time to gather stones together;
    A time to embrace, and a time to refrain from embracing;
    A time to get, and a time to lose;
    A time to keep and a time to cast away;
    A time to keep silence, and a time to speak;
    A time to love and a time to hate;
    A time of war and a time of peace.
God hath made everything beautiful in its time …..
I know that, whatsoever God doeth, it shall be for ever.

Ecclesiastes . Chapter 3, verses 1-7, 11 & 14.

TO THE VIRGINS, TO MAKE MUCH OF TIME

Gather ye rosebuds while ye may,
Old Time is still a-flying:
And this same flower that smiles today
Tomorrow will be dying.

The glorious lamp of heaven, the sun,
The higher he's a-getting,
The sooner his race will be run,
And nearer he's to setting .....

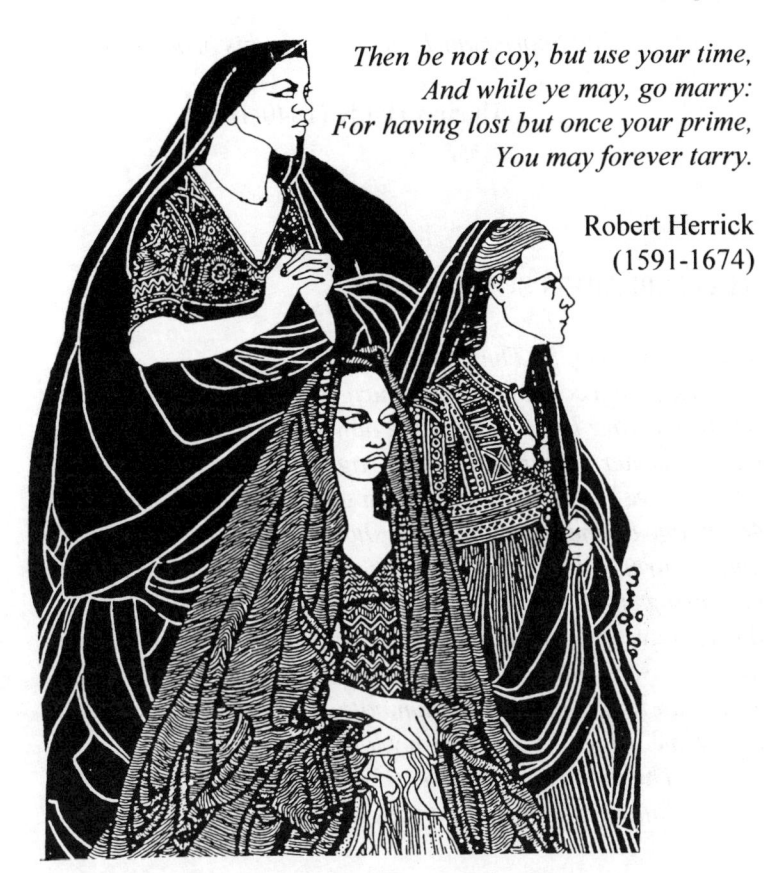

Then be not coy, but use your time,
And while ye may, go marry:
For having lost but once your prime,
You may forever tarry.

Robert Herrick
(1591-1674)

TIME IS A PREDATOR

Time goes by slowly, when you are bored -
Time is a predator hunting you down.
Time passes quickly, when you're having fun -
Time is a predator hunting you down.
Time's everlasting, as humans are mortal -
Time is a predator, hunting you down.

Guy Shidlo ©

The Sportsman Time but rears his brood to kill

Thomas Hardy (1840-1928)

SHAKESPEARE'S SONNET 64

When I have seen by Time's fell hand defac'd
The rich-proud cost of outworn buried age;
When sometime lofty towers I see down-raz'd,
And brass eternal slave to mortal rage;
When I have seen the hungry ocean gain
Advantage on the kingdom of the shore,
And the firm soil win of the watery main,
Increasing store with loss, and loss with store;
When I have seen such interchange of state,
Or state itself confounded to decay;
Ruin hath taught me thus to ruminate -
That Time will come and take my love away.
    This thought is as a death, which cannot choose
    But weep to have that which it fears to lose .

[This is from John Buchan's 1932 novel, *The Gap in the Curtain*. At a weekend house party, the enigmatic foreign scientist Professor Moe plans to conduct an experiment in manipulating time by getting the house-guests to 'read' the headlines in The Times for a year hence.]

Then he presented me with a theory of Time, for he had an orderly mind, and desired to put first things first. Here he pretty well bogged me down at the start. He did not call Time a fourth dimension, but I gathered it amounted to that, or rather that it involved many new dimensions. There seemed to be a number of worlds of presentation travelling in Time, and each was contained within a world one dimension larger. The self was composed of various observers, the normal one being confined to a small field of sensory phenomena, observed or remembered. But this field was included in a larger field, and, to the observer in the latter, future events were visible as well as past and present.

In sleep, he went on, where the attention was not absorbed, as it was in waking life, with the smaller field of phenomena, the larger field might come inside the pale of consciousness. People had often been correctly forewarned in dreams. We all now and then were amazed at the familiarity with which we regarded a novel experience, as if we recognised it as something which had happened before. The universe was extended in Time, and the dreamer, with nothing to rivet his attention to the narrow waking field, ranged about, and might light on images which belonged to the future as well as to the past. The sleeper was constantly crossing the arbitrary frontier which our mortal limitations had erected.

At this point I began to see the light. I was prepared to assent to the conclusion that in dreams we occasionally dip into the future, though I was unable to follow most of the Professor's proofs. But now came the real question. Was it possible to attain to this form of prevision otherwise than in sleep? Could the observer in the narrow world turn himself by any effort of will into the profounder observer in the world of ampler dimensions? Could the anticipating power of the dreamer be systematised and controlled, and be made available to man in his waking life?

TIME, THE SUBTLE THIEF OF YOUTH

How soon hath time, the subtle thief of youth,
Stol'n on his wing my three and twentieth year !
My hasting days fly on with full career,
But my late spring no bud or blossom shew'th.
Perhaps my semblance might deceive the truth,
That I to manhood am arriv'd so near,
And inward ripeness doth much less appear,
That some more timely-happy spirits indueth.
Yet be it less or more, or soon or slow,
It shall be still in strictest measure even
To that same lot, however mean, or high,
Toward which Time leads me, and the will of Heaven;
All is, if I have grace to use it so,
As ever in my great task-Master's eye.

John Milton (1608–1674)

from ODE ON A GRECIAN URN

Thou still unravished bride of quietness,
Thou foster-child of Silence and slow Time,
Sylvan historian, who canst thus express
A flowery tale more sweetly than our rhyme .....
With brede of marble men and maidens overwrought,
With forest branches and the trodden weed;
Thou, silent form! dost tease us out of thought
As doth eternity. Cold Pastoral!
When old age shall this generation waste,
Thou shalt remain, in midst of other woe
Than ours, a friend to man, to whom thou sayst,
'Beauty is truth, truth beauty - that is all
Ye know on earth, and all ye need to know.'

John Keats (1795-1821)

THE SHIP

Underneath the seventh sea, on the ocean's mattress,
At the bottom of the bowl of blue, lay the ship.

As time passed it sadly decayed, like an obnoxious tooth;
Dying in an unpleasant, sorrowful way; the ship aged.

Where once it was a great vessel, following the sun's rise and set,
Now its fame was stolen by life's enemies, and the ship died.

Time, most important in all of this change, for all was lost in an aeon,
Changing the four corners of the earth.
The ship was as if it had never been.

Irfaan Merali ©

DAYS

Daughters of Time, the hypocritic Days,
Muffled and dumb like barefoot dervishes,
And marching single in an endless file,
Bringing diadems and faggots in their hands.
To each they offer gifts after his will,
Bread, kingdoms, stars, and sky that holds them all.
I, in my pleached garden, watched the pomp,
Forgot my morning wishes ..... and the Day
Turned and departed silent. I, too late,
Under her solemn fillet saw the scorn.

Ralph Waldo Emerson (1803-1882)

THE FLIGHT OF TIME

Yesterday, yesterday, yesterday,
We thought it would always last;
Away, away it is moving,
And suddenly it is the past.

Today, and today, and today,
Is surely the here and now ;
But even this keeps shifting
Away from us all, somehow.

Tomorrow and tomorrow and tomorrow
Creeps on this petty pace;
But creep turns to rush, rush to fly,
And into the future we race.

TO HIS COY MISTRESS

Had we but world enough, and time,
This coyness, Lady, were no crime.
We would sit down, and think which way
To walk, and pass our long love's day.
Thou by the Indian Ganges' side
Shouldst rubies find: I by the tide
Of Humber would complain. I would
Love you ten years before the Flood:
And you should, if you please, refuse
Till the conversion of the Jews.
My vegetable love should grow
Vaster than empires, and more slow .....
But at my back I always hear
Time's wingèd chariot hurrying near:
And yonder all before us lie
Deserts of vast eternity.
Thy beauty shall no more be found;
Nor, in thy marble vault, shall sound
My echoing song: then worms shall try
That long preserved virginity:
And your quaint honour turn to dust;
And into ashes all my lust.
The grave's a fine and private place,
But none I think do there embrace.
Now therefore, while the youthful hue
Sits on thy skin like morning dew,
Now let us sport us while we may;
And now, like amorous birds of prey,
Rather at once our time devour,
Than languish in his slow-chapt power.
Let us roll all our strength, and all
Our sweetness, up into one ball:
And tear our pleasures with rough strife,
Thorough the iron gates of life.
Thus, though we cannot make our sun
Stand still, yet we will make him run.

Andrew Marvell (1621-1678)

*Alike for those who for Today prepare,
And those who after a Tomorrow stare,
A Muezzin from the Tower of Darkness cries
'Fools, your reward is neither Here nor There.'*

The Rubáiyát of Omar Khayyám
translated by Edward Fitzgerald (1809-1883)

SONNET 123

No! Time, thou shalt not boast that I do change:
Thy pyramids built up with newer might
To me are nothing novel, nothing strange;
They are but dressings of a former sight.
Our dates are brief, and therefore we admire
What thou dost foist upon us that is old;
And rather make them born to our desire,
Then think that we before have heard them told.
Thy registers and thee I both defy,
Not wondering at the present nor the past;
For thy records and what we see do lie,
Made more or less by thy continual haste:
    This I do vow, and this shall ever be,
    I will be true, despite thy scythe and thee.

William Shakespeare (1564-1616)

THE DEFIANCE

There's an experienced rebel, Time,
    And in his squadrons, Poverty;
There's Age that brings along with him
    A terrible artillery:
And if against all these thou keep'st thy crown
Th'usurper, Death, will make thee lay it down.

Thomas Flatman (1637-1688)

CHAPTER 6 : WHOSE BIRTHDAY IS IT ANYWAY? A SPIRITUAL PERSPECTIVE

It is not entirely certain on which date it took place, that miraculous birth in the manger in Bethlehem whose effects were to alter so much of recent history. A monk by name of Dionysius Exiguus ('Dennis the Small') devised a calendar in A.D. 525, placing Christ's birth on the December 25th - debatable in itself - just before January 1st of the year Anno Domini 1; but there is a body of opinion that believes it may have been four, seven or twelve years earlier, backed by astronomical evidence for an extraordinary star or comet in the sky, while further experts say it may well have been four to seven years later. What is indisputable and what rises above chronological squabbling, is the fact of the birth, and its meaning to so many people. We are celebrating the birthday of Jesus Christ; and whether you view Him as your Godhead, or as a supreme example of perfect man, or do not have any strong feelings at all, we must all acknowledge his earthly arrival as the starting point for modern history. Even to call our system of dates by the politically-correct 'Common Era' instead of 'Anno Domini' (Year of our Lord) acknowledges the significance of this watershed in time.

Over the last two millennia, the living standards of most people have improved dramatically. The lives of even the have-nots in society - which, as Hobbes noted, were *poor, nasty, brutish and short* - have improved dramatically through modern medicine and comforts, with soaring life expectancy levels: but has our spiritual development kept pace, or has it in fact begun to atrophy? Man has needed God throughout recorded history: the simple-living Australian Aborigines claim to have the longest-established continuous religious beliefs in the world, with rock paintings of a divine Rainbow Serpent dating back six millennia. Religious rituals were probably associated with the Sphinx in Egypt which can be dated back to 10,500 B.C. Has modern man, in gaining ease of living, neglected his soul and left God out of the equation?

Scientists believe that they have identified a particular part of the frontal lobe of the brain which pre-disposes us to spirituality; as though we have a physical, maybe even a chemical facility for belief. Defying it might be like saying that we will not get hungry, and do not need to eat - until hunger strikes. Maybe we ignore it at our peril. Surely the Millennium is an opportunity to do some sort of spiritual spring-cleaning, trying to decide where we are now, and where we might aim to be as our lives continue. It is in effect saying *Let's take stock and bench-mark where we are now; then consider where we can best move in the future.* This has to make sense - it is using the accumulated wisdom and experience of humanity, with God's aid, to try to reach some kind of peace with ourselves.

In striving for peace of mind, we can take inspiration from the mainstream Christian view that Man, though flawed and led astray by the temptations of free will, is nonetheless possessed of divine fire, and therefore there is always hope for us (unlike some of the deeply pessimistic millenarian cults, who view not only some of his actions but man himself as evil and without hope.)

We should acknowledge that the Christian Church has overcome some amazing obstacles to survive in to the third millennium. Its development from small-scale beginnings as a local movement in Palestine, to the greatest of world religions, has not always been straightforward. The struggles of the early missionary years, and squabbles between different factions; the schism between Western and Orthodox Christianity (one hopes for more co-operation after 2001 between East and West, when for instance the World Council of Churches' suggestion is taken up of having the same Easter Day for Western and Orthodox churches, though not however the same weekend year after year); the split between Protestantism and Catholicism; apparent blasphemies like the Avignon popes and the Taiping Son of God; and the move to secularisation in Western society.

The Millennium comes as a great opportunity for spiritual renewal; as a Church of England report terms it, it is 'A Chance to Start Again.' This report sees the millennium as *Christ focused - community engaging - other faiths sensitive - jubilee proclaiming.* We should start with clearing away some jumble from the lumber room of our souls, not waiting until the prospect of imminent death to bring the sad furniture of our past parading before us; but having come to some atonement on the past, we should then begin to make positive plans for our spiritual refurbishment, and pledge to seek for faith. The Church of England has three strands, all of which are important: the spiritual element; the body of its members, clergy and lay, and the fellowship they feel; and the historical heritage of its fabric.

It is estimated that about 36% of the world population are living in countries where the culture is historically Christian, albeit only a proportion of them (about ten per cent in Britain) ever darken the threshold of a church except maybe for weddings, funerals and the occasional christening. A recent survey of scientists in America, where church attendance is greater, found that 40% of them believed in God. Whether you are a formal church goer or not, isn't it curious that so few people ever question the cultural frame of reference which is the basis of their way of living? Often it is only in later years that people turn to faith: remember the old lady who was asked why she was reading her Bible, and answered *I'm studying for my Finals.* Perhaps the approaching Millennium - after all an indisputably Christian feast - can prompt us to seek for faith and work towards spiritual renewal. Prince Charles noted that unless the Church is involved, it risks becoming *a giant but essentially meaningless party.* The Bishop of Maidstone wrote in 'A Chance to Start Again':

> *Christians have adopted from the Jewish tradition the challenge to celebrate particular moments as jubilees. People in our society are familiar with the idea of celebrating anniversaries. A jubilee goes much further. It is a way of saying that this moment in time, this anniversary, reminds us of God's purpose and activity in our lives and in our world. The jubilee moment becomes an invitation to rededicate ourselves to the mission of Christ .....*

So there will be concentration on the signs of spiritual hunger and the demand for religious renewal, seeking for *new heavens and a new earth,* tying in with a national mood of reflection in 1999. With an evangelical

Archbishop of Canterbury, head of the 70-million strong worldwide Anglican Communion, there will be emphasis on witness and prayer. Sinners will not be damned to a fiery hell, more a deprivation of God's love. Worship in a public place, in church or in private should be more focused: maybe even school assemblies will be given the religious kiss of life. The church is adopting modern management techniques, including marketing the Cross as a 'brand image'. A 'Millennium Roadshow' with a round green logo proclaiming *New Start* has been touring under the aegis of the country's two archbishops and Churches Together in England, reminding the country that Christ is the centre of our celebrations. Congregations will receive new translations of the Bible, new hymns have been written (some in response to an initiative from St Paul's Cathedral), and there will be a plethora of new prayer books. A new Alternative Service of communion is expected (indeed, the 1980 version will be technically illegal after 2000), which has been widely debated in the Church's Synod. It aims to replace the rather prosaic language of its predecessor and return to more spiritual and poetic language reminiscent of the early church and the orthodox tradition of St Basil, along with more congregation participation. However, it won't matter how you pray - whether kneeling traditionally in church, sitting watching a candle, or whatever - but prayer may well become more contemplative and akin to meditation, than public reciting of ritual prayers. The important thing will be faith.

The Judaic jubilee, as outlined in Leviticus, Chapter 25, was proclaimed on the fiftieth year after seven cycles of seven years. It began on the Day of Atonement with the blowing of a trumpet (the word jubilee comes from the Hebrew word for 'ram's horn'), and was a time of celebration, liberation and the beginning of a year in which to sort out justice and to display mercy. This law was meant to prevent a permanent system of classes developing, and gave everyone the chance to start again. One particular aspect was of the forgiveness of debt; the Archbishop of Canterbury called for discussion of international debt, which he likened to the issue of the slave trade 200 years ago, at the Lambeth Conference in July, 1998, and a coalition called Jubilee 2000 have been fighting for it. Archbishop Tutu of South Africa said *The leaders of rich nations should look to the Bible for inspiration ..... You cancel any debts owed, if there are slaves you set them free.* There will be renewed respect for the other great religions of the world, many of whose adherents have a part to play in our multicultural society. The attention of many Roman Catholics will be focused on the Pope in Rome, who has declared that the millennium is a 'gran guibileo' while firmly rejecting the idea of the world soon coming to an end; and, as will also be considered later, Christians everywhere will turn towards the Holy Land. Let us look at what is happening here with the churches in the United Kingdom.

The Church of England has taken a lead - Archbishop George Carey calls it *a Christian party to which everyone is welcome* - but the same message has been strongly supported by other Christian denominations; often, in the encouraging modern spirit of ecumenism, coming together to plan millennial events both nationally and locally, such as those in Cardiff. Glasgow will still be basking in the glow of having hosted an exhibition in summer 1999 of the Dead Sea Scrolls on only their second visit to Europe; these were 800 manuscripts found in 11 caves in the Judaean Desert between 1947 and 1956, and are the oldest known Biblical manuscripts, many of which are still being deciphered. Meanwhile, the Church is involved to a certain extent in the National Exhibition in the Millennium Dome in Greenwich. There is to be a cycle of Millennium Mystery Plays performed in York Minster from June 22nd, 2000, and a newly-written cycle at Southwark.

Great plans are made for Christ-focused movements within public celebrations to welcome in the new Millennium on December 31st 1999. The Council of Church Bell Ringers has been restoring bells around Britain, some of which have been silent for two hundred years, and 150 new ones have been cast at either of England's two bell foundries, at Whitechapel and in Loughborough. A fully-glazed Bell Tower has been created in Basildon, Essex, with newly-tuned bells; the bronze Netherbow bell in Edinburgh is now in fine tune again after being silent for two hundred years; but the bells of St John's, Waterloo, in London, which were out-of-tune when Thomas Mears hung them in 1825, have been re-hung at the directive of English Heritage only partially tuned. A spokesman for the CCBR, who are busy training up new campanologists, promised that *all the bells throughout Britain will be sounding out at midnight on New Year's Eve, 1999*; these bells will be heard again at noon the following day, when the Open Churches Trust is planning a nationwide peal 'Ringing in the Millennium', together with a short act of prayer.

The Church Floodlighting Trust, backed by Lottery money of two million pounds, will light up 400 churches, this floodlighting to be ceremonially switched on for the occasion and some time thereafter (despite the protests of astronomers about light pollution.) One church that has relished their floodlighting for several years is St Andrew's in Butterwick, Lincolnshire. Other parishes like St Giles, Ickenham, will encourage the quieter light of candles in every window. Meanwhile, out in churchyards, the biologist David Bellamy has urged every parish to plant at least one yew tree, it being an ancient tree that can live a millennium or two, and originally kept out cattle and also provided the bows for English archers. Many churches have cleaned up old gravestones; or cleared them quietly to one side or placed plaques along a wall, to make a Garden of Remembrance. Raising one's eyes to the tower or the spire, if you are very sharp-eyed you may see the discreet grey bristle of telephone antennae; as some churches, including Ely Cathedral, have discovered a source of much-needed revenue by allowing mobile phone companies to put up their aerials on what might be the highest point in the neighbourhood. This mutually satisfactory arrangement has been dubbed by some *the great steeple chase.*

There will be further special celebrations at Pentecost. On Saturday, 10th June, there is a Global March for Jesus; on the Sunday, as suggested by the Archbishops' Office for the Millennium, there will be a nation-wide day of witness; followed of course by the bonus of the special Millennium Bank Holiday Monday.

In an interesting article in the 'Church of England Newspaper', the journalist Terry Warburton, having decided that celebrations even at

Pentecost were a little like celebrating the birth of a baby that has not yet been born, wrote:

> *Jesus enjoined his followers to 'Go and make disciples of all the nations', finishing with those amazing words of reassurance 'And know that I am with you always, yes to the end of time.' The question is, how can the Church follow his wishes on this occasion, without being seen to be triumphalist in relation to other faiths, without its message being overwhelmed by the tide of materialism or being left high and dry on the beach of the converted without touching the majority of society? Now, here is the opportunity and the challenge: to reclaim Christmas 2000 for Christ. New Year's Eve 1999 and New Year's Day 2000 will be largely secular celebrations, big business will see to that ..... (but) the Church can claim Christmas as its own. With a will, its voice could be heard at this time. Television coverage is almost guaranteed and its congregations are at their greatest. Christmas 2000: what a celebration that would be!*

This is getting one's priorities right, putting Christ back in to Christmas; and, as far as we know, as accurately as possible two thousand years after the event.

The buildings housing formal worship, which receive 35 million visits a year, should not be neglected. Despite disappointment about a planned Christian village in Battersea, Lottery money will have helped to extend St Edmundsbury Cathedral in Suffolk; London's Southwark Cathedral; Bradford Cathedral and its National Faith Heritage Centre; possibly new buildings in Canterbury and York; and the amazing religious centre in the form of a celtic cross at Cramlington, Northumberland. The 39 consecrated churches in the City of London have been revivified: St Ethelburga's, nearly destroyed by an IRA bomb, is now an ecumenical centre for peace and reconciliation, at another there is a newly-settled community of Franciscan monks, and others have become centres of meditation, relaxation and healing. Nearly 13,000 (about three-quarters) of the Church of England's churches are listed buildings; lottery money has contributed to their preservation, and the conservation of their beautiful interiors and fittings. Even churches built in this last century, which are more varied and exciting than generally supposed, need money for constant maintenance.

Faith takes many forms. A Sacred Land Project was announced in 1997 by the Archbishop of Canterbury to register the United Kingdom's five thousand sacred sites held in veneration by groups from neo-pagans through Baha'I and Jainism to Islam as well as by Christians. The sites are thereby listed and preserved for future generations. The Prince of Wales has given a moral lead in his relations to other faiths, especially with Islam, Hinduism and Sikhism. Bradford's all-faith centre is well-placed in a community of differing religions; Oxford's International Interfaith Centre is planned as 'a place where members of different faiths can meet and learn from each other on neutral ground', as is Peterborough's Hindu Concordia project. What a reminder that we are all brothers.

All religious institutions have an important part to play in social welfare; let us hope that succour can be found for all, for church-goers and non-churchgoers alike. Let us remember particularly those poor children growing up in moral poverty, where they may be surrounded by deviants and criminals trapped in desolate, chaotic, dysfunctional families, godless and jobless, where drug abuse and child neglect are twin curses. Rather, let us as a society take the opportunity of the Millennium to turn over a new leaf, and lead the benighted also to see that *Faith is a protest against meaninglessness* (Miguel de Unamuno), and a genuine alternative to despair and purposelessness.

What is indisputable about the millennium is that, while its significance concentrates some minds wonderfully along fairly conventional lines, for other people it beckons them along strange and weird ways. It is as though the roundness and apparent completeness of certain dates acts as an irresistible challenge to seekers after truth. Whether you are a stern millenarian or a gentle New Age dreamer, the year 2000 seems to be a chance to play God and (maybe) to write your own doomsday scenario.

At the last Millennium there were some who sold all their possessions and wandered away to find God. At the time of the Middle Ages' Black Death, victims engulfed by religious frenzy did a Dance of Death; people believed in the True Grail, and the Turin Shroud, and the liquefaction of St Gennaro in Naples. In the seventeenth century there were Diggers, Levellers, Ranters and Fifth Monarchy Men, whose dreams of social justice were inseparable from the idea of the great hereafter for the few but damnation for the many. Later, there were the Illuminati, who strove for rational enlightenment. Today at this significant point in time, we have Seventh Day Adventists, Jehovah's Witnesses, Christadelphians, Pentacostalists and other born-again Christians, Moonies, the Exclusive (Plymouth) Brethren, Scientologists, Mormons, the Jesus Army, the Celestian Church of Christ, the Rosicrucians, the Children of God, Moral Re-Armament, Zoroastrans, Hare Krishna, various voodooists, swamis and yogics, those who believe that even now the new Messiah is being brought up in London's Brick Lane, and many more exclusive cults and sects who believe the millennium will vindicate their faith. Damian Thompson, in his 1996 book 'The End of Time', noted

> *There are a number of unexpected parallels between the three main strands of apocalyptic belief - fundamentalists, Catholic and New Age. All of them predict natural cataclysms, (and) all of them deal in extra-terrestial communications whether outpourings of the Holy Spirit, apparitions of Mary or 'channelled' messages from other civilisations.*

Recently, there was an excellent radio series by the BBC's one-time religious affairs correspondent, Ted Harrison, on current religious issues called 'For God's Sake.' He explained to me later that it is a time of great interest in eschatology (that is, ideas of death, judgement, heaven and hell, *the doctrine of the last things*.) With millennial fervour gaining momentum, many are proclaiming that the end is nigh; or at least that sweeping changes are about to take place. One programme featured a member of the Aetherius Society, which thinks Jesus was an extraterrestial visitor from Mars, and that there is a new Aquarian age dawning when religion and science will come together. What such believers propound is that God will come again; or that He has come but that they alone have noticed. They claim that God's plans have been revealed to them in dreams (while they slept) or visions (while awake.) This leads them to prophesy, sometimes in audacious detail, exactly what will happen. Non-believers are made nervous by prophecy: should we pre-view the future, when it is not natural to draw aside the curtain of time and see what is revealed? What would we find, anyway? Supposing the future is a series of unpleasantnesses; can't we cope better by having them revealed to us gradually one by one? The Old Testament prophet's rôle, like that of Communist leaders in the tough years, was often to warn of coming trials and tribulations, while keeping up morale by assuring that it would all come out all right in the end, albeit in generations to come. Most of us nowadays are too impatient for that: and suppose, as with some doom-mongerers, there is no happy ending for the majority anyway?

It has to be admitted that most seers and soothsayers are just such masochists. They run the risk of ridicule and rejection with their gloomy prognostications, but have nonetheless a burning urge to get their message across. It can hardly have been fun being Nostrodamus or Joanna Southcott, hardly a comfortable option: but they had this burning compulsion to share their wild-eyed vision of gloom with the world. Some seers' forewarnings have been taken seriously: Joan of Arc's visions in fifteenth century France; the three secrets of Fatima in Portugal, revealed to three children in 1917; and those who see a message in the weeping statues of Knock in Ireland and in what was Yugoslavia. Some modern-day prophecies are being revealed, it is claimed, by modern technology, like the Bible Code (which indeed Isaac Newton is said to have laboured upon in vain in the early eighteenth century.) This involves running together all the letters of the first five books of the original Bible, in Hebrew, and then selecting letters in a certain sequence - following mathematical group theory - to spell out significant words.

Many prophets and their followers, today as before, take their ideas and vocabulary from the last book in the New Testament, popularly called Revelations. It is the startlingly vivid testimony of the apostle John, who when he was exiled on the island of Patmos received seven mystical visions from God. It contains references to astrology, numerology such as 666 (the Mark of the Beast, or Satan), magic, shamanism, and the Four Horsemen of the Apocalypse; and describes the final Battle of Armageddon, identified with a real place, Megiddo, in Palestine (although scientists believe that ancient civilisations were mainly toppled by natural disasters rather than by war.) In the best-known chapter, he sees a vision of Satan being cast in to the bottomless pit and chained there for a thousand years. He then breaks free to cause chaos; after which God triumphs and saves the faithful. Father Neil Horan, an outspoken priest from Ireland, points out that *Prophecy is an important part of the Gospel message, but has been almost entirely neglected by the church.* He wrote for 'Miscellennium':

> *The Bible book which is, above all else, a book of prophecy is the Revelations: it clearly predicts the end of the world, and the making of 'a New Heaven and a New Earth', when 'God shall wipe away all tears from their eyes.' Yes, the future is full of hope, not of gloom; full of joy, not sorrow. The end of the world should be a topic to cause uplift. Could the end of the twentieth century see the most momentous events in History, leading to the establishment of the Kingdom of God on earth?*

The trouble with many millennial thinkers is that they cannot satisfactorily reconcile the dilemma that in order to reach the radiant new dawn (probably only for believers), the titanic struggle of world-wide catastrophe first has to be endured. They alone will escape the flames which will consume the many, as they are flung in to the bottomless burning pit with Satan. Their escape may be by 'being raptured', a phrase beloved of American fundamentalists which indicates their being airlifted aloft in to the heavens. They huddle together in their cults, convinced of their own righteousness and flaunting the fact that they will be saved. Whether they are mainly religious cults or 'therapy' cults, they often use pretty sinister totalitarian ways of recruitment and retention. Believers are recruited with considerable guile, using techniques like 'flirty fishing' or love-bombing; they may then undergo a mixture of hypnosis, deprivation (sleep, privacy, affection, choice of food) and insistent peer pressure. The recruit 'snaps' in to acceptance or conversion, and experiences a drastic personality change, distancing themselves from family, friends or moderate ideas.

Do these cultists have no conscience about abandoning the rest of us not of their gang to perdition? Indeed, do some of the extreme sects actually plan to expedite matters, by fast-forwarding Armageddon? The end of the century has seen some acts carried out by cults which seem to the rest of us quite ghastly. In 1997, thirty-eight Heaven's Gate cultists died in California, perhaps trying to catch up with a 'spaceship' following the Hale-Bopp comet. 70 members of the Solar Temple died in Switzerland, France and Canada. In 1993, over 50 Vietnamese villagers killed themselves in a cult suicide pact. 1993's Waco siege in Texas despatched over seventy Branch Davidians to their form of heaven; in 1991, thirty Mexican churchgoers killed themselves. In 1978, the Rev Jim Jones led 914 followers to their deaths in Jonestown, Guyana. But it is when they take other people ..... It may have been cultists called Christian Identity who were behind the Oklahoma bombings in 1995; Japan's Aum Shinri Kyo sect killed twelve and injured 5,000 in the Tokyo subway in 1996. That is taking millenarianism too far .....

Let us move away from cults as such, and consider New Age ideas, where the worlds of spirituality and medicine often overlap as a healthy body is meant to lead to a calm mind, and vice-versa. These ideas sometimes better themselves by moving up from crankiness to alternative therapies or medicine, even in some cases like chiropractice to respectability. Some of the alternative ideas are good, or at least not harmful; but many of them remind you of the statement that when man gives up believing, he believes not in nothing but in anything. Of course we cannot know everything - gone are the days when one could aspire to being a polymath or scholar knowing most things - and certainly we should be open to new ideas in thought, in healing, about our environment, and in our spiritual lives, so maybe the millennium with its chronological 'roundness' is a time to try new ideas? Most people, however, still feel more comfortable with mainstream ideas, even at times finding it difficult to cope with everyday reality, let alone the taxing business of changing our lives and challenging the universe.

That to believers is part of the paradox of faith in Jesus Christ. He is one of the omniscient Trinity and commands complete belief (a hard task for some of us struggling with the free will God allows us); but He also provides a secure haven for those who can accept Him. Which is why Christians feel very strongly that the spiritual power of Christ should be at the heart of millennium celebrations, that it is not just the province of the tourist board/theme park/heritage industry. At this Millennium, we should acknowledge God's presence throughout time and space, reminding ourselves that materially-rich though we may be, we are often spiritually deprived. We should be rejoicing that He sent His beloved son to earth for us; which is why this chapter ends, as it began, in a cowstall in the little town of Bethlehem.

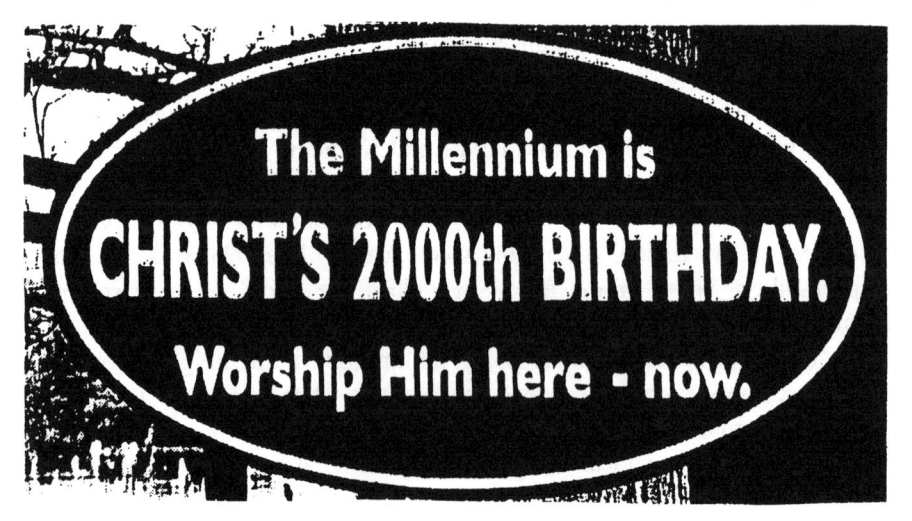

This sign, erected in front of his church, St Boniface's in Bunbury near Liverpool, by Canon John Bowers (who has also produced bumper stickers), was inspired by a sign he saw in Turkey. Hundreds of other churches have followed this example.

THE PILGRIM

Who would true valour see,
Let him come hither;
One here will constant be,
Come wind, come weather.
There's no discouragement
Shall make him once relent
His first avowed intent
To be a Pilgrim.

Who so beset him round
With dismal stories
Do but themselves confound;
His strength the more is.
No lion can him fright,
He'll with a giant fight,
But he will have a right
To be a Pilgrim.

Hobgoblin nor foul fiend
Can daunt his spirit:
He knows he at the end
Shall life inherit.
Then fancies fly away,
He'll fear not what men say,
He'll labour night and day
To be a Pilgrim.

John Bunyan (1628-1688)

*I was hungry, and you formed a discussion group to discuss my hunger.
I was imprisoned, and you quietly crept off to your chapel
and prayed for my release.
I was naked, and in your mind you debated the
morality of my appearance.
I was sick, and you knelt and thanked God for your health.
I was homeless, and you preached to me
the spiritual shelter of the love of God.
I was lonely, and you left me alone to pray for me.
You seem so holy, so close to God.
But I am still very hungry - and lonely - and cold.*

Reproduced with the permission of `Shelter` ©

ALONE WITHIN MANY AN ILLUSION

On earth a strange yet unmistakable incompleteness is sensed,
as if each knows there is part of himself from which he is somehow
mysteriously separated. This belongs to the human condition. Yet the
limitation and the yearning felt so painfully can be pointing all the
while towards the very thing from which one meanwhile feels so exiled.

from 'Hidden Man' by Paul Beard ©1986

GOD WHERE ARE YOU?

My pain falls like rain
And it's sending me insane...
It's causing my brain to strain -
I want to complain but the pain is in my brain.
And it won't let me.

Surely I am insane :
I cannot control my brain
The pain
Is in my dreams and in my thoughts.
I want to cut the pain
But it's in control
Of my heart, mind and soul -
Like a mole
It burrows in to every part
Of me.
I am doomed.

Peter Higginson ©

A PRAYER FOR FORTITUDE

God, at times I seem to be banging my head against a brick wall. No matter how I tackle a problem, I just can't seem to crack it. Perhaps I try too hard? Perhaps I should stand back and let life take its natural course? Perhaps I should release my prayer to You and let go?

I believe in solving my own problems in a hands-on way. Please teach me to appreciate that prayer is pro-active. Please help me to foster confidence in my prayers, and give me fortitude to do nothing - to leave it all to You in those times when Your help is truly needed. Teach me to know when I am licked!

Please help me in my meditation periods to grow in wisdom - to appreciate that man's self-induced sense of urgency is unnecessary; to appreciate the effective workings of nature - in its own time.

Ivan Sanders ©

THE UPRIGHT MAN

The man of life upright, whose guiltless heart is free
From all dishonest deeds, and thoughts of vanity;
That man whose silent days in harmless joys are spent,
Whom hopes cannot delude, nor fortune discontent;
That man needs neither tower nor armour for defence,
Nor secret vaults to fly from thunder's violence.
He only can behold with unaffrighted eyes
The horrors of the deep and terrors of the skies.
Thus, scorning all the care that fate or fortune brings,
He makes the heaven his book, his wisdom heavenly things,
Good thoughts his only friends, his wealth a well-spent age,
The earth his sober inn - a quiet pilgrimage.

Thomas Campion (1567-1620)
This poem appeared in a song book published in 1601.

from DOVER BEACH

The sea is calm tonight.
The tide is full, the moon lies fair
Upon the straits; on the French coast the light
Gleams and is gone; the cliffs of England stand,
Glimmering and vast, out in the tranquil bay.
Come to the window, sweet is the night air!
Only, from the long line of spray
Where the sea meets the moon-blanched land,
Listen! you hear the grating roar
Of pebbles which the waves draw back, and fling,
At their return, up the high strand,
Begin, and cease, and then again begin,
With tremendous cadence slow, and bring
The eternal note of sadness in.
Sophocles long ago
Heard it on the Aegean, and it brought
Into his mind the turbid ebb and flow
Of human misery; we
Find also in the sound a thought,
Hearing it by this distant northern sea.

The Sea of Faith
Was once, too, at the full, and round earth's shore
Lay like the folds of a bright girdle furled.
But now I only hear
Its melancholy, long, withdrawing roar,
Retreating, to the breath
Of the night-wind, down the vast edges drear
And naked shingles of the world.
…… We are here as on a darkling plain
Swept with confused alarms of struggle and flight,
Where ignorant armies clash by night.

Matthew Arnold (1822-1888)

*'Twas God the Word that spake it,
He took the bread and brake it ;
And what the Word did make it,
That I believe, and take it.*

Queen Elizabeth I (1533-1603)

Als die Nazis die Juden holten
habe ich geschwiegen;
ich war ja kein Jude.

Als sie die Kommunisten holten,
habe ich geschwiegen;
ich war ja kein Kommunist.

Als sie die Gewerkschafter holten,
habe ich geschwiegen;
ich war ja kein Gewerkschafter.

Als sie mich holten, gab es keinen mehr,
der protestieren konnte.

First they came for the Jews
and I did not speak out;
because I was not a Jew

Then they came for the Communists
and I did not speak out;
because I was not a Communist

Next they came for the trade unionists
and I did not speak out;
because I was not a trade unionist

Then they came for me, and there was no one left
to speak for me.

Pastor Martin Niemöller (1892-1984),
inmate of Sachsenhausen and Dachau

© Evangelische Kirche in Hessen und Nassau

ANTHEM FOR DOOMED YOUTH

What passing-bells for these who die as cattle?
Only the monstrous anger of the guns,
Only the stuttering rifles' rapid rattle,
Can patter out their hasty orisons.
No mockeries now for them; no prayers nor bells,
Nor any voice of mourning save the choirs -
The shrill, demented choirs of wailing shells;
And bugles calling for them from sad shires.

What candles may be held to speed them all ?
Not in the hands of boys, but in their eyes
Shall shine the holy glimmers of goodbyes.
The pallor of girls' brows shall be their pall;
Their flowers the tenderness of patient minds,
And each slow dusk a drawing-down of blinds.

Wilfred Owen (1893-1918).
This sonnet is an extended metaphor
for the death of a generation.

The Christian life is as
the turning of the sunflower to the Sun.

from the Sermons of Rev. Dr. Robertson,
Series IV, number 40, first delivered in 1852.

He said to me, 'It is done! I am the Alpha and the Omega, the Beginning and the End. I will give of the fountain of the water of life freely to him who thirsts.
'He who overcomes shall inherit all things, and I will be his God and he shall be My son.
'But the cowardly, unbelieving, abominable, murderers, sexually immoral, sorcerers, idolators, and all liars shall have their part in the lake which burns with fire and brimstone, which is the second death.'

'Blessed are those who do His commandments, that they may have the right to the tree of life, and may enter through the gates into the city. I, Jesus, have sent My angel to testify to you these things in the churches. I am the Root and Offspring of David, the Bright and Morning Star.'

The Bible, The Book of Revelations, 21. 6-8 and 22. 14,16

What is spirituality? Is it leading the good life, church on Sundays, jam making for the church fête, a pound in every collecting tin? Is it reading the Bible, studying the Psalms, writing letters to the Church Times? Is it sending a note to the bereaved, working in a charity shop, helping at hospital, sponsoring an overseas child, helping at Sunday school? Is it a smile on a wet day, holding a door open, taking a friend out for lunch? Is it an unexpected visit to a parent, an extra kiss for a spouse, an encouraging word to a child, a hug for someone who's troubled?

It is all these; but above all, it is a thoughtful mind, a caring heart, a twinkle in the eye and a merry smile.

I REMEMBER, I REMEMBER

I remember, I remember,
The house where I was born,
The little window where the sun
Came peeping in at morn;
He never came a wink too soon,
Nor brought too long a day;
But now, I often wish the night
Had borne my breath away!

I remember, I remember,
Where I used to swing
And thought the air must rush as fresh,
To swallows on the wing;
My spirit flew in feathers then
That is so heavy now,
And summer pools could hardly cool
The fever on my brow.

I remember, I remember
The fir-trees dark and high;
I used to think their slender tops
Were close against the sky;
It was a childish ignorance,
But now 'tis little joy
To know I'm farther off from heaven
Than when I was a boy.

Thomas Hood (1799-1845)

CHAPTER 7 : HOW GREEN IS MY PLANET ?

As society has moved from agricultural revolution through industrial revolution to the techno-computing world, in one sense we have moved away from our roots (a metaphor from Nature, of course); in another, with growing concern for ecology and green issues, we are learning to respect our world all over again. We return like naughty children to Mother Earth, apologising for spurning her and abusing the riches she entrusted to us. One attraction of New Age thought, as briefly mentioned in the last chapter, is concern for the environment: but even main-stream thought has begun to realise that if we are to be around in future millennia, we must husband the Earth's resources, and cannot with impunity go on squandering fossil fuels, putting pressure on biodiversity, polluting the seas and cutting down the rain forests. St Paul said *For whatsoever a man soweth, that shall he also reap*; literally, what damage we do to our world, will haunt our children and our children's children.

An observable phenomenon is that as the Millennium approached, it seemed collectively to focus people's minds on our treatment of the world. Just as, on contemplating Christ's birth, we might seize the opportunity to review our souls, it is also a particularly poignant time to view our environment. A microcosm of this might be our own little plot at home, our patio pots or garden, allotment or local park; or the wider lungs of green of the countryside, and the great fields of grain which provide our sustenance. It is not pure altruism to protect our green world, it is also a cold-blooded necessity. We must husband its resources for the sake of everyone who follows us, we must work with it in symbiosis - otherwise the planet will be brown, destitute and lifeless. If spring falls silent, crops cannot burgeon, animals waste away, seas become polluted and air unbreathable, won't it be disastrous for all? As the palaeontologist Richard Leakey pointed out recently, there have been five previous extinctions, the most recent catching the dinosaurs unawares: if we bring about a sixth extinction, it will be our own fault. We cannot all squeeze in to biosphere bubbles of artificial environments, even if one wanted to. We must re-use, conserve, re-cycle, and cherish our beautiful world.

Already we have considered the sunflower as a symbol of the fin-de-siècle, which is an extrovert flower, bold and cheerful, but also productive - that golden oil, those crunchy seeds. Seeds are of course the quintessence of new life, and consequently hope for the future. It seems particularly fitting therefore that one of the major recipients in Britain of lottery funding (one of the few Landmark projects of the Lottery to be ready on time), has been the Millennium Seed Bank project of Kew Gardens. Their Alison Mitchell wrote:

> We aim to collect seeds from the UK's 1,400 native plants, and by the year 2010 we plan to have collected 25% of the world's flora, approximately 25,000 species. All of these seeds will be stored in the Millennium Seed Bank at Wakehurst Place, Sussex, which is of global environmental significance. It is vital if we are to retrieve some species from the edge of extinction and preserve them for the use and enjoyment of future generations. Once in the Bank, seeds can be dried and kept at sub-zero temperatures for centuries or even millennia. They can be studied at length to discover how they can benefit mankind, and reintroduced in to the wild.

Patron of the Appeal is Sir David Attenborough, who has also been planning his year 2000 television production investigating the state of the planet. Another seed-lover, Hugh Stewart, reminded me that *Cereal grains recently found in Jericho, there at the time of its destruction, have been carbon-dated to be over three millennia old (1315 B.C.) ..... The dating seems consistent with known history, and supports the Biblical account.*

Parks will be renovated, such as Battersea and Coram Fields in London. Garden projects seem to be sprouting everywhere, either for renovation or to open up to the public. Tim Smit gained considerable fame with a 1997 television series on the renovation of the gardens at Heligan in Cornwall, and is now the moving spirit behind the Eden Project. This gained £50 million of lottery funding to transform a clay pit at St Austell in to 'the world's largest greenhouse', actually four in number, through which visitors will be able to walk and wonder. The so-called 'biomes', cunningly set in to the original topography, will house plant collections which will then represent a lush Indonesian rainforest, a flowering desert, the sub-tropics, and the Mediterranean, as a combination of permanent garden festival and botanical garden. It will probably feature on the series of expected Millennium stamps.

This country is blessed with some first-rate botanical gardens, of course, at Cambridge, Edinburgh, Kew and Oxford; another is the planned Botanic Garden for Wales, due to open on May 26th, 2000, at Middleton in Carmarthenshire. Originally a grand estate created in the 1770s, its six linked lakes will be renovated, as will its unique five-acre walled garden and arboretum. It will have a new domed glass-house designed by Sir Norman Foster, and educational areas known as the 'bioscope' and 'biosphere'. There is also to be a Millennium Coastal Park in Llannelli. In Doncaster, there has been quite a challenge to match lottery money to raise £125 million to create the imaginative Earth Centre straddling a 400-hundred acre site in South Yorkshire. This is to be a major centre for environmental research, uniting academic conservation with exploratory features for visitors, and a showcase for ecologically friendly, sustainable technology throughout the world.

Already much-loved is the Garden of the Rose outside St Albans. Their Development Secretary, Derek Palmer-Brown, explained to me that the Royal National Rose Society has been in existence since 1876. As well as organising the British Rose Festival, it has been creating and developing these amazing specialist gardens since 1960, to conserve and display their unique collection of 30,000 roses. It is truly a rose-lover's dream especially in summer time, and has particular Theme Gardens to interest certain groups. About a fifth of their visitors are from overseas. Their Rose 2000 development plan will extend and enhance the grounds and plantings and add a visitor centre, but above all, extend their work with the rose.

If instead of propagating gardens yourself, you fancy visiting other people's handiwork, a great treat for many people is to wander round the gardens opened for charity each year listed in the famous Yellow Book of the National Gardens Scheme. Although their Director, Col. Tym Marsh, told us that they have no special plans for the

Millennium (*We are holding our fire until our 75th anniversary in 2002*), if you enjoy visiting gardens from country mansions to twee backyards you will find all of them perennially fascinating. If you prefer walking through countryside rather than round gardens, you will be interested in Millennium plans for footpaths. In 1987, the then government promised to hike up the pace of improvements, so that by the turn of the century all 140,000 miles of public paths and bridleways would be clear, signposted and decently surfaced, reinforcing the 1990 Rights of Way Act, with stiff fines for obstructive landowners. Unlikely to be completed on time, nonetheless this is a commendable scheme which has the strong support of the Ramblers' Association.

..... Or riding through the countryside? Then find out more about the National Cycle Network promoted by Sustrans (short for sustainable transport), which has planned a national infrastructure of high-quality and attractive routes reaching all areas of mainland Britain. Financed in part by Lottery money, the so-called Millennium Routes (2,400 miles in all) are to be finished by 2000, with twice as many again ready five years later. A third of the population live within a ten-minute ride of one: for any owner of one of the twenty-one million mostly-unused bikes in this country, it will be an incentive to get out and explore these routes, like the delightful one from Padstow to Bristol over Bodmin, Exmoor and the Somerset Levels. Unlike W.S. Gilbert's nightmare of *crossing Salisbury Plain on a bicycle*, this will be good fun, and good exercise. Routes will be along derelict railway lines (i.e. mainly flat, because trains could not cope with huge gradients), canal towpaths, traffic-calmed roads, along the coast from Eastbourne to Dover, and for a 44 mile corridor along the Thames from Hampton Court to Dartford. It could be good for tourism, especially in beautiful country areas. In other countries, cycling has a more political significance: J.A. Viera Gallo of Chile said in 1974, *El socialismo puede llegar solo en bicicle (Socialism can only arrive by bicycle.)*

What are particularly English are our village greens. Part of our folk-memory of supposedly-idyllic rural communities from the past, they are still the attractive hearts of many villages. The aim is that around a thousand new ones are being created, thanks to Lottery money via the Countryside Commission, both in traditional villages and also as 'urban breathing spaces', giving a permanent focus to the conservation and outdoor leisure interests of a community. An example is Dormanstown in Cleveland, where a new green has been formed midway between a steel works and a chemical plant. Greens will be planted and registered under the Commons Registration Act (1970), and it is hoped that this will reverse the trend of enclosing or (as in Biggin Hill) building on our beloved village greens.

The greens lie so pleasantly; the stately homes of England, how beautiful they stand. Another great British institution is visiting National Trust properties, both for their fascinating houses and their varied gardens; and also to see the work they do on preserving our coastlines, countryside and woodland. The Woodland Trust was given money (£6.5 million) from the Millennium Commission to improve or establish 200 community woodlands throughout England and Wales. Additionally, there are two millennial projects particularly connected with trees. One is the National Memorial Arboretum in Staffordshire, at the epicentre of the country. Planted on over 150 acres of reclaimed gravel pits, it is creating a living, long-lasting tribute to those who have died in war in the century just passing, and as a gesture of hope for peace. The visionary project and its theme of 'Remembrance and Reconciliation' was inspired by Grp. Capt. Leonard Cheshire, V.C.. There will be a visitor centre, and a multi-faith chapel dedicated in December 1999, gardens themed around the various services and national icons like the Royal Family, a wildfowl reserve, but above all, trees. The centrepiece will be the Millennium Avenue, an imposing two-thirds of a mile long avenue of trees propagated from a 2,000 year old lime tree at Westonbirt arboretum.

The other arboreal plan is particularly appropriate as it originates from the University at Greenwich, on the Meridian. Dr Patrick Roper from the University wrote:
The Millennium Tree Line is a project set up to identify and conserve existing trees and plant trees along the Greenwich

Meridian (zero degrees longitude) to mark the arrival of the Third Millennium; initially in England (from North Humberside to East Sussex) then, as the project develops, in Europe and Africa. As the Tree Line becomes more continuous and mature it will be visible from the air and from space, as well as being an enduring and developing feature on the ground. Many of the trees will live for a thousand years, some species maybe for several thousand, and we believe that once the line is established, successive generations will want to keep it going. In addition to its general interest, the project has considerable environmental value and it is intended that it will generate a variety of environmentally-orientated associated projects.

France, Spain, North Africa and Ghana have collaborated to ensure that this is a really green millennial success. By definition, trees convey the dignity of maturity and ageing, so are fitting as long-term millennial initiative projects.

One way of using trees or box-hedges is in the creation of mazes. Combining the splendour of carefully positioned trees and the mystery of a treasure hunt, they were particularly beloved by the Elizabethans, such as the well-known one at Hampton Court Palace. There have also been stone ones, brick ones like the one in Henley-on-Thames, one in a maize field in Oxfordshire, Christian mazes, and pavement mazes laid in the stone floors of Gothic cathedrals in France to act as a 'memento mori'. When the previous Archbishop of Canterbury, Dr Robert Runcie, was enthroned, he used the maze as a metaphor to describe the human journey through life.

This has been a long, bracing ramble through the 'green' celebration of our Millennium. As we look back on our past, we can mourn the loss - through over-population, urbanisation, abuse of natural resources, greed and neglect - of so much of the world's green lungs; but we must take the opportunity to look forward, to commend and celebrate the riches of the earth, to breathe life in to those lungs, and by working at green issues, to give the kiss of life to our planet.

A POEM AS LOVELY AS A TREE

I think that I shall never see
A poem lovely as a tree;
Poems are made by fools like me
But only God can make a tree.

A.J. Kilmer (1886-1918)

NATURE'S DIURNAL ROUND

Dawn is the only time
Birds get for rehearsing new songs.

Day is when both people and insects
Buzz about their business.

Twilight could deafen you
If you could hear the shadows creeping.

Night is about the only time
That shy animals get to windowshop.

Kunal Desai ©

THE QUATRAIN OF THE BUSH

Do not dismiss the bush
As a plant with aspiration;
Nor see it merely
As a tree sans elevation.

Margaret Noone

THE TYGER

Tyger! Tyger! burning bright,
In the forests of the night:
What immortal hand or eye
Could frame thy fearful symmetry?

In what distant deeps or skies
Burnt the fire of thine eyes?
On what wings dare he aspire?
What the hand dare seize the fire?

And what shoulder, & what art,
Could twist the sinews of thy heart?
And when thy heart began to beat,
What dread hand? & what dread feet?

What the hammer? what the chain?
In what furnace was thy brain?
What the anvil? what dread grasp,
Dare its deadly terrors clasp?

When the stars threw down their spears
And watered heaven with their tears:
Did he smile his work to see?
Did he who made the Lamb make thee?

Tyger! Tyger! burning bright,
In the forests of the night:
What immortal hand or eye,
Dare frame thy fearful symmetry?

William Blake (1757-1827)

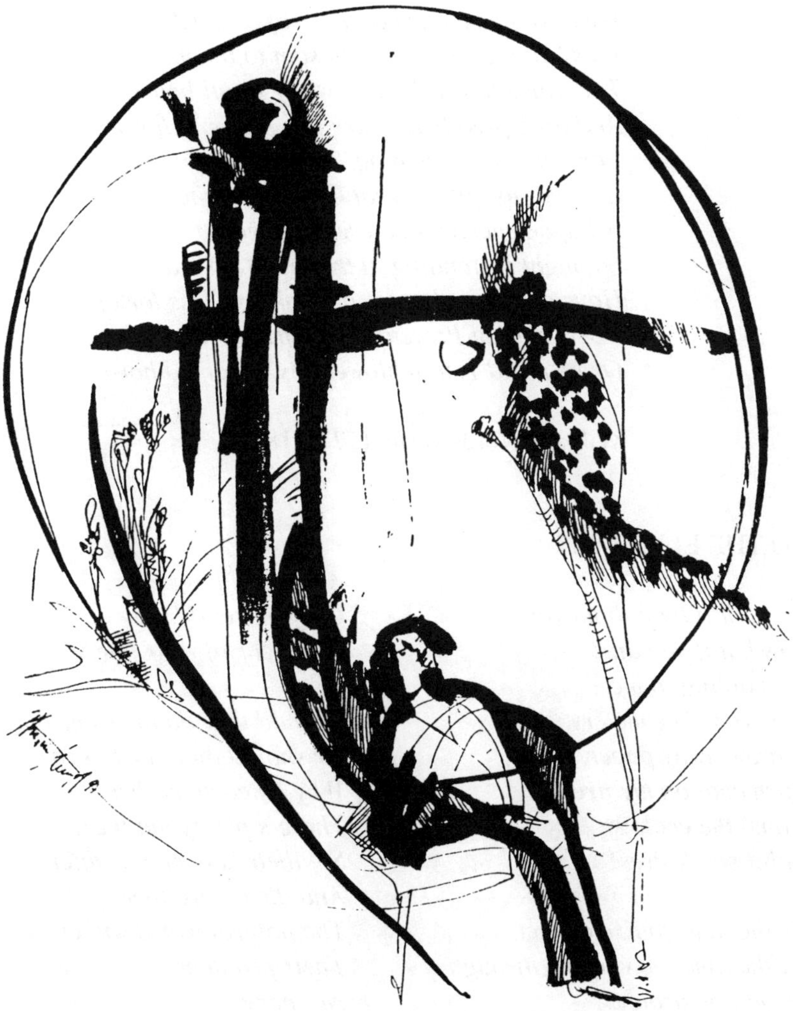

THE WORLD IS TOO MUCH WITH US

The world is too much with us; late and soon,
Getting and spending, we lay waste our powers:
Little we see in nature that is ours;
We have given our hearts away, a sordid boon!
This Sea that bares her bosom to the moon;
The winds that will be howling at all hours,
And are up-gathered now like sleeping flowers;
For this, for everything, we are out of tune;
It moves us not. - Great God! I'd rather be
A Pagan suckled in a creed outworn;
So might I, standing in this pleasant lea,
Have glimpses that would make me less forlorn;
Have sight of Proteus rising from the sea;
Or hear old Triton blowed his wreathed horn.

William Wordsworth (1770-1850)

TO THE ELEPHANT

So what if they shoot you?
So what if you die?
It's nothing to me,
You won't see me cry.
I throw away paper,
Burn coal on my fires,
Damn the ecology,
Fulfil my desires!

By the time you're extinct,
By the time the world's through
I won't be around
To care for you..
I'll be long gone
And so will my mate.
Only our children
Will hear of your fate.

Should they do the same thing?
Or should they start to care?
Why on earth bother?
There's plenty out there.
So, their kids might suffer,
And die before time.
The natural world wither;
Their problem,
Not mine!

Kate Saw ©

ENVIRONMENT MILLENNIUM

A thousand summers passed, and
Race after race of men were wiped out
For the sake of some land somewhere.
We also managed to make animals extinct,
(And travel to the moon), and even
Watch it on the box they call television.
Year after year became history and faded
Grey, but the sun still bothered to
Keep moving, and the sea and the sky
Remained blue, while we somehow
Had a higher power to do with those
Thousand years what we would, trying
Desperately to build monuments that would
Withstand time, but failing; while trees
Managed silently, and rocks did too.
We, with our power so great, were only
Servants to time, but wouldn't believe it.

Of course, in the hands of children,
The next millennium would be less wasted …..?

Alison Williams ©

> *I see the future as an unhappy place*
> *With a lot of problems and grief;*
> *The days hot and nights lonely,*
> *The rain poisoning the dead black sea,*
> *The birds flocking northerly.*
> *The future is around the corner -*
> *Dried-up beaches, dying lights.*
> *It is taking time for it to dawn on us -*
> *Cloudy days, murky nights.*
>
> Osman Mumtaz ©

GARDENS FOR THE MILLENNIUM

And should this be the last morning,
white light stretched to breaking point,
then we must find our gardens again,

leave the unbridled urban marshes
where tormentil and the little white weed
eke out, and all-night cats piss in the poison ivy,

through the commercial ogling
of hot-house tulips, the forced purples
they pretend are black

to come upon a muted place
where people pass twined under pergolas,
silent, sipping the cream of roses ;

beyond night's mythic flowers, stone fictions
watched by choirs of foxgloves trumpeting
in stucco to the leaning listening saints;

but the birds here are too big for the trees,
too allegorical with their jewelled eyes,
we don't believe in them, we have no simplicity,

not yet, though once a tulip tree reached up
to a castle window in the legendary Arthurian blue,
all summer it brought forth one pure white

just one white satin flower at a time,
high up, secret like a clandestine royal birth,
oblivious to impatience , disdainful of mass getting.

*It was there you watched without touching
or wanting in a float of non-desire until
that breeze came, came without premonition*

*from the locked night garden, and the water
plashed while you slept; where the syringa
would always be luminous
even without the moonlight.*

Judy Gahahgan ©

*The God of your father will help you, and the Almighty
will bless you with the blessings of heaven above;*
    Blessings of the deep that lies beneath,
    Blessings of the breasts and of the womb.
*The blessings of your father have excelled the blessings
of your ancestors, up to the utmost bound of the everlasting hills.*

                                                   The Bible, Genesis, chapter 49.

SONNETS 12 AND 124

When I do count the clock that tells the time,
And see the brave day sunk in hideous night;
When I behold the violet past prime,
And sable curls, all silver'd o'er with white;
When lofty trees I see barren of leaves,
Which erst from heat did canopy the herd,
And summer's green all girded up in sheaves,
Borne on the bier with white and bristly beard;
Then of thy beauty do I question make,
That thou among the wastes of time must go,
Since sweets and beauties do themselves forsake,
And die as fast as they see others grow;
    And nothing 'gainst Time's scythe can make defence
    Save breed, to brave him when he takes thee hence.

If my dear love were but the child of state,
It might for Fortune's bastard be unfather'd,
As subject to Time's love, or to Time's hate,
Weeds among weeds, or flowers with flowers gather'd.
No, it was builded far from accident;
It suffers not in smiling pomp, nor falls
Under the blow of thralled discontent,
Whereto the inviting time our fashion calls:
It fears not policy, that heretic,
Which works on leases of short-number'd hours,
But all alone stands hugely politic,
That it nor grows with heat, nor drowns with showers.
    To this I witness call the fools of time,
    Which die for goodness, who have liv'd for crime.

William Shakespeare (1564-1616)

The kiss of the sun for pardon,
The song of the birds for mirth,
One is nearer God's heart in a garden
Than anywhere else on earth.

The dawn of the morn for glory,
The hush of the night for peace,
In the garden at eve, say the story,
God walks, and His smile brings release.

Dorothy F. Gurney (1913)

THE PERFECT FLOWER

It's like the sun; but then you look closer and it's just a flower,
with petals so fragile, so amazing, you're scared to touch.
Each petal shines with light, and it feels now you've seen everything.
Place the flower close to you, and you can smell
the scent of life embedded in this delicate flower.
Then you realise that this sunflower
is the most perfect flower God ever created.

Jo Banger

from THE GARDEN

How vainly men themselves amaze
To win the Palm, the Oke or Bayes ;
And their uncessant Labours see
Crown'd from some single Herb or Tree.
All Flow'rs and all Trees do close
To wave the Garlands of repose.

Fair Quiet, have I found thee here,
And Innocence thy Sister dear!
Society is all but rude,
To this delicious solitude.

What wond'rous Life in this I lead!
Ripe Apples drop about my head;
The luscious Clusters of the Vine
Upon my Mouth do crush their Wine ;
The Nectaren, and curious Peach,
Into my hands themselves do reach;
Stumbling on Melons, as I pass,
Insnar'd with Flow'rs, I fall on grass.

Meanwhile the Mind, from Pleasure less,
Withdraws into its happiness :
The Mind, that Ocean where each kind
Does streight its own resemblance find ;
Yet it creates, transcending these,
Far other Worlds, and other Seas ;
Annihilating all that's made
To a green Thought in a green Shade.

How could such sweet and wholesome Hours
Be reckon'd but with herbs and flowers!

Andrew Marvell (1621-1678)

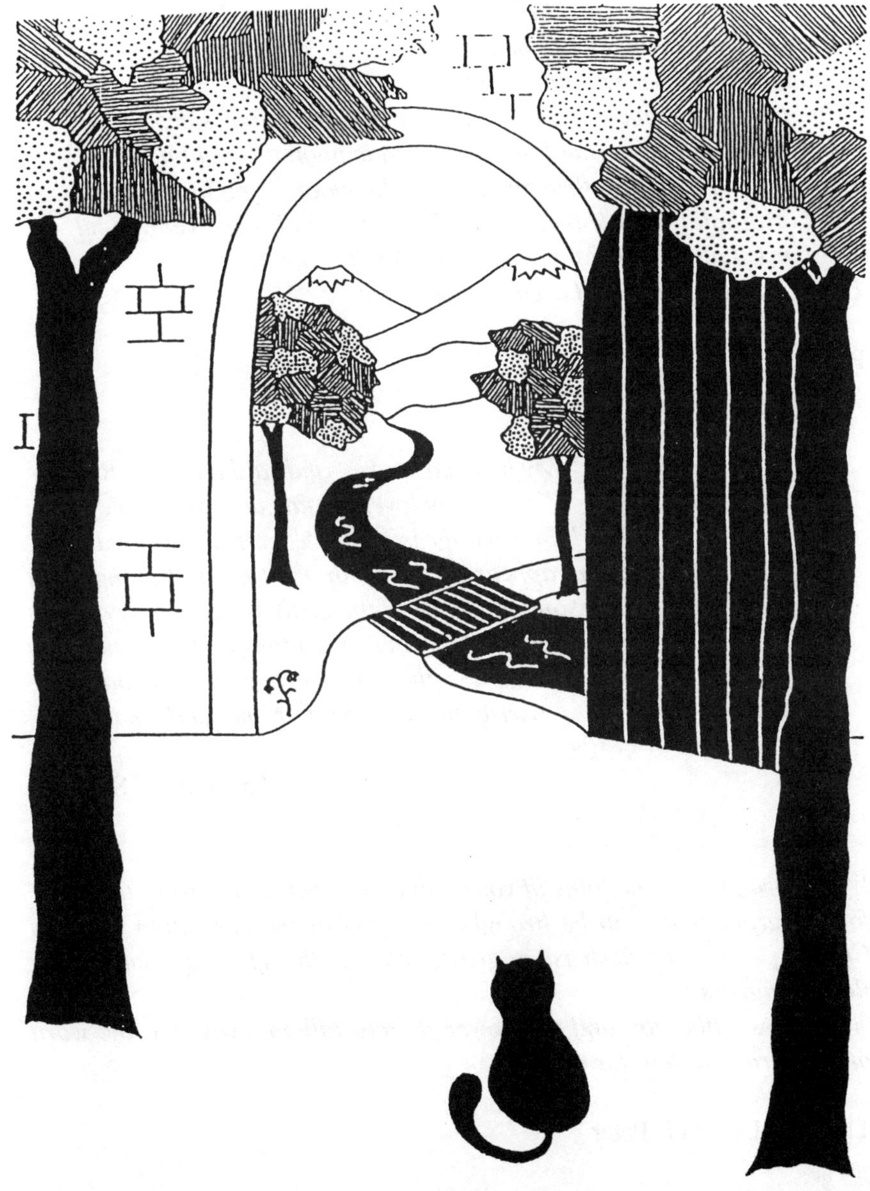

THREE EXTRACTS FROM THE BIBLE

I will lift up mine eyes unto the hills, from whence cometh my help.
My help cometh from the Lord, which made heaven and earth.
He will not suffer thy foot to be moved:
He that keepeth thee will not slumber.
Behold, he that keepeth Israel shall neither slumber nor sleep.
The Lord is thy keeper: the Lord is thy shade upon thy right hand.
The sun shall not smite thee by day, nor the moon by night.
The Lord shall preserve thee from all evil: he shall preserve thy soul.
The Lord shall preserve thy going out and thy coming in
From this time forth, and even for evermore.

Psalm 121

My beloved spake, and said unto me, Rise up,
my love, my fair one, and come away.
For lo, the winter is past, the rain is over, and gone.
The flowers appear on the earth, the time of the singing of
birds is come, and the voice of the turtle is heard in our land.
The fig tree putteth forth her green figs, and the vines with
the tender grape give a good smell.
Arise, my love, my fair one, and come away.

The Song of Solomon

Wherefore gird up the loins of your mind, be sober and hope to the end for the grace that is to be brought unto you at the revelation of Jesus Christ ….. For all flesh is as grass, and all the glory of man as the flower of grass.
The grass withereth, and the flower thereof falleth away; but the word of the Lord endureth for ever.

The First Letter of Peter.

THE WOODCUT

The grainy lines of a woodcut
Grate the blandness of being;
It catches at silken certainty,
And offers a new way of seeing.
Black on white, black on black,
Snag and tear, snag and catch,
The tool - and inspiration - bite,
Picture emerging as you scratch.
There's the plump shape of a pear,
Leaf in front quite like a fan;
But plumb centre now emerges
The shapely watering can.

THE TREE

The tree stood there,
boldy, without fear or apprehension,
of being lonely,
at the foot of the volcano.
The smooth rubble surface
interlocked with the ground,
where three hundred years of life had sprouted.
The tree was nature's slave,
and lifeblood for the volcano;
the irregular, shaped tree,
withstood years of wars,
and has witnessed many eerie cries for help.
It was distorted at its inability to move.
The tree was so important,
yet treated with so little respect.
Until one day,
one stormy day,
the clouds advanced overhead,
turned black
like a vivid charcoal drawing,
till the wick of the candle
had died out;
the tree was dead.
Nature mourned,
as the volcano erupted -
its life drained -
and the clouds burst;
the tree had died,
like a vibration,
affecting the neighbouring cities.
 Slowly, all life forms were
absorbed into the ground.

Romit Bhandari ©

SONNET 18

Shall I compare thee to a summer's day?
Thou art more lovely and more temperate:
Rough winds do shake the darling buds of May,
And summer's lease hath all too short a date:
And often is his gold complexion dimm'd;
And every fair from fair sometimes declines,
By chance, or nature's changing course, untrimm'd;
But thy eternal summer shall not fade,
Nor lose possession of that fair thou owest;
Nor shall Death brag thou wander'st in his shade,
When in eternal lines to time thou growest;
So long as men can breathe, or eyes can see,
So long lives this, and this gives life to thee.

William Shakepeare
(1564-1616)

from SONGS OF EXPERIENCE

In futurity
I prophetic see
That the earth from sleep
(Grave the sentence deep)
Shall arise and seek
For her Maker meek;
And the desert wild
Become a garden mild.

William Blake (1757-1827)

NEW MILLENNIUM

A dead flower,
An unread book,
A cut-down tree,
A toxic brook.

Asthmatic kids,
A poisonous car,
Polluted sea,
It's not for me .....

A new-born baby,
An open gate,
A turned-over leaf,
A clean slate,

The just-opened bud
Of a laburnum .....
Let THIS be the beginning
Of the new millennium!

Tilly Maxwell ©

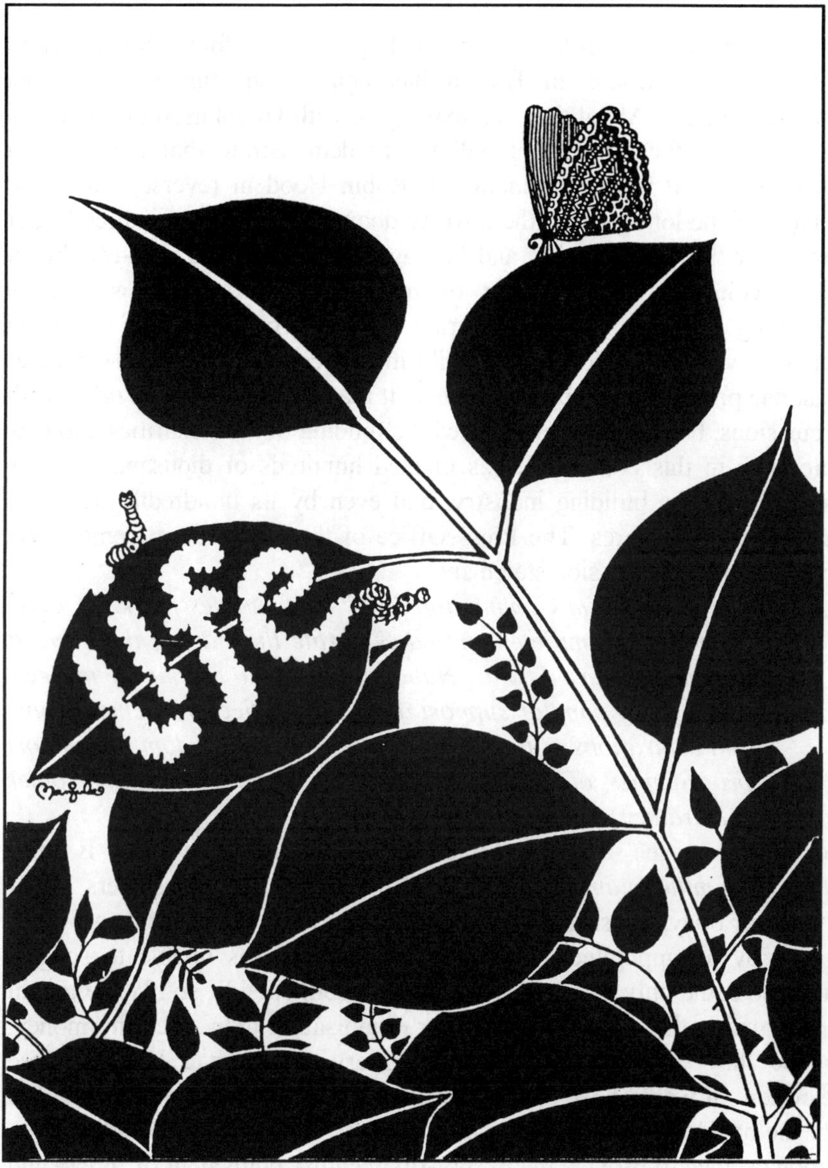
Life

CHAPTER 8 : THE MILLENNIUM COMMISSION

About two-thirds of the funding for the four billion pound millennial celebrations in Britain has come from funding from the National Lottery. Albeit that you may agree with Dr Johnson that lotteries are a tax on the ignorant, I will try to demonstrate that this was an inspired idea. It is not the tactics of Robin Hood in reverse, where the players of the lottery from the poverty-doomed masses pay indirectly but surely for the opera houses and heritage artefacts of the well-off; but a major voluntary redistribution of national wealth which is already benefiting us all in many ways, rich or poor. By the end of 2000, on average every man, woman and child in this country will have visited at least one project funded by the Lottery. It may be nothing but a raffle with pretensions, but it has revolutionised the funding of arts, charities and new enterprise in this country. It has created hundreds of thousands of jobs especially in the building industry, and even by its hundredth draw had made 280 millionaires. The Press Office of the Millennium Commission sent the following mission statement :

> *The Millennium Commission helps communities mark the close of the second millennium and celebrate the start of the third. It uses money raised by the National Lottery to encourage projects which enjoy popular support and which reflect the achievements and aspirations of the people of the United Kingdom; to support programmes of awards to individuals; and to support other celebratory activities in the Year 2000.*

For those on the net, the Millennium Commission website is on : *http://www.millennium.gov.uk.* The Millennium Commissioners, their governing body, consists of three political and six independent members, served by an appointed staff. The Commission was unable to suggest ideas, so could only act on ideas submitted from outside, so if you thought it was unfair that your pet charity or organisation didn't get any money, maybe they did not apply? If the lottery money had been diverted elsewhere, it would have paid for fifteen 800-bed new hospitals, or wiped out the backlog of maintenance on the country's schools; instead we as a nation decided to provide the twenty-first century equivalent of 'bread and circuses' to mark a time when (to quote the Millennium Commission again) *People looked to the future by revitalising cities, renewing rural communities, and promoting science and technology.*

The National Lottery was established by Parliament to raise money for worthwhile causes. The five good causes - arts, sports, charities, heritage and celebrating the Millennium - were chosen by Parliament; later a sixth category, the New Opportunities Fund was added, to cover areas like out-of-school clubs and training in technology for librarians and teachers. There are eleven distributing bodies responsible for giving grants to these good causes: they are the Sports and Arts Councils of England, Scotland, Wales and Northern Ireland, the National Lottery Charities Board, the Heritage Lottery Fund (dealing with conserving the best of our past), and the Millennium Commission. The Millennium Commission also funds the Millennium Experience based at the Greenwich Dome; supports the Millennium Festival, for celebrations around the country during the year itself, which may include arts, sports and religious events; and runs the Millennium Awards scheme, enabling individuals to contribute to the community through such organisations as the Prince's Trust, Raleigh International, Arthritis Care, Earthwatch, Mind and Help the Aged. The Lottery's regulations decree that projects should be inside the UK, although it had been hoped at one stage to divert some funds to Commonwealth projects like the restoration of rajahs' palaces in India. However, some of the Charities Board awards are for British volunteers to help in countries such as Chile, Namibia, Chile, Indonesia and China; medical emergency relief; and special projects like solar-powered hearing aids and livestock for Africa. The Scottish Cultural Resources Access Network is available to anyone around the globe free on the Internet. In case you thought money was handed out willy-nilly, in early 1997 two projects (the Giant's Causeway railway, and the Thames Marker scheme), had their joint funding of £3.5 million withdrawn for failure to deliver.

The whole business was set up under the National Lottery, etc., Act (1993) under the then-Conservative Government. The money generated was intended to pay for new projects, not replace subsidy from taxation; the Prime Minister, John Major, and his Heritage Secretary,

Virginia Bottomley, promised not to use the lottery for things the government were already funding, warning of the example of New Zealand where the government has virtually bowed out of funding the arts, and leaves it to their lottery. The policy director of Camelot was quoted as saying that *(It is) a time when people look to the future by revitalising cities, renewing rural communities, and promoting science and technology.* He continued: *The central criterion is that a project should be in the public interest. That means schemes are primarily not commercial.*

In 1997, lottery tickets worth £4.72 billion were sold; and it is estimated that by the time it will be wound up in 2001, around £9 billion will have been raised for the good causes. To show the widespread nature of the projects, by 1997 a third of that sum had already been distributed, to almost 20,000 projects big and small; and over half the awards are for less than £25,000, as the Commission believes that small amounts of money do a lot of good to a lot of people. Out of every pound spent, the money is divided as follows :

Prizes	50 pence
Lottery duty	12 pence
Retailer commission	5 pence
Operating costs	4 pence
Profit	1 penny
Good causes	28 pence

This precious 28 pence is given to the five good causes, meaning they get 5.6 pence each to spend on their allotted business. Originally, the rules of funding meant that most of the money went on capital projects, not revenue funding for staff to run them nor associated consumables. This resulted in two potential problems: the plethora of building projects starting up, with over-ambitious funding, some of which might never be completed; and secondly anomalies such as the Royal Academy of Dramatic Arts (RADA) being given £22 million - coincidentally, about the same sum of money as the largest jackpot that has been won - in 1995 to repair its buildings, at a time when many young people were finding it impossible to get the funding actually to attend as a student. This was changed, and new funding rules meant that from then on

Lottery funds could be invested in people, as well as in building projects. The Sports Council was then able to provide revenue funds for talented athletes, for instance, and the Arts Council could give grants to increase access and participation in the arts particularly for young people. All these bodies that disburse lottery money, except the Charities Board, come with fairly challenging demands for the recipients to raise funding themselves, from as little as 10 per cent but more usually 50%, which was expected to come not only from the private sector, but also the public sector such as local authorities and quangos. The Government Minster in charge now is the Rt. Hon. Chris Smith of the Department of Heritage.

A consortium called Camelot Group plc won the licence to operate the National Lottery for seven years until 2001 in a competitive tendering process as a result of its lowest bid (although the process was not without subsequent controversy). An American company called Gtech is one of the consortium members; it was set up in 1976 by two mathematicians called Victor Marowicz and Guy Snowden, which now runs 70% of the world's lotteries, including national lotteries in 43 countries including Iceland and Estonia. Our Lottery is a bigger operation than any other lottery in the world, making £77.5 million pre-tax profits in its first year. Its high point was £128 million ticket sales in a week for the double roll-over in January 1996; and though it has not achieved that since, it has deeply embedded itself in the national consciousness. Surely, even more so than the television franchises of which it was first said, it has been 'a licence to print money.' Indeed, BBC Television paid Camelot about half a million pounds a year to show the Lottery draw on the screen; it may be cheap programme-making for the BBC, but it also gives enormous free advertising to Camelot.

The first ticket was drawn on Saturday, November 19, 1994, with scratchcards beginning five months afterwards, and then two years later a mid-week draw as well. In February 1998, a new two-pound scratchcard, TV Dreams, was brought out (which offered not only instant wins but also the chance to appear on the National Lottery Big Ticket Show.) The top prize in any week - many people feel that it is too large, changing people's lives not always for the better - is called a 'jackpot', an expression from the card game poker when money is put in to a pot not to be touched until a player has pair of jacks or better. At the beginning, it was a far greater success than anticipated; two-thirds of the adult population bought an average of nearly three cards each per week, but of course this tailed off somewhat except in weeks of a large 'rollover' (i.e. when prizes not won one week would be held over for the next) jackpot, when five million tickets an hour were being frenziedly bought in the hours beforehand. The operation was at first overseen by a single Regulator from OFLOT, the Office of the National Lottery, which regulates and licenses individual games promoted as part of the lottery, but later this was changed to a five-person team. The Department of National Heritage, which in addition to its other duties for tourism, broadcasting, and conservation of ancient buildings, is the government department responsible for the Lottery.

By 1999, the National Lottery had come through certain controversies about the granting of the franchise, actions of some personnel both in Camelot and OFLOT, and various way-out grants, to be seen as a force for good at the end of the millennium. After 2001, the Government has pledged that the lottery will continue on a non-profit-making business under the control of the National Lottery Charities Board with the continuation of bursaries but with other changes (e.g. the Millennium Celebrations Fund will be replaced by a new Information and Communication Technology fund.)

The Millennium Commission announced that it was to further the cause of *People Power : ordinary people doing extraordinary things.* It created the logo of the '**M**' mark, a navy letter above an orange curve they call a 'strap line' to celebrate Britain's new dawn, so that when people see the Millennium Mark on a project or scheme they know where their money has been spent (although some people were sorry it didn't feature a cuddly animal so that furry souvenirs could be made.) The Ordnance Survey, Britain's national cartographic agency, plotted a map showing 185 capital projects at over 3,000 locations which in total cost three billion pounds -

only a fifth of which will be going on the great Greenwich Experience, of which more later.

One can still have a fair sense of unease about the encouragement of people to gamble; and indeed the churches and Gamblers' Anonymous have expressed their disquiet about the incidence of addictive gambling associated with it (one man is said to have sold his car to buy more tickets on a roll-over week). It was a humbling sight to see a simple young man in a small post office bring out his last three pounds for yet more scratch-cards, and hear the motherly soul behind the counter suggest gently that he put his money away. Baruch Spinoza said in his 'Tractatus Politicus' in 1677:

> *Sedula curavi, humanus actiones non ridere, non lugere, neque detestare, sed intelligere.*
> *I have made a ceaseless effort not to ridicule, not to bewail, nor to scorn human actions, but to understand them.*

Sadly, the gambling inherent in the lottery does not seem to bring out the nobler side of man. A lottery is just a system where people pay for a chance to be part of the division of spoils by random chance, whether that be by lottery ticket, by turn of a card, or drawing straws of different lengths, their 'lot'. The dictionary reminds us that 'lottery' is also used figuratively for things that defy calculation, as in one's lot in life.

The popularity of this type of gambling has always risen and fallen over the years. The Emperor Augustus two millennia ago helped finance building projects(!) that way, and they became popular in Europe from the fifteenth century. In 1567 Queen Elizabeth established a National Lottery to raise money for 'Good Workes'; from 1698, lotteries had to be licensed. Surges of interest throughout the seventeenth and eighteenth centuries ('The London Spy' in 1699, exactly three centuries ago, reported that *All the Fools in Town were busy employed in running up and down from one Lottery or another*) gradually declined until the last draw in 1826. Thomas Love Peacock in his novel 'Crotchet Castle' written in confident Victorian times says : *Modern literature has attained the honourable distinction of sharing with blacking and Macassar oil the space which used to be monopolised by razor-strops and the lottery,* implying that the lotteries were a completely dead issue. The mid-nineteenth Italian statesman Count Cavour called them *a tax on imbeciles.*

Is its modern resurgence a sign of malaise in society? Is excessive gambling associated with times of economic hardship, as a promise of escape; or when society is in turmoil? In the bleak world of '1984', said George Orwell, the lottery was for millions of 'proles' the principal if not the only reason for remaining alive. If Marx were alive today, he would truly decide that the LOTTERY is the opiate of the people. It is an expression of desperate hope in the immediate future, which in the world of work was ever associated with the feckless working classes, rather than the quiet confidence of planning for long-term financial stability by deferment of pleasure, shown by professional people. Logically, it does not make sense: only 50% of the money invested is repaid, and to win a major prize means overcoming odds of 14 million to one (and you are 500 times more likely to be run over on the roads), or to put it another way, if you 'invest' £5 a week, it would take you over 53,000 years before you are statistically due for the big win ...... (Odds can be shortened, apparently: those Thais who took the advice of a monk Phra Khru Sangkharak about winning their national lottery were so successful, that the organisers will only pay out half-winnings if he has been involved.) Surely the best advice is still - unless you happen to enjoy the ritual of filling in pieces of paper - better by far to ignore mystic monks or Megs, and save the money instead.

There is no real justification, for one to have a flutter on the lottery; but it is a bit of fun, and the whole ritual of buying the ticket has changed the pattern of many people's Saturday nights, where traditionally the pattern was take-away Chinese noodles followed by canoodling; now some people are getting their orgasmic thrill watching a superior form of housey-housey. At least you may feel that the majority of the non-prize money is going to good causes, many being small improvements in your community, as well as providing major changes in great national institutions. The wealth it has generated is creating the greatest millennial changes of any country on the globe. It will be interesting to see if it continues to influence our way of life in years come, or whether after the Millennium it will have come to the end of its natural product life-cycle.

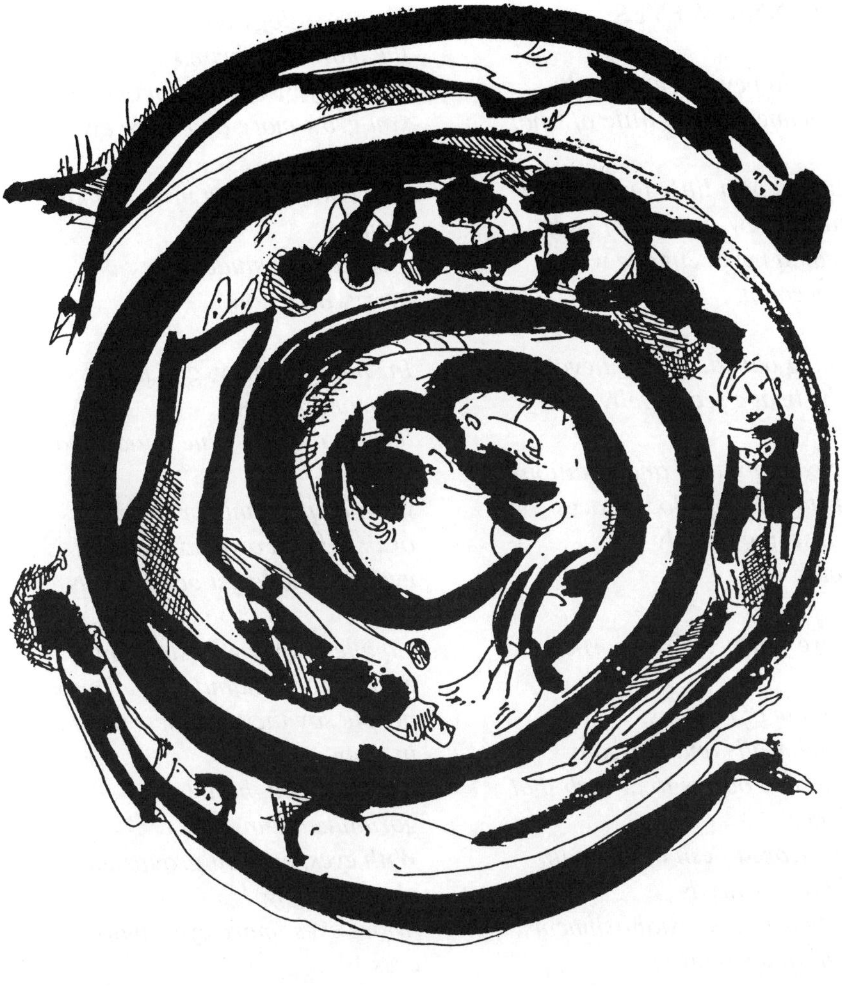

MILLENNIUM EYES

*We could never see enough.
We gleaned only a little of what
is.
A hidden past little understood
a future view still out of sight
we could never engage with a
full account.*

*Nothing outside was believable
as the image seen. Delivered
words
carried omissions and additions
and stayed with closed faces
when seeing exactly was
crucial.*

*And we yearned. We yearned to
see
to bottom of reasons,
through walls and horizons.
We needed others to absorb that
violence
in the seared flesh of our pain
and see our needs
and their rooted establishments;
see all of a situation,
all of an outcome
with all its angles, way back to
source.*

*Now astrology tells us
the millenium brings new eyes:
makes eyes, wear them openly,
you grow more and more eyes
inwardly.
And colleges start up eyemaking
courses -
a craze with students
everywhere now.*

*In shades of grey, green and
diamond,
brown, orange, blue, black and
purple,
worn as pendants or bracelets
or as a band around the head,
eyes are the latest adornments.*

*Couples newly wed stare into
each other's manufactured eyes:
people say they see their future
in them.
And crowned, bangled,
garlanded, hung
With eyes, student groups go
about singing
'More eyes, more eyes, more
eyes !
The millennium brings new
eyes.'*

James Berry ©

Nineteenth century artificial eyes were auctioned recently by Christie's.

FORGOTTEN GLORIES

In dim corners of cool cathedrals
these ancient standards hang.
Faded colours stirred
only by the drum of cold stone footsteps,
or the hum of Sunday choirs.
Weary banners, torn fragments
threaded with dusty motes of remembrance.
And only hushed whispers,
woven like so many prayers
for old griefs and forgotten glories.

Linden Sanders ©

IS LIFE A GAME OF BAGATELLE?

Is Life a game of bagatelle?
The Ball's blind way, none can foretell;
Yet once the cue has struck the ball
No-one can change where it will fall.
It may bounce aimless, nail to nail,
And end up on the bottom rail,
A stone in Fate's unseeing sling,
Destined to be a worthless thing,
Unhonoured, void of skill or art;
Or else a pin may just impart
A nudge, a fraction off the true
And guide the errant ball into
A home, mid others of his kind
To anonymity consigned,
And yet of worth, a part to fill
In the game's - and Life's - unending spill.
But, rare as truth, some fateful chance
May lead the ball in Luck's brief dance,
Till by haphazard ricochet
It sweetly drops and gains the day,
To universal loud acclaim!
Yet Fortune blind has won the game .....
Tell me, is life mere bagatelle?
We do not know - 'tis p'rhaps as well
The ball's blind way none can foretell.

Bill Jarvis ©

I DO, I DO, I DO

Who controls the British Crown?
Who keeps the metric system down?
I do, I do,
Who keeps Area 51 off the maps?
Who keeps the martians under wraps?
I do, I do,
Who says there will be no end?
Who drives others round the bend?
I do, I do.
Who made Super Mario a star?
Who holds back the electric car?
I do, I do.
Who keeps gremlins out of sight?
Who rigs every Oscar night?
I do, I do.

Peter Cronogue ©

IMMORTALITY

Mortal man has hungered
Since the dawn of time
For the secret of immortality,
And the secret is mine.

A comfort to know I can not die,
Life for me has no time;
Yet I am damned,
Yes, the secret is mine.

To walk the earth alone,
For all eternity,
And yet not age
In complete solidarity.

And yet you all complain,
That there's not enough time,
You don't want to die......
The secret is mine.

Ruth Burke ©

from THE RUBÁIYÁT OF OMAR KHAYYÁM

Helpless pieces of the game He plays
Upon this chequerboard of Nights and days,
Hither and Thither moves and mates and slays,
And one by one back in the closet lays.

The Rubáiyát was written by the Persian poet Omar Khayyám, who died in 1123, and was memorably translated by Edward Fitzgerald in 1859. The translator said of the writer: *And this, I think, especially distinguishes Omar from all the other Persian poets: That, whereas with them the Poet is lost in his Song, the Man in Allegory and Abstraction; we seem to have the man Omar himself, with all his humours and passions, as frankly before us as if we were really at the table with him, After the Wine has gone round.*

from THE CHARIOT by Emily Dickinson (1830-1886)

Because I could not stop for Death,
He kindly stopped for me;
The carriage held but just ourselves
And Immortality.
We slowly drove, he knew no haste,
And I had put away
My labour, and my leisure too,
For his civility.
We passed the school where children played,
Their lessons scarcely done;
We passed the fields of gazing grain,
We passed the setting sun.
Since then 'tis centuries; but each
Feels shorter than the day
I first surmised the horses' heads
Were toward Eternity.

Sonnet

How do I love thee? Let me count the ways.
I love thee to the depth and breadth and height
My soul can reach, when feeling out of sight
For the ends of Being and ideal Grace.
I love thee to the level of every day's
Most quiet need, by sun and candlelight.
I love thee freely, as men strive for Right;
I love thee purely, as they turn from Praise;
I love thee with the passion put to use
In my old griefs, and with my childhood's faith.
I love thee with a love I seemed to lose
With my lost saints, - I love thee with the breadth,
Smiles, tears, of all my life ! - and, if God choose,
I shall but love thee better after death.

Elizabeth Barrett Browning (1806 – 1861)

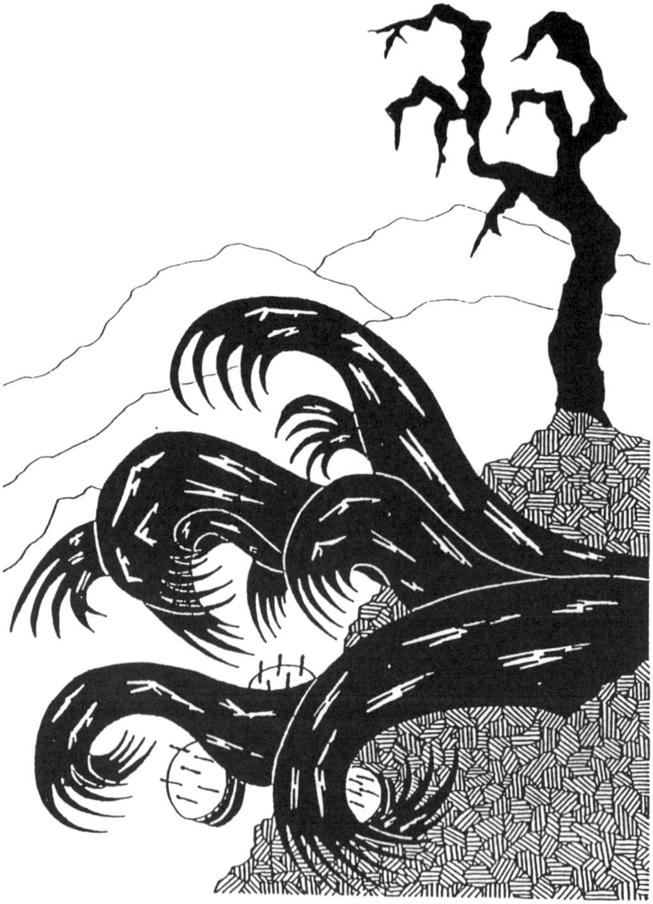

GERMAN JABBERWOCK

'S war schummricht, und die Wolper kreisen
Gar bohrlich norgelnd Wurzelmoos;
Die Parmazieben mümfen Quengelweisen,
Und Gründelschnüffen scheuchen bloss.

'Hüt' dich vorm Schlabberwork, mein Kind
Es reisst sein Zahn, es kratzt sein Klau!
Hüt dich vorm Vogel Jüberjüp und flieh geschwind
Vorm Banderschmatz so schaurigschlau!'

Sein Balmungschwert nahm er zu Hand
Folgt mählich Weil dem Unhold Kühn
Bis unterm Bongbaum süße Rast er fand,
Und träumend ward sein Sinn.

Wie er in hehrem Traum so stand und sann,
Der Schlabberwork mit Aug wie Feuersglut
Naht brimsche aus dem talgen Tann
Und schnorgelt seine Wut!

Eins, zwei! Eins, zwei ! Durch Horn und Bein
Der Balmung scharf in Hieb und Stich gradaus
Trifft tief ins Schlabberherz hinein! -
Das Haupt am Knauf er trirumtrabt nach Haus.

'Ist hin der Schlabberwork? Sag's hurtig an!
Komm an die Vaterbrust, mein trutzger Sohn
Oh, gloriglicher Tag! Halli! Hallan!'
Die Freudenzähr ihm voran.

'S war schummricht .....etc

The human body is perfectly fashioned for all its functions. It is meet and right and suitable; it has evolved to a state of near perfection. It breathes alone after birth; as it matures it gains true independence from its parents. It grows slowly to a certain pattern and also a certain strength and matures as years go by. Its skins is elastic and self-regenerates; its eyes give it binocular vision; its hair provides protection from the elements; I would say truly that its wonders continue.

CHAPTER 9 : MILLENNIUM PROJECTS

The very idea of a project is something that you are hurling in to the future, and indeed it comes from the Latin word 'to throw'. Also it has the idea of something rather making an exhibition of itself, in the nicest possible way, as in someone projecting their personality or making their mark on something, or maybe a cinema projector, flashing up before our eyes a vision of a world different to our everyday milieu. So this little word, that we take quite for granted, is actually extremely appropriate for us when we come to celebrating the Millennium. We will celebrate it by thought, word and deed; but this chapter is mostly about deeds planned, in progress, and best of all, in place. Some particularly major projects have Lottery funding; but many individual, school and group efforts do not. It is just people wanting to share together an important historical landmark. Many of them are architectural, some quite innovatory and exciting, making one pleased that the Millennium did not happen a few decades ago when concrete blocks were de rigeur.

Everyone is likely to be aware of the 27 major capital projects funded in three rounds by the Lottery, which awarded them between £15 million and £50 million pounds, the Millennium Dome in Greenwich being in a category of its own. They are New Technopolis of Norwich; the National Space Science Centre in Leicester; the Tate Gallery of Modern Art at Bankside, London; the British Museum Great Court; the Centre for Life, Newcastle upon Tyne; the Lowry Centre at Salford; the National Discovery Park, Liverpool; the renaissance of Portsmouth Harbour; the Millennium Seed Bank, Wakehurst Place, West Sussex; Bristol 2000 Science World and parks; The Earth Centre, Doncaster; the Magna Centre at Rotherham; Millennium Point, Birmingham; the Eden Centre in St Austell, Cornwall, which has the biggest site of any of the projects ; the Deep, Hull's aquarium-plus; Sheffield City Centre; the Odyssey Project in Belfast; the Glasgow Science Centre (X-Site); the University of the Highlands and Islands, the most northerly project; the Millennium Link between the Forth & Clyde and Union Canals; Hampden Park Stadium, Glasgow; Dynamic Earth in Edinburgh; new stadium at Cardiff Arms Park; Wales Millennium Centre, Cardiff; the National Botanic Garden of

Wales; Changing Places, the Groundwork Foundation; and the National Cycle Path called Sustrans. Some of these projects are at the time of writing seriously behind schedule, partly because of delays in getting Lottery funding, and then in raising the further private funding necessary; some like the Doncaster project have trimmed their sails a bit to achieve their target, others will open sometime around the Millennium.

In addition, there are other exciting projects financed in part by Lottery money, such as the Royal Opera House, Covent Garden, and Sadler's Wells Ballet. Others include the new Gothic tower to 'finish off' Bury St Edmunds Cathedral; SUZY, a model of sustainability for the 21st century, being set up in Middlesborough; a new Spa Centre at Bath, opening the Roman baths again after eighteen years of neglect; and the Royal Gunpowder Mills at Waltham Abbey, coincidentally right alongside the Meridian. Manchester city centre is being pedestrianised and renovated; Croydon's Skyline project will be the largest single lighting installation in the world, using energy efficient lighting.

Other money has been allocated for the rejuvenation of our public spaces (it is reckoned that over three billion visits are made to them in a year), with grants for park-keepers, drinking fountains for people and their pets, cafés, boating lakes such as in Lister Park, Bradford (which will also boast a Mughal garden), and new flowerbeds. Stranraer's seafront park will be transformed. Some parks have a distinguished history, like the Voysey-designed Emslie Horniman walled garden in Kensington, Humphrey Repton's Russell Square, and the park in Halifax, Yorkshire, laid out by Joseph Paxton of Crystal Palace fame. Other park projects have received money, including six new parks in Belfast and a glass-covered park in Liverpool; Wales is getting a marvellous Coastal Park around Llanelli, regenerating old spoil tips from the mines. Other monies will go to war memorials, public monuments, village halls (like the Grade II* listed hall in Stebbings, Essex, in use since 1674, and the most southerly one at Lamorna in Cornwall), rural churches, and community centres.

On the cultural front, ten million pounds from the Millennium Commission has gone to secure Somerset House on the Embankment as a home for major art collections, including restoring its river terrace to the eighteenth century plans, and improving the courtyard. Money has also gone to the Marx Memorial Garden in Clerkenwell Green. The Royal National Theatre gets a big chunk, as does the Royal Court Theatre, and Sam Wanamaker's loving recreation of the Globe Theatre on Bankside. John Ruskin's library in Lancaster is being restored; and the Arts Theatre in Cambridge supported. A large pantechnicon will literally take theatre around the Scottish Highlands. The Everyman Library will be sponsored to donate 245 classic titles to 4,500 state schools, and create a website for youngsters all over the world. There is money for educational awards and bursaries, some through the National Endowment for Science and Arts, which will continue after the Millennium Fund has stopped giving to bricks-and-mortar in 2001. Some money will specifically go to fund meaningful travel and work with charities; some for dance and drama scholarships, and also arts education generally, like TS2K (originally Trafalgar Square 2000) which will encourage 12,000 youngsters from deprived areas of London to join in arts projects.

Museums have benefited. The museum 'superleague', like the British Museum and the Walker Art Museum in Liverpool, have had great injections of cash; and also the Wallace Collection, the National Portrait Gallery, and the Tate's original site on Millbank, some for buildings and for acquiring the Oppé collection. Smaller sums have gone to Dulwich Picture Gallery, and the Serpentine Gallery, and the I.C.A. Plans are under way for a Museum of British History in St Bartholomew's Hospital. Then there is Ceramica in the Potteries, Staffordshire; the Welsh Slate Museum; the Roald Dahl Gallery in Aylesbury; and the Stanegate Inheritance, Northumberland. Money has funded the great extension to Duxfield Air Museum, Cambridgeshire; Weather Watch Discovery Centre, Bracknell; for wetlands conservation in Slimbridge, Gloucestershire; Island 2000 (built to resemble a dinosaur) to show palaeontological collections on the Isle of Wight. A quarter of a million pounds went to provide archaeological record-keeping. Support has gone to the National Museum of Photography, Film and Television in Bradford;

£14 million to the British Film Institute; and money put up for four film studios and 43 projects. Some has gone to owners of stately homes like Stoneleigh Abbey (£7 million) in Warwickshire, on condition that they extend public access. A new art gallery is being built in Walsall, partly to house Jacob Epstein sculptures, and money has gone to the Snape Maltings. Sheffield has a centre for more modern music, the National Centre for Popular Music, designed to look from afar like a pair of drums. In Ayrshire, there is The Big Idea, a museum of discovery.

There is something special about the combination of land and water which as a sea-faring, water-girdled nation we have in our blood. Piers are defiant fingers of land stuck boldly in to the enveloping sea, and have a sort of primitive fascination - paddling for adults, without getting your feet wet - apart from the fact that many of them were built beautifully and lovingly of Victorian ironwork. Sadly the ravages of the storm have battered several in to ignominious wrecks. Margate Pier, built in 1855, devastated by storm in 1978, was finally demolished in 1998. There are practical reasons for piers: they provide a focus for tourism; they may support a variety of 'end-of-the-pier' shows, arcades and slot machines; and some-times ships like steamers still stop there, such as at Clevedon Pier in Bristol which has received Lottery money. Where there were 85 piers a century ago, there are only 43 in Britain, half of them privately owned, many requiring enormous renovation; but there are millennial plans to rescue five (including Swanage and Penarth) and build two new ones (in Bognor Regis and Minehead.) The Lottery has given fifteen million pounds for the restoration of the 1866 Grade 1-listed, 100 foot long, West Pier in Brighton (which also has the nearby Palace Pier), mothballed for a quarter of a century and then gutted by fire. Others, like the Hastings Pier which is Grade-2 listed and 130 years old, Morecambe Bay, Blackpool, Ramsey (IoM), the Mumbles, Colwyn Bay, Porthcawl, the newly-built one at Weston-super-Mare, Teignmouth, Cromer, and Bridlington have to keep up the struggle against salt and tide by their own devices (indeed, Southend's survival seems dubious at the moment.)

Many other millennium projects feature water. There is to be the National Maritime Museum on the waterfront in Falmouth. There are the canals, of which 122 miles will be re-opened for navigation, like the Kennet and Avon restoration, and half of the £5 million pounds for restoration of the Ribble Link on the Lancaster Canal. There will be a lock on John Constable's River Stour, and the regeneration of Bristol's Harbourside and Liverpool's waterfront. Bridges are by definition high profile, and there are already ten major ones planned with Millennium funding. In London there is the Millennium Footbridge of Sir Norman Foster, Sir Anthony Caro and the Ove Arup Partnership, the first pedestrian bridge built in London this century, to be ready by May 2000. It has been described as 'an elegant blade' to link the commerce of the City and the cathedral of St Paul's on the north bank, and the arts (the New Tate with its 'light box', and the Globe) on the south bank. An estimated four million people will make the five-minute crossing each year. The new generation of 40 tonne lorries hitting the streets in 1999 will be limited to only 11 bridges strong enough to bear them, but three more strong road bridges are due, one of them possibly inhabited. On Tyneside, the breathtaking futuristic 'S' shaped bridge links the Baltic Flour Mills (now a modern art gallery), and can open when required like a giant eyelid.

Money will go to sport. In addition to the two stadia in the 'major 27' at Glasgow and Cardiff, Wembley Stadium will get £100 million. Other money will go to such things as the Football Museum in Preston, and awards for athletes called the World Class Performance Programme. Hampshire will have a marvellous rounded cricket ground, London's Royal Albert Dock Rowing Club won over £5 million to extend the dock to form a standard 2km course, and the Royal National Orthopaedic Hospital at Stanmore has gained a sports centre. Golf clubs have on the whole missed out, because as private clubs they have tended to exclude certain categories of people.

Not every endeavour to mark the Millennium had Lottery funding, of course. The National Trust has received some for small parts of their work, but has mainly been generating its own funding. They wrote:
> *The National Trust plays an enormous rôle in helping to safeguard the best of our coastal landscapes. More than 570*

miles of coastline are protected by the Trust, and this continues under the Enterprise Neptune campaign ..... as part of its millennium celebrations, the Trust will therefore be focusing on that. There will be exhibitions, competitions for children, musical evenings, coastal cruises, and many opportunities to see the Trust's conservation practices including going 'off the beaten track' with our coastal wardens (a sighting of a puffin or a seal becomes a memory for life.)

In Budleigh Salterton, Devon, a new centre will open in honour of Sir Walter Raleigh. He would have been interested in the millennial plans of the world's sailing boats, whose Tall Ships Races 2000 will visit Southampton, Genoa, Agadir, Puerto Rico, New York, Halifax (Nova Scotia) and Amsterdam.

The Royal Society of Arts launched Project 2001 six years before, to create new social capital by investing in education and training. In Leeds, the Leeds Tapestry - a Bayeux for our time - has been created in 24 panels stitched by over 300 volunteers. Stonehenge, denied the Lottery money first time, is proceeding with much-needed improvements. In Magor, Monmouthshire, the biggest theme park in Britain called Legend Court is taking shape. The Royal Festival Hall has been running its series of concerts by the City of Birmingham Symphony Orchestra under Sir Simon Rattle called 'Towards the Millennium', covering one decade at a time. The BBC is to televise a 2,000 year history of Britain, exploring the experiences of figures involved in the central events of the last two millennia. The British Library, opened to the public in 1998 and whose move cost £511 million pounds, is becoming established in St Pancras with its 150 million books, CDs, etc.

And what about individual efforts? Alan Rogan from Burnham in Buckinghamshire planned two huge 50-storey high globes linked by a walkway, costing £30million; Margaret Noone is determined to complete her publishing project; Clair Hobson of Sugarcraft is planning a millennial project in sugar. For other people, it will be a year of non-stop, unbreakable resolutions ..... what will yours be ?

The Dynamic Earth project in Edinburgh starting to take shape against the silhouette of Arthur's Seat.

from THE PROBLEM

The hand that rounded Peter's dome
And groined the aisles of Christian Rome,
Wrought in a sad sincerity;
Himself from God he could not free,
He builded better than he knew
The conscious stone to beauty grew.

Ralph Waldo Emerson (1803-1882)

A RED RED ROSE

O my Luve's like a red, red rose,
That's newly sprung in June;
O my Luve's like the melodie
That's sweetly play'd in tune.

As fair art thou, my bonnie lass,
So deep in luve am I;
And I will love thee still, my Dear,
Till a' the seas gang dry.

Till a'the seas gang dry, my Dear,
And the rocks melt wi' the sun:
I will love thee still, my Dear,
While the sands o' life shall run.

And fare thee weel, my only Luve!
And fare thee weel, a while!
And I will come again, my Luve,
Tho' it were ten thousand mile!

Robert Burns (1759-1796)

A POEM OF SEVEN WORDS

Different people everywhere,
Different dreams and beliefs.
Dreams and beliefs,
Make people everywhere different.

Everywhere people dream,
Everywhere people believe, and
Everywhere different dreams and beliefs
Make different people everywhere.

Brian Smith©

from ALASTOR, OR THE SPIRIT OF SOLITUDE

By solemn vision, and bright silver dream,
His infancy was nurtured. Every sight
And sound from the vast earth and ambient air,
Sent to his heart its choicest impulses.
The fountains of divine philosophy
Fled not his thirsting lips, and all of great,
Or good, or lovely, which the sacred past
In truth or fable consecrates, he felt
And knew. When early youth had passed, he left
His cold fireside and alienated home
To seek strange truths in undiscovered lands
(And) the awful ruins of the days of old:
Athens, and Tyre, and Balbec, and the waste
Where stood Jerusalem, the fallen towers
Of Babylon, the eternal pyramids,
Memphis and Thebes, and whatsoe'er of strange
Sculptured on alabaster obelisk,
Or jasper tomb, or mutilated sphynx,
Dark Aethiopia in her desert hills
Conceals. Among the ruined temples there,
Stupendous columns, and wild images
Of more than man, where marble daemons watch
The Zodiac's brazen mystery, and dead men
Hang their mute thoughts on the mute walls around,
He lingered, poring on memorials
Of the world's youth, through the long burning day
Gazed on those speechless shapes, nor, when the moon
Filled the mysterious halls with floating shades
Suspended he that task, but ever gazed
And gazed, till meaning on his vacant mind
Flashed like strong inspiration, and he saw
The thrilling secrets of the birth of time.

Percy Bysshe Shelley (1792-1822)

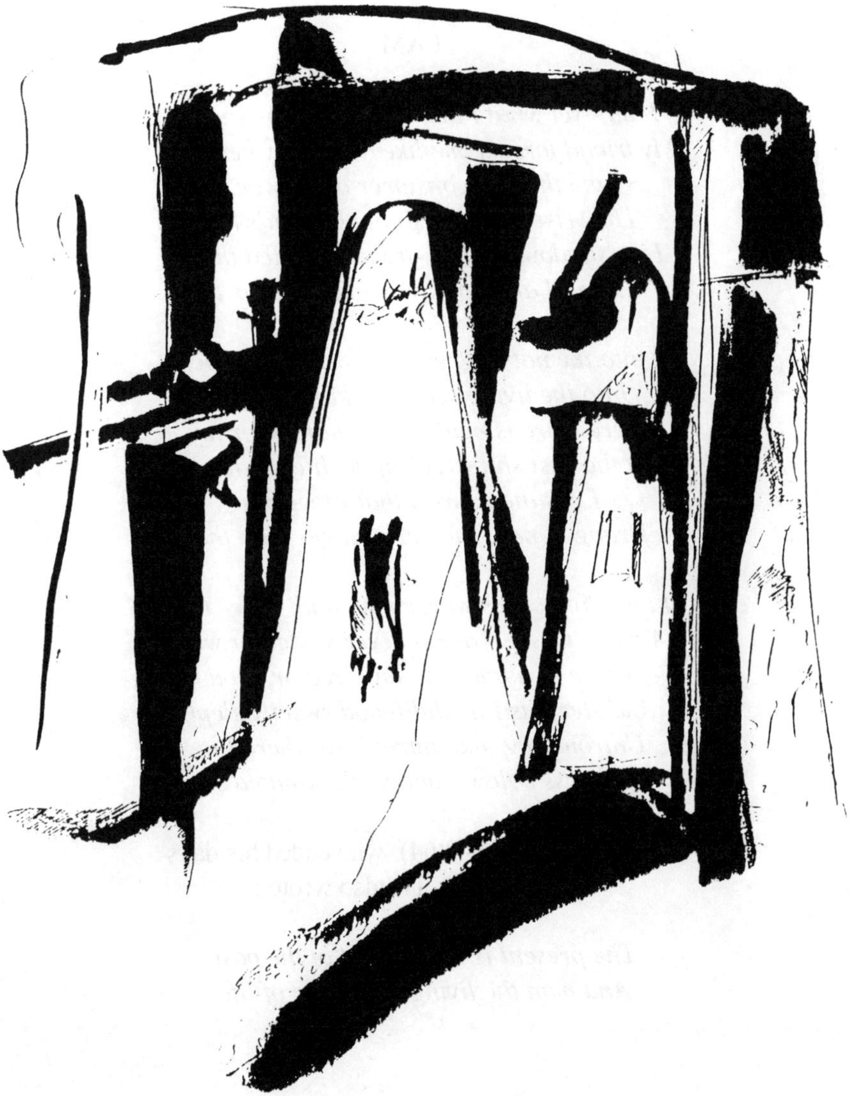

I AM

I am - yet what I am, none cares or knows;
My friend forsake me like a memory best lost:
I am the self-consumer of my woes -
They rise and vanish in oblivion's host
Like shadows in love-frenzied stifled throes
And yet I am, and live - like vapours tost

Into the nothingness of scorn and noise,
Into the living sea of waking dreams,
Where there is neither sense of life or joys,
But the vast shipwreck of my life's esteems;
Even the dearest that I love best
Are strange - nay, rather, stranger than the rest.

I long for scenes where man hath never trod
A place where woman never smiled or wept
There to abide with my Creator, God,
And sleep as I in childhood sweetly slept,
Untroubling and untroubled where I lie
The grass below - above, the vaulted sky.

John Clare (1793-1864), who ended his days in an asylum. He also wrote :

The present is the funeral of the past,
And man the living sepulchre of life.

HAIKU OF THE SEASONS

Spring; dogwood blossom;
Mother wakes, finds child alert,
Happy in the sun.

Summer sunflowers rise,
Strongly blaze; defiant that
Time will wither them.

Autumn daisy field
Is blessed with sun; my mother's
Spirit smiles on me.

Winter waves are calm,
Sated by a glut of storm;
Now they are at peace.

Satako Namino ©
translated by Mariko Hosumi

Silbener Reiher
im nahen Blau des Frühlings
zieht den Fluß hinauf.
The silver heron
in the dense blue of springtime
moves up the river.

Im Herbstgold Wespen
dürsten nach trügrischem Saft
am Abend der Tod.
Wasps, in autumn's gold,
thirst for the deceptive juice ;
in the ev'ning, death.

Reinhild Hensle ©
translated by Brigitte von Peinen

AFTERWARDS

When the Present has latched its postern behind my tremulous stay,
And the May month flaps its glad green leaves like wings,
Delicate filmed as new-spun silk, will the neighbours say,
'He was a man who used to notice such things'?

If it be in dusk when, like an eyelid's soundless blink,
The dew-fall hawk comes crossing the shades to alight
Upon the wind-warped upland thorn, a gazer may think,
'To him this must have been a familiar sight.'

If I pass during some nocturnal blackness, mothy and warm,
When the hedgehog travels furtively over the lawn,
One may say, 'He strove that such innocent creatures should come to no harm,
But he could do little for them; and now he is gone.'

If, when hearing that I have been stilled at last, they stand at the door,
Watching the full-starred heavens that winter sees,
Will this thought rise on those who will meet my face no more,
'He was one who had an eye for such mysteries'?

And will any say when my bell of quittance is heard in the gloom,
And a crossing breeze cuts a pause in its outrollings,
Till they rise again, as they were a new bell's boom,
'He hears it not now, but used to notice such things'?

Thomas Hardy (1840-1928)

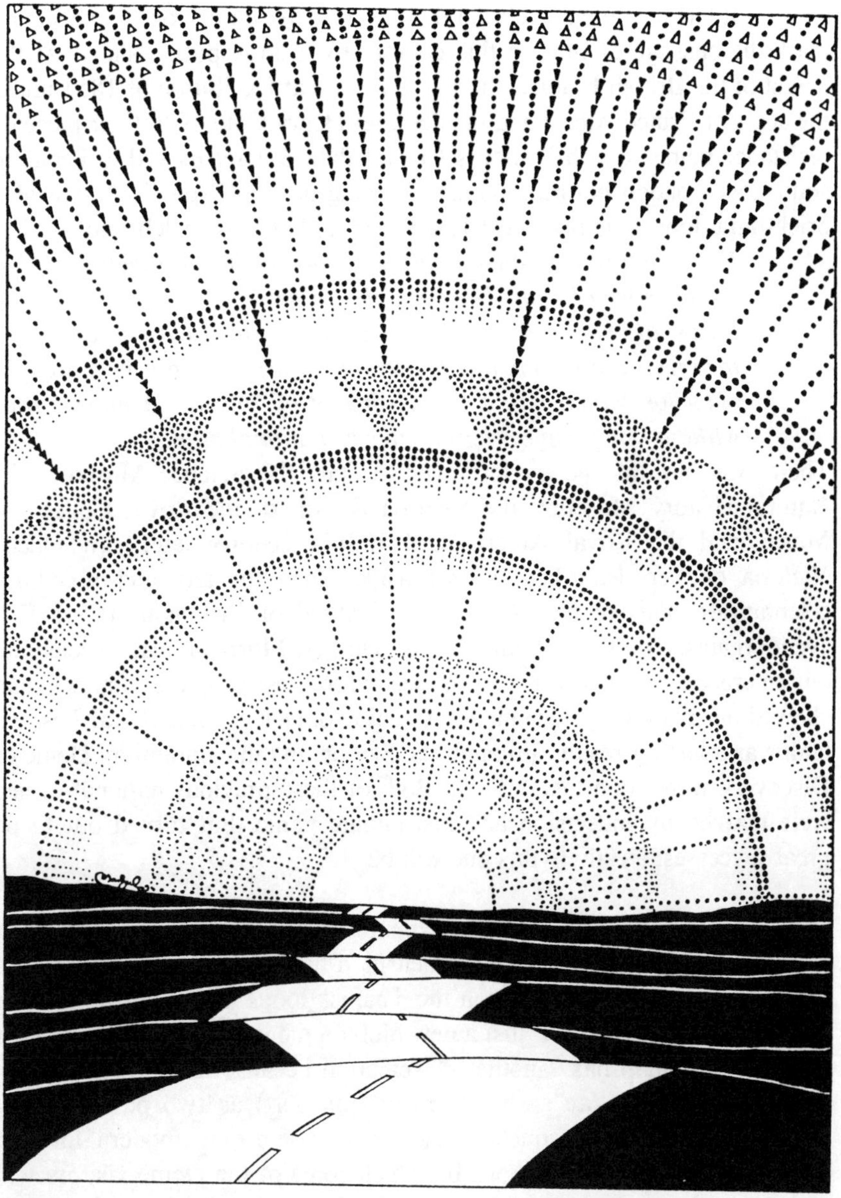

CHAPTER 10 : THE GREENWICH DOME AND LONDON

It has become a tradition that, every half-century or so, we should mark the passage of time in this country by a large public show. At the height of the British Empire, there was the Great Exhibition of 1851 under the aegis of Prince Albert and his designer Henry Cole, with their pièce de résistance being Joseph Paxton's Crystal Palace, later moved to Penge in south-east London before famously burning down. (Brunel's design of a brick-built dome was rejected.) The Times said of those celebrations:

> *Never before was such a vast multitude collected together within the memory of man. The struggles of great nations in battle, the levies of whole races, never called forth such an array as thronged the streets of London on 1st May ..... but here was an occasion which might be celebrated by the whole human race without one pang of regret, envy or national hate.*

There was surplus money left over to start the Science Museum, the Natural History Museum, the Victoria & Albert, the Royal College of Music, and the Royal Albert Hall! Half a century later saw Queen Victoria on her death-bed, so set aside plans for any end-of-century celebrations, and we move on to the Festival of Britain in 1951. This event organised by the Labour Minister Herbert Morrison was to celebrate our emergence from world war, the second in most people's lifetimes, and showed our national determination to enjoy ourselves. The Royal Festival Hall was a lasting result, although the Skylon and the aluminium Dome of Discovery were soon taken down. Both of these previous national events were marked by indecision and last-minute panic, but turned out to be great successes; as surely this one will be.

So, to celebrate the Millennium half a century later, a great architectural folly shaped like a pincushion has been built, nestling in a peninsular of land around which the Thames loops past what used to be Docklands. The site is not just a new blob on the map at the start of 'East Enders'. This map has another fascination because it shows the Royal Docks to the east (an earlier form of transport) as two parallel lines, between which is now squeezed the runway of a very modern form of transport, London City Airport, by which some of the Dome visitors will come. Others may use the Docklands Light Railway (another example of recycled transport, because it used many bridges which were originally built for dock freight.) The DLR runs across the Isle of Dogs, so-called as it was where Henry VIII kept his hunting dogs; and where lottery money is supporting a new Museum of the History of the Port of London costing sixteen million pounds, being built in a Grade 1 listed warehouse on West India Quay.

The Docks had thrived for hundreds of years, till a combination of restrictive union practices and a failure to embrace containerisation, led to their severe decline in the 1960s and '70s, with the last ship unloaded in 1981. Much of the whole area was poor, and parts of it had failed to recover from the severe World War II air-raids, the secret having been kept from German High Command that its bombs and doodle-bugs were often falling short of their intended targets further west. The great nineteenth century building of underground railways had not ventured far south of the river, for want at the time of the technology to cope with the difficult south London soil. Add to that brew the influx of new immigrants, often settling near the docks of their arrival (Huguenots being replaced by Jews, Jews by Chinese, Chinese by Asians, Asians by Somalis) until they began to prosper and move away, and it explains why you found to the east of London, some pockets of real poverty. But the Greenwich area just south of Docklands also embodies this extraordinary paradox: alongside all the neglect, were reminders of a more prosperous age. The naval tradition and its imposing architecture gave us the buildings of what has just been designated England's latest World Heritage site, notably the magnificent Royal Naval College, Queen Anne's House, the Seamen's Hospital, the National Maritime Museum including the Old Royal Observatory, the Cutty Sark and St Alphege's Church. Add to this the modern infrastructure brought by the Docklands redevelopment from the 1980s on, and the millennium improvements, the third great element of London metropolitan life - along with the West End and the City - is at last emerging from its chrysalis.

The site, originally known as the Blackwall Peninsula, was chosen for the Millennium Dome (after a brief flirtation with the National

Exhibition Centre in Birmingham) in early 1996. The actual site had been occupied by a toxin-producing gas works, and the topsoil was terribly polluted (though beneath that it is likely, as archaeologists pointed out, that the waterlogged peat subsoil of the whole Greenwich peninsula contains intact some interesting artefacts.) Next to the gasworks, appropriately I think, was the old Phoenix Wharf. The land area of 300 acres, of which 130 are for the Millennium Park, is surrounded by water on three sides. Positioning it there will bring great benefits to the local area (including a nearby purpose-built village); and also improve communications, with the essential £2 billion extension of the Jubilee Line tube eastwards (travel time 14 minutes from central London) and the improvement of commuter river traffic. Above all, it is in Greenwich, home of time, and a natural focus for the Millennium.

As a classic 'brownfield' site, contaminated and unhealthy, those responsible had to spend a lot of money cleaning it up. British Gas, no longer needing the site they had had since the late nineteenth century because of the use of North Sea gas, spent over £22 million on clearing it before they sold it to the current owners, English Partnerships, in early 1997; but it is alleged that the beneficent ghost of one of the old gasworks proprietors is still occasionally to be seen. The London Borough of Greenwich spent the early years of that decade overseeing the cleaning, digging nearly a thousand pits, 30 gas probes and 21 boreholes; then removing 200,000 tonnes of topsoil contaminated by coal tar, lime waste, cyanide and heavy metals to registered sites in the Midlands. Much of it was, however, cleansed on site, with foul water being extracted, purified and returned; areas impossible to clean have been securely capped and topped with a huge orange membrane. The whole preparation of the site has come to £200 million.

The Dome's first champions were the then Conservative Government, whose Heritage Secretary Virginia Bottomley was responsible for getting it going; but this rôle was passed on the change of government in May 1997 to Peter Mandelson, Minister without Portfolio (who is Herbert Morrison's grandson), with Michael Heseltine from the previous regime. The Dome itself covers ten acres; a million square feet of floor space, twice the size of Wembley Stadium and as big as 13 Albert Halls, being 1,000 yards across and 170 foot high at its centre. The Richard Rogers Architectural Partnership designed the dome, which as a structure is planned to last up to sixty years but could well reach its centenary. It is roofed with a light translucent rain-cleaning fabric called PTFE (that is, Teflon-coated glass fibre) from a company called Birdair, who had already roofed the largest existing dome in Atlanta, Georgia, and has cost £14million. It is so strong that a jumbo jet could safely land upon it. It is suspended from a ring of twelve 100 metre high steel lattice masts projecting through the fabric, supporting a forest of tension wires; these are meant to look from afar like the points on a clock. The canopy has specially-shaped panels to surround one of the huge ventilators of the Blackwall Tunnel, which will be well-hidden backstage. When the weather is fine, 24 'petals' can open in the roof. In high winds, there will be some movement in the fabric, but said not to be noticeable from the ground. Once the cover was up, then the foundations, central arena, lifts and escalators were installed. The actual building has taken about forty per cent of the overall budget.

So what will be going on inside this giant whoopee cushion for the 12 million visitors expected during AD 2000, its sole year of operation? The content was approved and selected by the New Millennium Experience Company, the state-owned enterprise planning the events and their Creative Review Committee, headed by Michael Grade; with their agent being Mark McCormack's International Management Group. Initially criticised by a Government committee for its secrecy, it made the unveiling of the first stage of the plans by Peter Mandelson in February 1998 all the more exciting.

The twelve zones are mainly sponsored by the British companies who have backed the project. In the centre is a giant piazza 386 feet across, wide enough to assemble a complete symphony orchestra and move them around on a mobile stage. It was originally to have been the scene of a huge theatre, but the logistics of audience crowd control forbade that; now it is to have raised semi-circular seating (thereby still leaving series of open vistas across the Dome).It will hold spectacular shows created by Peter Gabriel and Mark Fisher for around 12,000 people six times a day, starting with their New Year's Eve special, on the theme of man, the environment and technology, for which circus performers and acrobats have been recruited and trained. Each zone will exemplify one aspect of the whole exhibition's theme 'Time to make a difference':

- *The Mind*: discover the creative power inherent in us all.

- *The Body Zone*: voyage in to the human machine, containing the ten-storey figure and baby.

- *Spirit Level*: experience a moment of peace and reflection.

- *The Work Zone*'s two areas are called *Licensed to Skill*: match your hidden skills to the new world of work; and *The Learning Curve:* open your mind to life-long learning.

- *TransAction*: how money and finance are changing your life.

- *Dreamscape*: dream, imagine and return refreshed.

- *Serious Play*: how leisure can reactivate your life.

- *Shared Ground*: learn what the future holds for your community.

- *Living Island*: choose how to protect your environment.

- *Atmosphere*: experience the wonder of your planet.

- *Time to Talk!:* learn better ways of talking to each other.

- *uk@now*: decide what being British means for the future of all of us.

It is hoped each area will feature examples of good British design and innovation.

Two areas have been particularly controversial, the first being the large figure. Starting as quite female (she was modelled on 22-year-old dancer Naomi Crouch) and vertical enough to scrape the roof, with visitors wandering around inside her, it became more androgynous, and for safety reasons it became more horizontal for ease of escape in an emergency. The other area whose rôle changed was the Spirit Level, after claims that it neglected the Christian tradition, and separated Christianity sharply from other religious experiences. It should finally be inspirational; there is a glass tent in the middle for meditation, holograms of famous religious works of art, and displays of religious ritual from around the world. In the area will be Christian drama from schools backed by the charity JC2000.

Circling the central area will be the Millennial Pathway, passing under the great legs of the masts. Around 300 different food outlets, including top restaurants and six three-storey food courts, including one with genuine ethnic food. There's twenty souvenir shops, and the loos are innovatory cone shapes. Alongside, outside, will be the 'Baby Dome' or 'Domelet', which is a concert space for 6,000 people. The Dome will have two operating sessions a day, each with a capacity of 35,000 people who will have pre-ordered and paid for their tickets (a clever wheeze, this) by Camelot, the very company whose successful Lottery has raised so much of the money.

All this should be in place for the year 2000, at which point the public - by then having their initial scepticism overturned by the hype for the Dome, and gathering millennial fever in general - will be able to see what they have got for their money. This money will by then be nudging £1,000 million (of which private/corporate sponsorship raised £150 million), plus entrance fees from 12 million visitors - a sixth from overseas - in the one year of operation; with the vast bulk coming from Lottery money, a fifth of the total proceeds of which has been allocated to it. Interest will also be whipped up by the use of marketing logos similar to the Boadicea figure chosen in 1998. The Dome will have a Royal opening on Friday, December 31st under the gaze of television cameras from around the world, to be the party of the Millennium. Details are still emerging (will Oasis be there?) but the countdown will be by Swatch. It will certainly feature a giant games show that night, whose preliminary heats will have taken place earlier in clubs, schools and through the internet; there will also be on-going competitions in the different zones, maybe under corporate sponsorship (such as the trading game for children sponsored by the London International Futures Exchange.) Later in the year starting on April 23rd, the Michael Bogdanov cycle of all 37 of Shakespeare's plays will be there.

Meanwhile, the whole area surrounding the Dome has been landscaped. To ensure their continued healthy growth, some of the trees on the Dome part of the site have been planted on artificial banks to keep their roots from going down into the old soil. Even the shoreline has been improved, with hundreds of metres of land cut back to allow the river more space to flow around the Greenwich loop, the shingle cleaned up, the terraces seeded with traditional river plants to encourage wildlife to return, and a boardwalk built.

Tethered nearby, it is hoped, is Richard Branson's static balloon, which will lift people over the site twice as high in the air, as the planned Ferris Wheel further upriver. Other people will be swishing past 250 feet in the air as they arrive in the gondolas of the Meridian Skyway cable car system, taking three minutes to get from East India Docks station of the DLR over the Thames.

Although cars will be strongly discouraged from the site, with a two-mile exclusion zone to the south, there will be parking space for 400 coaches, and some parking for the disabled; but 77% are expected to arrive by public transport.. The original plan for a huge park-and-ride carpark on Falconwood Field abutting Oxleas Wood was abandoned at an early stage, because of opposition from environmental campaigners; there will be five other carparks, with some people having to park up to twenty miles away at Kempton Park and Wembley Stadium. Two existing piers on the peninsula will be renovated, to which ferries and river-buses will come via 'Cutty Sark' from Westminster Bridge ('park and sail' plans were not pursued.) Overseas visitors, of whom it is estimated there will be over two million in total, might choose to travel to Waterloo by Eurostar, to Bank station and then by Jubilee Line straight to Greenwich.

South of the Dome is the new urban village called Millennium Village, just below the knuckle joint of the 'thumb' that is the Blackwall Peninsula, off Horn Lane and the delightfully-named Bugsby's Way. Designed by veteran Anglo-Swedish architect, Ralph Erskine, it has the highest standards of architecture for the homes, and the most exhaustive soil clearance for their back gardens. The village will also have a school, hotel, parks and offices, and a light industrial area.

At times during the Dome's genesis and development, it seemed a very doubtful affair. Would it be the spectacle it was planned to be - or a spectacular failure? In the words of Peter Mandelson, how sad it would have been, when all the eyes of the world were on Greenwich at the turn of the Millennium, *If all we had to offer was bunting and 300 acres of contaminated wasteland.* Only as years pass can we know for sure, but most opinion is that it truly will be one of the marvels of the next century. In years to come, with the dome itself maybe by then a sports centre or entertainment arena, the Millennium Village thriving, and the area's transport infrastructure permanently improved, people will agree that it has left a worthwhile legacy for the next millennium.

* *

As far back as February 1995, the Millennium Commission warned that the capital city of London was going to miss out on Lottery money in comparison with other areas, if it did not co-ordinate and submit its bids correctly. This was in part because since the abolition of the GLC there had been no overall local government, until the plans for a Lord Mayor. Of course, that is not how other parts of the country see it, because of two factors. Firstly, the average Londoner spends £78 a year on lottery tickets, but 70% of that amount was returned to the region; whereas in Scotland, where the average person spends over £100 a year on tickets, they only get back an average of about £30 per head in grants to that region. Secondly, of course, they are quite rightly dazzled by the big investment in the Dome. If one sets the Dome aside as a 'national' investment - which should anyway attract a lot of money-spending foreign visitors to this country - then it is true that London has not had much more than its fair share. It is a central location, and the capital, after all; for instance, of the nineteen national museums, ten are in London. Also, much money has been awarded to organisations which may have their headquarters in London, but through the multiplier effect, quickly disburse their money out to the provinces. Possibly also it was less than tactful (say) to promise the whole £55 million to the Royal Opera House in one go; to have paid it out in several stages might have defused criticism. In the 1980s, the main awarder of money to the arts was the Arts Council, and it was sometimes said that actually they favoured the provinces at the expense of the capital (though probably not so.)

As we approach the historical tidemark of the Millennium, what emerged was that London at last started to appreciate once again one of its most neglected assets, the River Thames. John Burns said in 1943: *I have seen the Mississippi. That is muddy water. I have seen the St Lawrence. That is crystal water. But the Thames is liquid history.* In Celtic and Roman times, it was the very reason for the capital's existence, being the first convenient crossing place. Nick Raysnford, the then Minister for London, said: *The river is (still) this city's lifeblood, the landmark by which people define the part of London they live in.* The river was broad (the Strand really was on the edge of the water) but shallow; but over the years it became channelled in, narrower and deeper, and increasingly cut off from the populace who had used it, by embankments, roads and earlier ugly flood barriers along the banks. Naval ships disappeared, where once there was, according to Tobias Smollett, *Such a forest of masts for miles together that you think all the ships of the universe here assembled.* For years, as the docks declined and bomb sites on its eastern margins left neglected, London seemed to turn its back (some difficult metaphorical usage here) on the heart of the city, the river running right through it. Now, the Thames is coming to life again, partly thanks to the Thames Barrier. The water is clean enough to allow fish (shad, Dover sole, bass, whitebait, smelt) to swim as far as the tidal reach and further; and one of the Lottery's early grants was for fish ladders in eighteen weirs on the River Kennet which should result in a self-perpetuating stock of salmon in the River Thames such as it used to have until the mid-eighteenth century.

There are more and more exciting buildings on its margins, not forgetting the Dome, and new bridges straddling it. In 1996 the then-Government's John Gummer launched a strategic plan for the river up as far as Windsor, both requesting developers to incorporate public uses (such as shops and restaurants) at ground-floor level of new developments, as well as encouraging the continuation of working wharves: but he re-iterated that *The Thames must remain a working river and not degenerate into gentrification.* In 1997 a £10 million flood defence scheme was launched by the Deputy Prime Minister John Prescott, with the additional aim of creating a 'wildlife superhighway' along 2,400 metres of the Thames foreshore. The Environment Agency claims that this plan would not cost more, but would bring greater environmental advantages; maybe once again the Cockney mudlarks will paddle on the shore? There should be more boating for pleasure and business, recalling the days when the king would go by barque to Hampton Court Palace, and little ships and ferries would buzz across the river all day. There have been river cruises, but these will increase as there is more to see and enjoy, feeling more like Paris' *bâteaux mouches*. What must not be forgotten, though, is that what seems charming on a summer's evening may not be so on a dark blustery February one; it is a tidal river, with all its unpredictability.

What makes a great difference to the feeling of life on the river after dark is its lighting; so far, only Albert and Tower Bridges had been were lit, but plans are afoot for lighting bridges and famous architectural landmarks along the riverside. By the Millennium these landmarks should include the already-mentioned foot bridge from Bankside, with its vista of St Paul's; and possibly the cable car from Covent Garden to the Royal Festival Hall.

The Globe will also be linked by the Millennium Mile via the Oxo tower and the South Bank complex to County Hall. The South Bank, whose Festival Hall was the centrepiece of the 1951 celebrations, had with the other great concrete cultural monoliths of the South Bank (Royal Festival Hall, Hayward Gallery, Queen Elizabeth Hall, Purcell Room, Royal National Theatre) become somewhat out of date in their facilities, and also unpleasant to reach on foot by the walkways because of the poor unfortunates in 'cardboard city' (many now rehoused to make way for a huge wrap-around cinema.) The RFH will be restored, and the approaches cleaned up to Waterloo Station, itself renovated and with the spanking new Eurostar terminal; but other parts of the controversial plan by Richard Rogers involving a transparent canopy placed over the rest of the site, seem unlikely at the moment.

County Hall, no longer the administrative focus of London, is by now a collection of prestigious flats, two hotels and a huge aquarium. Outside in Jubilee Gardens is the base of the Ferris Wheel, the most significant millennial project built without state funding or lottery money, which has planning permission to be there for five years. It is suspended actually over the river itself, and has superb views over Westminster, a panorama of London, and over the hills to Tunbridge Wells 30 miles away. It is ecologically friendly, its turning powered by floating tidal-driven turbines; and at 500 foot high, two-fifths as high again as the highest existing wheel in Japan and twice the size of Vienna's famous *Third Man* wheel at the Reisenrad. Originally designed with 60 cars, so from the side it will look like a clockface, now it has forty; each will hold sixteen people, and as it turns so slowly - it takes 20 minutes - you can walk on and off. It will run for eight hours a day. The egg-like cars are heated or cooled by solar panels, and within them will be headsets describing the views in a choice of languages. What is not yet known is the ultimate fate of Battersea Power Station, that up-turned table of a building about which rumours have circulated since it ceased to be a power station in 1983. Would it be renovated by Michael Jackson, or the Parkview Company with money from Hong Kong? Battersea Park, however, is benefiting from some well-deserved investment.

Around this time, there is to be a cultural festival called the String of Pearls, co-ordinated by Dylan Hammond with the support of the Minister for London, involving all the places mentioned above and over forty more, all within ten minutes of the river, to celebrate the Millennium. The two UNESCO World Heritage sites in London (in addition to Historic Greenwich) are the Tower of London, and the Palace and Abbey of Westminster, and they will especially be involved; also Lambeth Palace, the Royal Courts of Justice, St Paul's Cathedral, the Tate Gallery, City Livery Halls, Guy's and St Thomas' Medical Schools, and Southwark Cathedral, for whom (like York) a new cycle of mystery plays is being prepared.

Additionally, there are ambitious and more permanent plans for central London. In 1996 the architect Sir Norman Foster was chosen to produce a plan for improvements to Trafalgar Square, Parliament Square, Whitehall and the Victoria Embankment, which will feature extensive pedestrianisation. Sir Norman has also been involved in the Great Court Scheme, the imaginative plan to install a translucent roof over the two-acre space around the British Museum's Reading Room (from whence the Library has moved.) At the moment it is a clutter of odd-shaped bookstacks; it will become an extension of the Front Hall, a major public concourse open all day with a Centre for Education, a restaurant, and Information Centre. The whole complex will be the centrepiece of a new London Heritage walk , linking St Pancras with Covent Garden.

Although it has some of the world's greatest buildings, surprisingly (partly because of its period without a local authority) London is not so good on conference facilities. Unlike Glasgow or Birmingham, it still has no large international convention centre capable of hosting more than 10,000 delegates. The Council of Science and Technology Institutes is trying to get one off the ground as early as possible in the new millennium.

Let us finish this round-up of London's millennium plans at the Royal Albert Hall, once described by someone affectionately as *the world's largest jelly mould*, but which likes to call itself 'the nation's

Village Hall'. It has received £40 million from the Lottery, to which they have added half as much again to renovate the building totally. There is something very fitting about this, as the hall was built with the proceeds of the Great Exhibition of 1851 centred on the Crystal Palace, which was then situated just down the road in Hyde Park; and of course pioneered by and named after the Prince Consort himself, who died ten years later and whose Memorial opposite has recently been renovated and re-opened.

from PROTHALAMION

At length they all to mery London came
To mery London, my most kind nurse,
That to me gave this Lifes first native sourse,
Though from another place I take my name,
An house of ancient fame:
There when they came, whereas those bricky towres
The which on Themmes brode agèd backe do ryde,
Where now the studious Laawyers have their bowers,
There whylome wont the Templer Knights to byde,
Till they decayd through pride:
Next whereunto there standes a stately place,
Where oft I gaynèd giftes and goodly grace
Of that great Lord, which therein wont to dwell,
Whgose want tto well now feeles my freendles case;
But ah! Here fits not well
Olde woes, but joyes, to twll
Against the Brydale daye, which is not long:
    Sweet Themmes! Runne softly, till I end my song.

Edmund Spenser (1522-99)

This was a 'Spousall Verse' to celebrate the double marriage of the Lady Elizabeth and the Lady Katherine Somerset, daughters of the Earl of Worcester, in 1596.

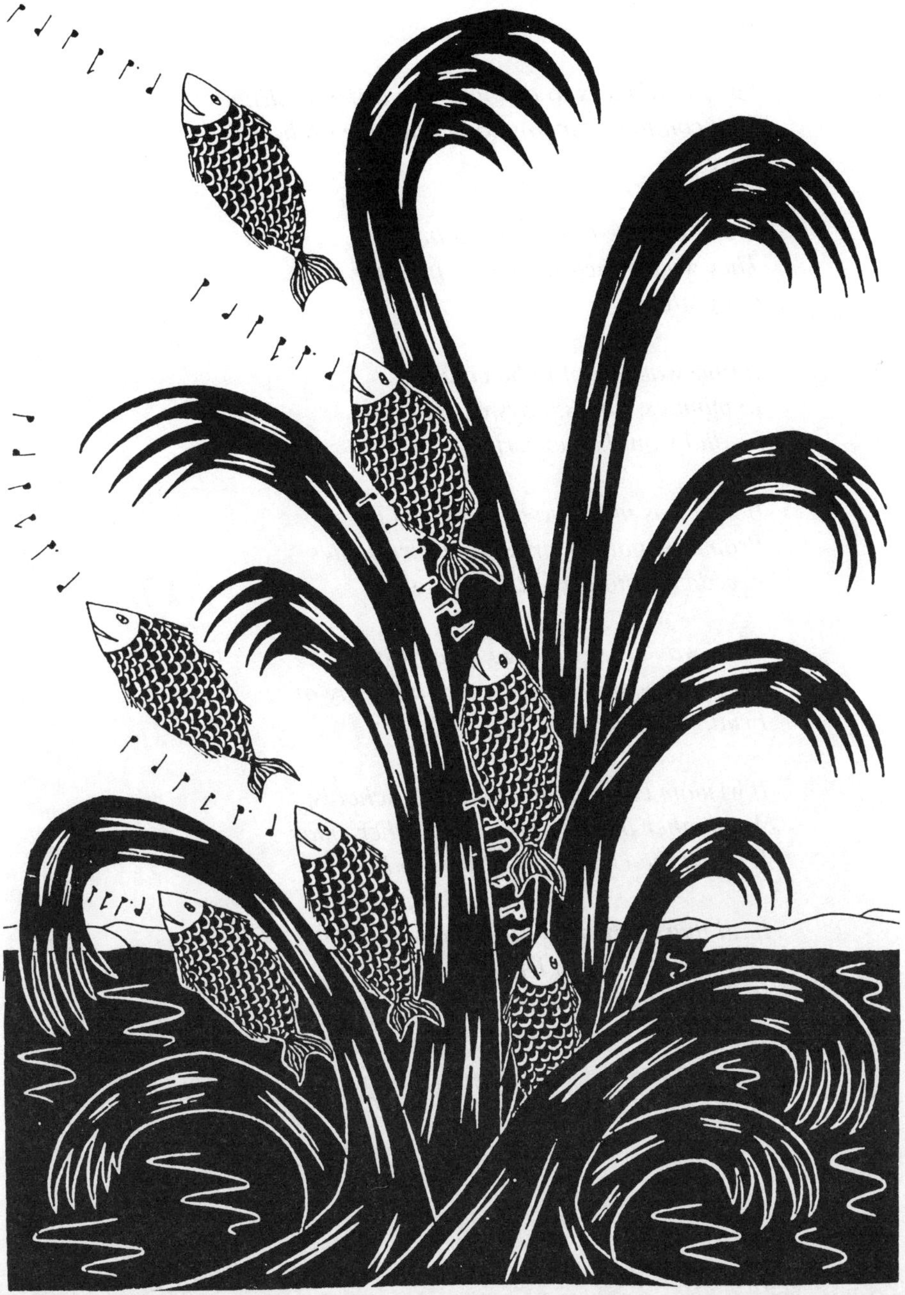

IF

She who dances to the beat of a different drum
Will continue dancing long after the orchestra
have left.

If words were to have meaning
They would need neither paper, nor air,
Only silence.

If time was meant to be counted
In minutes, hours, days or years
Its dial would be experience.

If love was meant to be captured by
Promises, golden rings, and certificates
Freedom would count for nought.

If life was given to forge a harvester
Then her basket should carry a bounty of
Fruit, not gold.

If wisdom can only be gained in schools
And higher places of learning, where may
We find the University of the Gods ?

If all that we have is ourselves
In a timeless sea of learning, then
We must study the tides well.

Ivan Sanders ©

TWO EXTRACTS BY PERCY BYSSHE SHELLEY (1792-1822)

ODE TO THE WEST WIND

Thou dirge
Of the dying year, to which this closing night
Will be the dome of a vast sepulchre.

ADONAIS

The one remains, the many change and pass,
Heaven's light for ever shines, Earth's shadows fly;
Life, like a dome of many coloured glass,
Stains the white radiance of Eternity
Until Death tramples it to fragments.

MILLENNIUM XANADU

*In Greenwich town, the government
A stately pleasure dome decreed;
Where Thames, the smelly river, ran,
Past wasteland mucked about by man,
Down to a soggy sea.
So twice ten miles infertile ground
Of gas-slag rubbish heap was found:
A dome was planned, to celebrate
Two thousand of our years A.D. -
For Christians, 'tis a telling date.
Mandelson seized it with glee.
He was a man who little feared,
And so the ground and soil were cleared.*
'We'll have a most distinguished Dome',
He told his chums,
'The natural home
Of lots of jolly things to do.
*There's statue gilt and baby too,
Who live within the* Body Zone*;
You enter it via the backbone.
The* Work Zone *has no snakes, no adders,
But lots of rather clever ladders;*
Learning Curve, Licensed to Skill,
Will both educate and thrill.
The Spirit Level's *special angle
Is in displays in a triangle.
You and children spend all day
In area known as* Serious Play*;*
Living Island - *like the sea -
Will be a super place to be;
On 'floater-coaster' (what a jape),
You'll glide along the fun* Dreamscape.
Later, other plans come clear:
The Mind, TransAction, Atmosphere,
Time to Talk!, uk@now,
*Stay while time will allow
And lastly, with its thoughts profound,*

*Will be the show called
Common Ground.
And outside place a Baby
Dome,
A sort of mini-hippodrome,
Where concerts, bands and
opera be
And other kinds of revelry.
We all will see project
millennial
Providing us with joy
perennial;
It must succeed, it really
must,
So I say - Greenwich or
bust!'*

Margaret Noone ©

from ENDYMION

A thing of beauty is a joy for ever:
Its loveliness increases; it will never
Pass into nothingness; but still will keep
A bower quiet for us, and a sleep
Full of sweet dreams .....
Some shape of beauty moves away the pall
From our dark spirits. Such the sun, the moon,
Trees old and young, sprouting a shady boon
For simple sheep; and such are daffodils
With the green world they live in; and clear rills
That for themselves a cooling covert make
'Gainst the hot season; the mid-forest brake,
Rich with a sprinkling of fair musk-rose blooms:
And such too is the grandeur of the dooms
We have imagined for the mighty dead;
All lovely tales that we have heard or read:
An endless fountain of immortal drink,
Pouring unto us from the heaven's brink.
Nor do we merely feel these essences
For one short hour; no, even as the trees
That whisper round a temple become soon
Dear as the temple's self, so does the moon,
The passion poesy, glories infinite,
Haunt us till they become a cheering light
Unto our souls, and bound to us so fast,
That, whether there be shine, or gloom o'ercast,
They always must be with us, or we die.

John Keats (1795-1821)

SHAKESPEARE'S SONNET 60

Like as the waves make towards the pebbled shore,
So do our minutes hasten to their end;
Each changing place with that which goes before,
In sequent toil all forwards do contend.
Nativity, once in the main of light,
Crawls to maturity, wherewith being crown'd,
Crooked eclipses 'gainst his glory fight,
And Time that gave doth now his gift confound.
Time doth transfix the flourish set on youth
And delves the parallels in beauty's brow,
Feeds on the rarities of nature's truth,
And nothing stands but for his scythe to mow:
    And yet to times in hope my verse shall stand,
    Praising thy worth, despite his cruel hand.

INVICTUS

Out of the night that covers me,
Black as the pit from pole to pole,
I thank whatever gods may be
For my unconquerable soul.

In the fell clutch of circumstance
I have not winced nor cried aloud;
Under the bludgeonings of chance
My head is bloody, but unbowed.

Beyond this place of wrath and tears
Looms but the Horror of the Shade,
And yet the menace of the years
Finds and shall find me unafraid.

It matters not how strait the gate,
How charged with punishments the scroll,
I am the master of my fate:
I am the captain of my soul.

William Henley (1849–1903)

CHAPTER 11 : OTHER COUNTRIES

Just because Britain is the centre of world celebrations of the Millennium, reassuring those of us in these post-imperial times that we are still the centre of something, does not mean that other countries are not also producing exciting, creative and imaginative celebrations for the Millennium. Naturally, they too will start most events on Friday, December 31st, 1999; so let us dodge their champagne corks and side-step their party poppers to see how they are going to mark the arrival of the twenty-first century; and also consider more long-term arrangements for the Millennium in other countries.

So, how will New Year's Eve be celebrated in traditional ways overseas? We could start by visiting the Continent by one of the century's most amazing engineering feats, the Channel Tunnel, where it is planned that Eurostar trains starting in London and Paris will pass each other on New Year's Eve sweeping guests to parties in the respective countries. At the end of the C.19, the Bureau de Longitudes in Paris declared that the new century would not begin until 1st January 1901, but the French do not like to be left behind, so have fallen in with the fin de siècle being the end of 1999 with the rest of us. In Gaullish days of druid-worship, France celebrated the tradition of 'au gui l'an neuf', 'gui' being mistletoe. The New Year may be of either gender, either le Nouvel An or la Nouvelle Année, and is usually marked by dancing with friends in a confetti-and-party-hats way, with lots of kisses and champagne at midnight. On New Year's Day you visit families to exchange 'étrennes', small packets of money, as good luck. Food may be like Christmas: oysters, 'boudin blanc truffé' (special veal sausages with truffles), turkey and 'bûche' (yule log), with variations from region to region. This year we could be, as Jeremy Baker suggested, dancing in the streets along the Meridian from Greenwich to Le Mans and Angoulême.

In Paris, whose city centre will be all floodlit, we could visit the Place de la Concorde, temporarily turned into a vast sundial with its

Egyptian obelisk at the centre, or the amazing new exhibition space underneath; or the newly-renovated Pompidou Centre, and listen to the bell weighing 30 tons which will be heard nearly twenty miles away. On the Grand Arche of La Defense will be projected a mosaic of images chosen by the French public called 'Expoterrestre'. To highlight French literature, there has been a giant 'book' alongside the Hôtel de Ville; and museums will be putting on special displays, like the joint 'Tableau du fin de Siècle' between the Louvre and the Musée d'Orsay. The Maritime Museum is being moved to a more central position on the banks of the Seine. A giant laser clock, whose points will be the twelve avenues leading up to it, will centre on the Arc de Triomphe in the Place Charles de Gaulle Etoile, showing the meeting-point of east and west. Laser beams of 300 metres will act as the hour hands, and the minute hands will be 500 metres, with the seconds ticking away on December 31st on a great digital display on the Arc itself. As midnight approaches, street lighting will be dimmed but the lasers intensified to daylight proportions; at the same time, additional lasers from high points in each of the twenty arrondisements will be beamed upwards back to the Arc de Triomphe. On the banks of the River Seine will be the new 650' wooden structure, Tour de la Terre; and in the river itself will be two thousand 10-feet plastic fish in all the colours of the rainbow bobbing about. The river will be especially perfumed, as part of the Route du Parfum to be established from Paris to Grasse, which will also pass through eight other towns connected with perfume. The Eiffel Tower, itself a reminder of an earlier celebration, had an electronic meter ticking off the days as the century ended. The tower is due to lay a luminous egg at 11.00 to the sound of 2,000 drums from five continents, which when midnight comes will glow an intense white, throwing light on to the tower, and crack open to reveal hundreds of television screens relaying pictures of other parties around the globe in places like the Marquesas Islands. Other events during the millennial year will be an international music festival on June 21st; and an extra-special celebration of July 14th with tree-planting along the meridian line and associated festivities. Avignon, renowned for its Roman 'pont' and its summer theatre festival, will be one of the European Cities of Culture 2000. In the Haute Vienne region, events to mark the death of Richard the Lionheart in 1199 will have been going on all year.

On to Germany, maybe, where in Berlin we could see Sir Norman Foster's new Parliament Building (now the Government has moved there from Bonn) near the Reichstag and join in partying to live bands round the Brandenburg Gate, or opera at the Komische Oper, the Friedrichstadt Palast or the Konzerthaus. Maybe instead you will go to the enormous Expo 2000 at Hanover lasting five months and costing £1 billion, with new British-designed trams to speed you around there. The theme of this, the first expo in the unified Germany, is 'Mankind - Nature - Technology', which will feature both futuristic events like a link-up with the Mir Space Station and a vast virtual-reality cityscape, as well as 160 national pavilions. Later at Eastertime, over a million and a half pilgrims will flock to watch the Passion Play in Oberammergau in southern Bavaria, played once a decade since 1633. European Football Championships will be jointly hosted by Belgium and the Netherlands; and Amsterdam will have a visit by the Tall Ships in August, 2000.

In Denmark, as in other Scandanavian countries and all of Germany, there is a curious obsession with a 1963 English film lasting 17 minutes called 'Dinner for One', in which Freddie Frinton, an actor from Grimsby, plays the butler at the whim of his employer, Miss Sophie. He enacts the parts of many of her old friends, now dead, at a dinner party, drinking more steadily as the evening wears on, until he carries her off to bed. This has become very much part of the northern European New Year's Eve ritual, and is shown on nearly every television station on December 31st to howls of delight. Some people celebrate by watching it on video, with traditional accompaniment of mulligatawny soup, North Sea shellfish, and roast chicken, the menu in the film.

In Iceland, people bathe outdoors at midnight on New Year's Eve in the hot sulphurous volcanic pools, searching the night skies for the shimmering aurora borealis, before drying off by dancing in the streets. Over the year, their capital Reykjavik is one of the nine Cities of Culture 2000; and will be celebrating a thousand years of Christianity in Iceland, and Leif Eriksson's discovery trip to America in 1000A.D. There will be a World Millennium Threshold Observance in the summer in the natural amphitheatre used by early Icelandic governments at Thingvellir.

In the Pope's home country, Poland, there will be celebrations all round, partly to welcome Krakow's selection as a further one of the nine Cities of European Culture (the official publicity spoke delightfully of it being 'the navel of the world'.) There will be rock concerts in steel works and salt-mines; at Easter, Krakow will be the venue for the Beethoven Festival. Helsinki in Finland is another named City of Culture (the other Northern European ones are Bergen and Brussels) and will mark the Millennium with an international cultural programme and later, a larger-than-usual Autumn Festival of Light.

Russia after communism is experiencing a religious revival, so many people will be in church. In St Petersburg in Russia there are plans for a Gala Dinner at the Grand Hotel Europe; and the annual black-tie dinner at one of the royal palaces. The Austrian capital Vienna will lay on its perennially wonderful Imperial Ball and Opera at the Hofburg Imperial Palace, to which it is best to arrive in the local horse-drawn carriages. The Viennese cheer up the hangovers of the world with their New Year's Day concert; the city was of course the setting of Johann Strauss the Younger's delightful opera *Die Fledermaus* (1874) actually set on New Year's Eve.

In Spain the time is called 'Nochevieja', that is literally 'old night'. Large gatherings of family and friends get together usually at home for a grand dinner with many courses. This usually features fish (sea bream or salmon) and/or lamb, followed by sweets as at Christmas like the traditional marzipan turron, dried fruits and 'piñones' (pine nuts); the sparkling white wine Cava is drunk. At midnight a grape is eaten with each of the twelve chimes to assure a happy and prosperous new year; you eat the last on the stroke of midnight, standing with the right foot forward and making a wish. This often accompanies following the celebrations on radio or television live from Puerto Del Sol, Madrid. You then dance the night away at hotels or clubs, picking up 'churros' (like doughnuts) and chocolate on the way home. This year, the sister ships *Black Prince* and

Black Watch will be cruising off the Canary Islands to catch the New Year. Over the Christmas/New Year period, the state lottery known as 'El Gordo' (The Fat One) pays out draws worth £154 million, often to syndicates involving whole villages. So far, despite checks with all sorts of reputable sources within the country, the *mañana* habit seems to reveal little other planning ahead for the Millennium; but as a Catholic country there will be special services. None will be greater than in the pilgrim centre of Santiago de Compostela with its immensely impressive ornate cathedral, especially over 'semana santa' (Easter week), Corpus Christi in early June, and St James' saints day on July 25th. St James of the Field of Stars is credited with ousting the Moors from Spain, and his city will be one of the European Cultural Cities 2000.

At Portugal's 'ano novo', wearing blue underwear under new clothes, you go to the highest point of the hall and jump, eat sultanas to the accompaniment of a wish, and exchange greetings. Special foods include a fish dish called 'bacalhau' with potatoes called 'perú', or turkey and rice, followed by cakes and savoury pastries.

At New Year the citizens of Italy's beautiful city of waterways, Venice, eat the traditional dish of lentils and cotechino (boiled sausage). It normally has ten million visitors annually, but its Mayor thinks there will be an extra fifteen million over the year 2000. Bologna will be another of the European Cities of Culture, when it will open up several museums, including one of the history of Judaism. Assisi is expecting twelve million visitors (three times as many as usual) to see the opening up of the Upper Church of the Basilica of St Francis, devastated by earthquake in September 1997. In Turin, the famous Shroud which may have wrapped the body of Christ, is to be displayed in its own chapel in Turin Cathedral from April 29th until June 11th. On April 1st, the port of Genoa will see the start of the Tall Ships 2000 race to Agadir, Morocco, across the Atlantic to Puerto Rico, New York and Halifax, and back to Holland five months later.

Rome will of course be the centre for many religious events. Although eighty years old, physically frail and suffering from tremors,

Pope John Paul is determined to survive in to the third millennium, and ever since his apostolic letter *Tertio Millennio Adveniente* of 1995, has referred to it often. During what he sees as the year of 'Giubileo' or Great Jubilee, the Pope has many plans for reconciliation and reunification (Vatican officials called it an attempt to 'square accounts with history'), with moves to free third world countries of debt and to hold an ecumenical service in the Holy Land that would bring together the leaders of the world's monotheistic religions. Millions of pilgrims are expected to visit Rome and the Vatican City over the year (estimates vary from ten million to six times that number), swamping the regular population of three million. Over twenty new churches are being built, some in outlying suburbs, the most prominent being the Church of the Year 2000 designed by the American Richard Meier. The government has planned for £1.4 billion of public works, including improvements to the road from Fiumicino Airport and upgrading the ring road, a £27 million underground carpark beneath the Janiculum Hill next to the Vatican, two complete tramlines, new bus facilities and over eighty other works; but probably the only ones to be finished will be the city's third underground line from the Coliseum under the Tiber to St Peter's Square and the restoration of the Coliseum. Access will be improved to pilgrimage sites like San Lorenzo, and the Basilica of St Peter, where the tomb of St Peter in the crypt will be renovated and specially lit.

In Israel there is an enormous refurbishment programme, of course, partly because the Vatican stated that it was 'a sacred duty' to visit the Holy Land in the years 1998-2001, and the Pope's aforementioned ecumenical service. This would centre on the cities of Bethlehem, Jerusalem and Nazareth, where the leaders may gather for a series of events whose emphasis would be on worship during the last two weeks of 1999. Bethlehem 2000 has plans for building restoration, and a programme of cultural events running from January 1999 to Easter 2000, with an opera festival and pop concerts, to which four million visitors will come. The Roman Catholic mayor, Hanna Nasser, UNESCO and the Palestinian authorities plan to spend £150 million; a Swedish architect has redesigned the town's Manger Square. There are even rumours of a Three Wise Men visitors centre and planetarium …..

Nazareth, the home town of Jesus, will also have millions of tourists for their festival, Nazareth 2000, when £60 million-worth of restoration will take place on the old buildings, connecting religious sites by a scenic walk-way, erecting eight new hotels and restoring the market. It is the largest Arab town in Israel; its population of 60,000 is 60% arab. Jerusalem's festivities will centre on Temple Mount and the Dome of the Rock , but be wary of friction with Muslims because the latter is a holy place for them too. At Megiddo, the site of the terrible prophecy by Joel in the Old Testament that gave us the word 'Armageddon', the tourist authorities are preparing an exhibition of holograms.

There is a lot going on in Asia. In India there will be various celebrations, some centred on an ancient observatory called Jantar Mantar. In the Amritsar area, where Sikhs call the new year 'Nava Saal', people will assemble in new clothes - women in their finest, flashiest jewellery - to give gifts of sweets and money to children, and dance bangra. Food for that time is barji, ladow, grajnella, jalebi, pakoras, samosas, puree, chale, ladoos and kheer. Sikhs will have spent 1999 in marking the 300th anniversary of the formation of the Khalsa, the pure community of Sikhs. In Delhi and Bombay, with its larger population of Christians, many people will spend time in church. In Thailand it will be the year 2543, that being the number of years since the death of the Lord Buddha; no great celebrations are planned. In the Seychelles, people will be eating dishes of rice with fish or curry, and enjoying street parties.

China, whose children are given money in red purses at such times, plans to start the Millennium with a bash on the Great Wall; or reliving the legendary glamour of the 'Paris of the East' at a costume ball in Shanghai. On February 16th 1999, they will have moved from the Year of the Tiger to that of the Rabbit; and on 5th February 2000 dancing will welcome in the Year of the Dragon. By January 24th, 2001, it will be the Year of the Snake. This vast country is planning entertainment beyond the millennium at a £30 million theme park called Oriental Studio 2000 in the southern city of Guangzhou. Many eyes will still be on Hong Kong, whose freedoms were guaranteed for fifty years from 1997.

You could visit Japan, home among other things to a range of religions which many people follow in pluralistic fashion, as well as some weird millennial sects. It will be the year Heisei 12 (the twelfth year of Emperor Akihito) and will be celebrating with the best of us, as they have their annual holiday for three days away from work for family gatherings. Each house will be spotless, decorated with pine branches and hand-printed 'nengajo' New Year cards. New Year's Eve in Japan is called 'òmisoka', 'misoka' being the last day of the month and 'ò' being 'big'. The special tradition is the Joya-no Kane (= watchnight bell), when the temples around Japan ring their ceremonial bells 108 times. According to the teachings of Buddha, mankind is plagued by 108 sins, so each clang of the bell banishes a particular fault. They ring 107 bells before New Year and the final bell after midnight. Some people go to a temple to observe this ceremony; or they watch it transmitted live on television from a famous temple in Kyoto, the old capital. Families may wear beautiful traditional costume to visit the shrines together on New Year's Day for the 'hatsumōde' (= first visit), and again next day when visiting friends. Special foods to eat at this time include 'toshikoshi' or buckwheat noodles, with the hope that one's life will be as long as the noodles, and 'o-mochi' (round rice cake) or 'o-zoni' (ditto, plus vegetables and soy sauce soup.) With a population which is approaching 150 million by the Millennium, people will start to live in huge cloudscrapers like the planned Aeropolis Centre, planned home to 300,000 people. Sports fans will be looking forward to co-hosting the 2002 World Cup Soccer League, with South Korea.

Countries not part of the Christian tradition may have their official new years at other times, but as part of the global village they will no doubt be well aware of the Millennium. Unfortunately, Muslims cannot do much celebrating at first, as the month-long Ramadan will have started on December 12, 1999, so they will have to wait until the following New Year (not a time of Ramadan) to celebrate. In Afghanistan, the new year is a time for visiting your family and friends, and patching up old quarrels. On New Year's Eve, every family is in their own house making special dishes with fresh fish from the sea, followed by cake made with seven types of fruits called Haft Mawa. More sophisticated fare will be offered to guests of the Ritz-Carlton hotel in Dubai - they will go on safari in to the desert and dine under the stars.

It will be interesting to see if the planned party at the Pyramids in Egypt (guests invited included Margaret Thatcher, Ronald Reagan and that millennially busy man, the Pope) comes off, it being an American-backed charity events to raise money for educational scholarships. In Ethiopia, to celebrate 'Adis amet wazim', families come together wearing their traditional clothes, sing a special song, and light a bonfire; children distributing flowers sing songs around the neighbourhood. Food for this time is enjer, doro wet, buna and a special coffee.

Christian communities in Africa will be celebrating. In Ghana, the churches have been preparing a mission to their youth for some time; families will gather to eat yam with palm oil, and sheep soup. The country will have its portion of the north-south Millennial Tree Line to show off. In Nigeria there are no unique traditions, except eating special foods like yams, jollof rice and fried fish. In Kenya, 'Mwaka Mpiya' is marked by beating drums, wood fires in the home, traditional costume and special songs, to accompany huge feasts of ugali, pilau rice, roast meat and chicken washed down by local beer. In Harare, while waiting for Millennium midnight to be marked (as each year) by the sound of car horns and drums, the Zimbabweans will be eating festive dinners of samosas, pork or lamb from the spit, and carrot rice or yellow rice. Africa will be the crossing-point of two huge trekking groups, who will set off from New Zealand or Greenwich respectively, keeping in touch by e-mail. There is a luxury fortnight's tour going from Luxor to watch the millennial sunset over Victoria Falls, then to Zanzibar, the Serengeti and the Masai Mara.

In Bermuda they will be celebrating as usual with the visit of the Gombeys, carnival figures who revel in the streets. Jamaicans will be holding beach parties or street parties, dancing to reggae and calypso bands and visiting each home along the way. Energy to celebrate the so-called 'extra special reggae sunsplash' of 31.12.99 will be provided by curried goat and rice, fried fish, jerk pork, ackkee, bammy, manish water made from goat's liver, and johnnie cakes.

In America, some wild things will be going on. Probably the biggest will be in Times Square, the centre of New Year revelry for many years, now sanitised in to some sort of respectability by the Times Square Business Improvement scheme; where huge television screens will follow the twenty-four time zones as up to a million people welcome the Millennium, this affair being hosted for the twenty-fifth time by Dick Clark. Everyone cheers the 'Lowering of the Ball', six foot in diameter, 500 pounds in weight, clad with rhinestones and containing 144 strobe lights, which is lowered down the 77 foot flagpole on the top of the *New York Times* building, to the accompaniment of flurries of fireworks and ticker-tape (and possibly snow.) The city has pledged to stage a year-and-a-half-long celebration from July 1999 to January 2001. Boston began the tradition of alcohol-free First Night celebrations, a tradition which has now spread to over two hundred cities; but they have also planned special millennial visual and performing arts events. In South Carolina there is a $500 million theme park opening called 'God's Wonderful World'. Floating over the Arizona desert will be some people watching the Millennial dawn from a balloon. In Texas, there will a large gathering at the 'Meet in the Middle Festival.' Further west, some people are hoping to close the Golden Gate Bridge in San Francisco for a party; and there will be another huge one in California's Mojave Desert with spectacular drumming. Los Angeles will be opening their new cathedral named after St Vibiana; the city is home to the new Getty Centre, and also the focus of a round-the-world cycle race. Up in Canada, there's been a movement to divert funds away from the ephemera of fireworks and so on, to environmental projects under the umbrella title of 'The Will for the Earth'. Halifax, Nova Scotia, will be celebrating the 250th anniversary of its foundation, and hosting the Tall Ships in July 2000. Latin American countries will be enjoying themselves with massive parties, especially at Copocabana Beach in Brazil where it is also the feast of Iemanjá, the goddess of the sea, in whose honour lighted candles are placed on the shoreline. Preparations will already be under way for their famous Carnival in early March.

The really determined - and rich - pleasure seekers will be those who try to 'follow the sun'. On Concorde, it would be possible by flying from London to New York and back to catch three dawns ..... that is, if you trust that air traffic controllers world-wide are actually at their desks, and are not facing a Millennium Bug melt-down. The thrill to search for, is to be the first to see the dawn on January 1st, 2000 (the fun to be repeated again for 2001, no doubt), but that is not as simple as it seems; it all depends over where that will actually be. Many people can only think in terms of the Pacific, where the International Dateline is. That was arranged so that the date is altered to compensate for the gain or loss of time (one hour per 15°) which occurs when circumnavigating the globe. However, purists will tell you that the 1884 International Meridian Conference decreed that the day does not start world-wide until it reaches the dark hour of midnight at Greenwich. When that moment comes on January 1st, the Pacific will already be at noon that day; so where is sunrise at that very moment? At 12 midnight here, the sun will apparently be rising over the Nicobar Islands (which are not touristy places) halfway between Sri Lanka and Malaysia.

Even the actual Dateline is not clear .....It is no longer exactly straight down 180 degrees Longitude. The Meridian Conference bent the line so that all parts of New Zealand would be together in the same time zone, but did not consider the case of Kiribati, which at that time (1884) was a collection of independent islands whose inhabitants knew nothing of the 24 hour clock! Thus, Kiribati (pronounced, curiously 'Kiribass'), in the South-West Pacific where the Dateline dissects the Equator, re-drew the line in 1995 in a great 1,000 mile loop to ensure that all the 36 islands that belonged to its group should all be in the same day west of the Dateline. In an interview with Michael Walsh, Honorary Consul for the Republic of Kiribati in Britain, he said :

> *Caroline Island is the easternmost of eight islands which form the Line Islands group. Under the previous dateline, both that group and the Phoenix Islands group were in a time zone a full day ahead of the Gilbert Islands and Banaba, which are the remaining part of the country. It was a nonsense that one part of*

the nation was located in a different day from the rest; the action of the President in remedying it was long overdue.

So now all parts of the Republic of Kiribati are in the same day, which allows the uninhabited Caroline Island (especially renamed Millennium Island) to be acknowledged by many to be THE first place to welcome January 1st's happy dawn at 05.43 GMT; swiftly followed by sunrise on Kiritimati (their way of saying 'Christmas') Island, which was once used for nuclear tests and is now preparing to be the Japanese space landing site in 2005, but is a bit lacking in comfortable hotels. A commercial company called 'The Billennium©' will be marketing T-shirts and is planning a satellite link-up with Kiribati. Even those who settle for Tarawa, the main island in the group, may not find all the luxuries to which they are used.

Other contenders for the 'first' trophy are the Chatham Islands, a New Zealand dependency 500 miles east of Christchurch which has a permanent population of only 750 people, and will have a large airship floating over it; nearby Pitt Island where the sun will arise 14 seconds before 4.45 a.m. local time on January 1st 2000 (when it will still only be Friday teatime of December 31st in Britain); and Tonga, who will go ahead anyway with 'the bonfire of the century' at a huge beach party with feasting and *lakalaka*, the traditional Tongan dancing in grass skirts, and entertaining planeloads of Americans. The King of Tonga intends to send a message of peace to all the world from his capital, Nuku'alofa, on the Internet. You could be on Fiji watching its local fire-walking ritual, at a special millennial gathering of tribal people from around the world, at a dawn-to-dusk concert party, looking at the newly-built wall that marks the new millennium from the old, or on one of its romantic blue lagoon islands. If you are a desperate Millennium chaser you will go for a travel package that will fly you from one place to another like Fiji to the Cook Islands; or from Tonga (which is 120 miles west of the Dateline), and Apia in Samoa, eighty miles east, whose Cape Mulinu'u beach will see the very last sun of the old Millennium.

On mainland New Zealand is the city of Gisborne on the north island of New Zealand, which will be the first major settlement to see the

Millennium at 4.46 a.m, with a planned 100,000 guests; 2,000 people will have cycled from Auckland, and there will be Christian groups, hot-rodders and motor-bikers, and at the same time a fleet of ocean-going canoes will arrive from seven Pacific nations. The craft from Pacific Tall Ships 2000 (including a replica of Captain Cook's *Endeavour*) will also have arrived from Wellington, on their way to join the America's Cup celebrations in Auckland in March. Slightly further south, but with Te Mata Peak possibly putting their view of sunrise sooner, is Hastings, where there will be parties to watch the hang-gliders and paragliders trying to catch the first glimpse of the sun as they take off from the peak.

On the South Island, Christchurch is in centenary mode in 2000. Christopher Godley, great great grandson of one of the founders of the city, writes as follows:

> *Millennium plans currently being planned for Christchurch are likely to run longer than anywhere else in the world. For them, the celebration covers not only the moment when the C.20 passes into the 21st, but the sesquicentennial of its founding by John Robert Godley in 1850. Planned by a committee, many from Church College, Oxford, almost uniquely it was a planned community which sought to organise a balanced collection of emigrants capable of establishing a whole society based on the three ideals of community, church and college. It is planning a huge millennial party in Cathedral Square and Hagley Park on New Year's Eve 1999 which will progress directly in to the 'Karaunga', a unique Maori/Christian service to welcome the dawn of the new Mmillennium on Godley Heads. Many events are planned over the year, including a regatta, and a June Winter Ball to celebrate the Maori New Year. The year culminates with special waterborne celebrations in December.*

Australia will be looking forward to marking the centenary of the Federation of Australia in 1901 (it is possible by then that Australia will be a republic.) Australians too will be taking advantage of the fact that their New Year starts in summertime, not (as with us) in sometimes dreary winter. There is to be a gourmet New Year's Eve barbecue in the bush looking up to sunrise on Ayers Rock. Preparations will be in train for a Conference on Pacific Green Issues (at Easter) and an International Garden Festival in New South Wales (in August.) The whole country will already be in a frenzy about the Sydney Olympics, which runs from Friday, September 15th to Sunday, 1st October, with the Paralympics from 18th to 29th October, all run by the Sydney Organising Committee for the Olympic Games (SOCOG.) Proud of being the only Olympics of recent times to be ready on time, and also built on ecological principles, it will be built on old Aboriginal wetlands at Homebush Park, 14 km west of the city centre, site of half the 28 Olympic sports. Other events will be in the Sydney Harbour precinct or nearby (such as beach volleyball at Bondi.) The budget of nearly A$2.3 billion will pay for the immense building projects; and for the workforce of two and a half thousand to organise over ten thousand athletes and 5,000 officials from 200 different countries. The Olympic torch will be carried around Oceania (the Pacific) beforehand; the torch will feature on the logo, and there are also no less than three mascots, a platypus called Syd, a kookaburra named Olly, and an anteater, Millie, named of course after the Millennium. There had been associated cultural festivals since 1997, the last featuring Antipodean Kiri Te Kanawa.

There is one really good reason to be afloat and away from land, because the millennial melt-down will not be a worry (though watch that navigation equipment as you near shore.) Cunard has several Millennium cruises: to Java and the Spice Islands, to Panama and Mexico, but best of all a 23-night cruise from Southampton stopping at New York, Fort Lauderdale, Mexico, Costa Rica, Cartageña, Aruba, Grenada and then celebrating the actual Millennium in Barbados. There is a cruise on the *Marco Polo* from Buenos Aires via the Falkland Islands to Antarctica; or around the Galapagos Islands on a three-masted schooner.

So, this ends our trip around the world in eighty ways (or so). You did not need a faithful servant like Passepartout to make arrangements for you, you just had to sit back and read all about it ..... The world will be *en fête* for the Millennium, particularly on Friday, 31st December, 1999, but also all through the year 2000 and in to 2001. There are of course bound to be some people and countries who will lavish stupidly extravagant sums of money on the occasion's entertainment; as a British pharmacist Chandy Patel said, *Maybe too much money and effort is being spent on having a big party, especially by the richer countries of the world; the poorer countries may feel they need to follow suit, something that they can ill-afford.* What would be nice would be if everyone felt they were included, whether their celebration were a bottle of Dom Perignon at the Dome, or a bottle of fizzy drink with the family in kraal, favela or igloo. It would be a triumph of Christian values, if marking the birth of Jesus Christ was able to unite in spirit the peoples of the world; and if at this time, the brotherhood of nations managed to drop its sibling rivalry to make a the world united.

MILLENNIUM

Paris is hatching an egg,
Greenwich is building a dome,
America's having a party,
And I'm staying at home!

Millennium comes in two thousand,
Or is it two thousand and one?
If the bug's gonna get us before then,
Let's just go out and have fun.

So much has happened to earth
Two thousand years of change,
From virgin birth to Virgin trains
And comet tails to Concorde planes.

A new era's about to begin,
The sand has started to run;
The clock is ticking away,
We need a starting gun!

Sarah Packman ©

A GILBERTESE PRAYER TO THE SUN

O, Sun, thou art reborn out of darkness;
Thou comest out of deep places,
Thou comest out of the terrible shadows;
Thou wast dead, thou art alive again.
O, Sun, behold me, help me!
The word of power died in my heart,
Let it be reborn again as thou,
Let it fill me with light as thou,
Let it soar above the shadows,
Let it live !
So shall I be eloquent.

from **A PATTERN OF ISLANDS** by Arthur Grimble © John Murray (Publishers) Ltd. This book was about the Gilbertese Islands, now known as Kiribati, which will see the Millennium's first dawn. This photograph was taken at dawn on the main Kiribati island of Tarawa.

TO MARGUERITE

Yes: in the sea of life enisl'd,
With echoing straits between us thrown,
Dotting the shoreless watery wild,
*We mortal millions live **alone**.*
The islands feel the enclasping flow,
And then their endless bounds they know.

But when the moon their hollow lights
And they are swept by balms of spring,
And in their glens, on starry nights,
The nightingales divinely sing;
And lovely notes, from shore to shore,
Across the sounds and channels pour;

Oh then a longing like despair
Is to their furthest caverns sent;
For surely once, they feel, we were
Parts of a single continent.
Now round us spreads the watery plain -
Oh might our marges meet again!

Who order'd that their longing's fire
Should be, as soon as kindled, cool'd?
Who renders vain their deep desire?
A God, a God their severance ruled;
And bade betwixt their shores to be
The unplumb'd, salt, estranging sea.

Matthew Arnold (1822-1888)

THE TIMING OF NEW YEAR?

The new year is known to bring happiness
And light into people's lives.
They say it makes a fresh start with a lot of promises.
But when the gusty winds come with a chill
In the air, it's the same old story ......

The new year begins with sadness and gloom,
With wintry showers, the frosty mornings and foggy days. This is
In concord with soggy moods;
With bare trees there isn't much to hope for.
(Only one little sparkle which shows on everyone's faces is
The white soft snow, which lightens up the dull day.)

With this start to the new year, all the promises
Are broken, and the fresh start slides
In to the old ending.

I wonder, if the new year started in the summer
Would life be different; and would the promises
And the fresh start be kept?

Osman Mumtaz ©

My brief sweet life is over, my eyes
no longer see.
No summer walks - no Christmas trees -
no pretty girls for me.
I've got the chop. I've had it.
My nightly ops. are done.
Yet in another hundred years I'll still be twenty one.

R.W. Gilbert (inscription in the RNZAF museum in Christchurch, N.Z.)

Japan in the 21ˢᵗ Century

The calligraphy by
Kaneyoshi reads
ni jù i sei ki no ni hon

二十一世紀の日本

ZUKUNFT

Zurück?
Voraus?
Bleiben?
im leeren Raum
dazwischen?
Mir ist so kalt
und wage nicht mich zu bewegen ~
jedes Rühren an die Schwellen
ist schmerzhaft.
Wann und wo beginnt die Zukunft?

Backwards?
Forwards?
Stay?
In empty space between?
I'm so very cold,
don't dare to move ~
every touching on the borders
gives pain.
When and where does the future start?

Reinhild Hensle © translated
by Brigitte von Peinen

'So, how are *we* going to celebrate the Millennium?'

CHAPTER 12 : THE FUTURE

It is a bit like Christmas; well, of course the Millennium is a lot like Christmas, except we are celebrating Christ's birthday on a year marked out of other years, as opposed to a day marked out of other days. Just as before Christmas, we think of events in the autumn as being 'before Christmas' or 'up to Christmas', but when it comes you suddenly note that life goes on afterwards; similarly, as this book is being prepared everyone is only concentrating on the Big M itself, but also we should be looking at what will follow. Having survived the Millennium, what then? Whither Mankind?

It is difficult even to think about the immensity of the universe, and therefore where it might be heading. Trying to contemplate the great imponderables of time and space leaves the brain reeling and helpless. It is sort of comforting that Somebody has an overview of all this, that maybe Somebody or some force is in charge. St Matthew tells us in his Gospel that though there are many sparrows, none fall to the ground without the knowledge of God, and that He knows all about us - who are of infinitely greater value to Him than the sparrows - to the extent that the very hairs of our head are numbered. When we look up in to the night sky and marvel at the mass of stars and planets wheeling about, when we look at a drop of water under a microscope and see the myriad of little swimming things therein, we realise how little of the universe we personally know. Even as a race, man cannot fathom more than a fraction of anything; but one prediction can surely be made without fear of argument, that the coming millennium will not stop man trying to find out more and more.

Puzzling about the future seem irresistible to humanity. It is as though we are impelled to do a caesarian on the womb of time, too impatient for events to take their course, and desperate to see what time will give birth to. Albert Einstein proved that he was not as other men when he said in 1930 *I never think of the future; it comes soon enough;* the rest of us, however, cannot wait. The Bible counsels patience, as when in the Old Testament book of Proverbs we are told *Do not speculate about tomorrow. For you do not know what a day may bring forth;* and in the New Testament Book of James, the writer says :

> *You do not know what will happen tomorrow. For what is your life? It is even as a vapour that appears for a little time and then vanishes away.*

The good thing about the future is that it comes one day at a time. Whatever the horrors that one day may bring, the next day may bring happiness again; with the unquenchable optimism of human nature, most of us spend sufficient time on the sunny plateaux with the occasional lifts to the peaks, to balance out our time in the valley of depression. In his infamous 'Devil's Dictionary' (1911), the American humorist Ambrose Bierce wrote tongue-in-cheek of the future as a rosy time when *Our affairs prosper, our friends are true, and our happiness is assured;* but early in life, most of us are resigned to the fact that such pie-in-the-sky whimsy is unlikely to happen, and inure ourselves to the reality of a mixture of good and bad. The future, as someone once truly said, is the past in preparation; and often it turns out to be much the same as the present, only more so. Until it comes, we cannot know ..... and mostly we are desperate to know.

Divination took many forms in times past, and people still try to prophesy or influence the future by means of reading signs, observing superstitions and performing rituals. You could interpret dreams, or read the arrangement of entrails in a sacrificial animal; you could 'read' the stars, open a book at random, read cards or throw rods in a certain way (a sort of spiritual version of Pick-up-sticks). You could study crystals, or the way minerals reacted on a red-hot axe. You could write predictions on leaves, and 'see which way the wind blows'. You could avoid seeing an owl in daytime, or a single magpie anytime. You should avoid walking under ladders, or giving the name of 'the Scottish play'. You could search for auspicious auguries in comets, thunder, lightning, fire, air and water.
However, this chapter is not an Old Almanack predicting the glorious future that surely you personally deserve; rather, it is a casting of a line in to the uncharted waters of time to see if we can land a few predictions about what is likely to come about in the next few years in society in general. Is the future likely to be rosy, or terrifying, or a mixture of both?

In the past, as so much change was brought about by science, predictions of the future over the years tended to be in the form of science fiction. Much that was thought as fiction has actually - like the man on the moon - come to pass. (Some predictions have not of course turned out as expected, like the nineteenth century guess that London's traffic would grind to a halt in the twentieth century because of the increase in the amount of manure from carriage horses .....) Science fiction makes you think of rogue boffins making discoveries with which to terrorise whole nations with phials of deadly bacteria, or people floating about dressed in silver-foil clothes and travelling in phallic-shaped cars, or the UFOlogists' dream of little green men with antennae on their heads. One is longing to ask, why these extra-terrestrial visitors should travel all the way to earth then only show themselves hovering for ten minutes in a ball of fire in New Mexico or wherever? There certainly are inexplicable things in our world, of course, and we may agree with Hamlet that *There are more things in heaven and earth, Horatio, than are dreamt of in your philosophy.*

Mainly, though, it will be to the realm of real science that we turn when we think of the future. As a country, we have produced outstanding and original scientists over many generations, from Sir Isaac Newton to Stephen Hawking, even if they have had to struggle for recognition. World-wide, there is still so much actually to be discovered, such as quantum gravity; but probably the science of the immediate future will be not so much amazing leaps like Einstein's amazing theory of relativity which overturned scientific thinking in 1925, but careful evolution of existing theories in areas like electrons, bio-engineering, genetic research and so on.

One enormous area of scientific research is of course the space/time continuum, which not only looks back across the aeons of millennia that have passed before us, as briefly surveyed in the first chapter, but will look forward to millennia to come. As the biologist J.B.S. Haldane said in 1927, *My suspicion is that the universe is not only queerer than we suppose, but queerer than we can suppose.* In the past, Ptolemy, Copernicus, Galileo and colleagues searched the skies and beyond for knowledge and inspiration; today we view space also as an extension of humanity's back-yard. With future cosmology research, will come space probes ever-deeper to find what is out there, like the so-called Pistol Star which is ten million times more powerful than our sun. There will naturally be exploitation of its resources (Hilton International have already started planning a 5,000 bed hotel on the moon), and increased interplanetary travel; such as the first man on Mars by 2020, maybe sent into hibernation to while away the time getting there, and an unmanned spacecraft to Mercury. Information sent back from the spacecraft such as Voyager 1, and Pioneer 10 (which in twenty-five years travelled nearly seven billion miles out of our planetary system but would still need another 100,000 years before it hit the nearest star to our solar system), combined with theoretical astrophysics, indicate that we still have another five billion years - that is, many millennia yet to celebrate! - before Earth is swallowed up by the expanding Sun. Any danger we may actually be in is collision with asteroids, which may have been the cause of some the previous great extinctions of life here on earth; it has now been recognised that at the end of every June, Earth's orbit takes us in to the path of a disintegrating comet called Encke, which troubles us little now but may be very serious in about 3,000 A.D, the next millennium. Astronomers have revised their opinion and now think it unlikely that we might be grazed by the mile-wide asteroid 1997 XF11 in 2028. More positively, other scientists from the Space Regatta Consortium are working on plans to beam light on to major cities from space during dull winter months.

Meanwhile, Earth's own deep space is being explored as core samples are taken from as deep as 750 metres under the ocean bed several miles below sea level, where, amazingly, worm-like animals and microbes manage to live.

Neither ocean nor space exploration would have been possible without the formidable calculating power of computers. Starting as little more than large electric abacuses, they are now infinitely complex cyber brains that do achieve more than we could ever imagine. The mechanical inventions of Pascal and Leibnitz were developed by Charles Babbage in his 1835 'analytical machine'; in 1946 came the first electronic computer, from the work of Alan Turing, and in 1948 the Mark 1 machine called 'Baby' with which Tom Kilburn and the late Fred Williams launched the digital computer. In 1971 came the first microchip, and thereafter they have been getting smaller and more powerful, so that even today's PC is more powerful than a computer that filled a room in the 1950s. Mini-computers in the form of microchips will be everywhere; ICL forecast that in half a century there will be the equivalent of 1,000 for every person, some of which may be implanted under your skin for medical checks, or in clothing or jewellery.

The huge mainframes now crunch unbelievable numbers; a gigaflop computer is thought to be capable of a billion floating-point operations a second, and a teraflop can do a trillion. Recently, over a thousand computers were linked together to crack an encryption code, which took 53 days and involved over 200 million million calculations. Back in the home, many a youngster's bedroom resounds to the 'zap' of an electronic game being played, and computers are used by all the family for accounts, writing homework assignments, preparing work (our next computer will have SuperDisks capable of holding as much as 83 floppies), assembling genealogical research or writing letters. There are networks to link and support people world-wide who share rare diseases, or an interest in esoteric hobbies. The computer can already achieve neural network technology, whereby after seeing many examples (say, of one face) it can learn to recognise that person in another photo. Touch-screen computers are in use in museums, shops and so on; and voice recognition systems, whereby you can dictate to a machine and have it typed straight up, are currently emerging. There may soon be wearable computers in the form of waistcoats. It is all amazing stuff; although, by what has been termed the 'Productivity Paradox', some experts argue that it has produced little net benefit to business and has made no increase in productivity. It does things nicer, but does it do them *better*? The PC has made Bill Gates the richest man on earth (with an estimated fortune of $18 billion a year) and enriched some people's lives immeasurably, whilst at times driving us all to distraction.

A welcome development of computing is its use for communication on the Internet - the information super-highway - and therefore electronic missives (e-mail) and the world-wide web. The Internet was developed in the 1960s, as America planned to keep ahead of international competition through its Advanced Research Project Agency (hence an early version was called the ARPANET).In the following decades, it developed from a system to share files and resources mainly in the office situation, through the means of packets, gateways and bytes, to become a truly global information system. It spawned e-mail, starting in a small way in the early 1970s in America and then spreading around the globe; and the World Wide Web (www) which was developed at CERN, the European Particle Physics Laboratory in Geneva in 1991 by the Briton Tim Berners-Lee, who developed a global hypertext project to be available on the Internet at large. This has meant that the Internet has been adapted in to the world of PCs (personal computers) and network computers. It all works extremely fast (when web insiders talk about a 'web year', they mean three months); and cleverly. When the web breaks down, as it did memorably in April 1997 for 36 hours in a stoppage known as a 'brown-out', the web simply knits itself back together. This is good news for communications (and could in theory survive global disasters) but makes it difficult to police or censor, and so there will be an increase in defamation and copyright cases arising from its free use. Some countries try to curb its use; in China every one of its 600,000 or so users has to register with the police, and even in New Zealand there is the legal right to censor it.

There are now 2,000 Internet Service Providers, and more than 90,000 people go on the net worldwide every day. By the millennium there will be nearly three million home internet accounts in the UK and 200 million world-wide. Not surprisingly California, home of Silicon Valley, accounts for 80% of world usage; and thanks to a donation from Microsoft, every American library is connected to it. Libraries here are beginning to incorporate it, thanks to Lottery funding; bibliographies, indexes, reference books and journals and newspaper archives are already on computer. Now anyone with a PC, a modem and a telephone line to plug in can be linked to the world. In the future the connection may be the power supply that serves street lamps; via fibre optic cables, laboriously laid under our streets; by our existing telephone lines or ISDN lines, or the coming ADSL (Asynchronous Digital Subscriber Lines). This is a system BT will introduce whereby down its existing copper wires, can be sent high-quality television pictures (including interactive television) and high-speed computer data including of course the Internet. Via the Internet we can access complete libraries, surf the net, do banking and shopping (for instance, Avon cosmetics, Amazon books) and communicate with our on-line friends, even if this can in business mean that everyone in a company receives everything, and at home we get unwanted bumph and suffer information overload! We will read books on it; in 1997 the author John Updike started an interactive 'relay short story' on line. It can mean we may actually work from home by 'teleworking.' In coming years there will be V-mail, for sending video clips. The Internet is truly the amazing offspring of the computer.

A big problem looms for computers, which is unfortunately linked with the millennium; that is, the so-called Millennium Bug. For ease and cost, dates were coded into programs and installed on microchips embedded within computers (and other things) as just two numbers, e.g. '95' for '1995', and it is thought that when the Millennium comes, the double nought at the end will be interpreted by machines as 1900. This potential disaster, nicknamed Y2K, may be foreshadowed by problems on September 9th, 1999, when computers could be muddled by '9/9/99', and exacerbated on February 29th, 2000, a leap year which 1900 was not. The whole thing, which The Times in a leader in 1996 claimed was the mistake of the Millennium and said would send the world tumbling in to a time warp, may cost the world (by an American estimate) £180billion to sort out. Neither the government nor insurers will bail businesses out. The bug has enormous implications, such as centenarians being summoned to the baby clinic and 'losing' their pension, and thousands of other problems for everyone in society. As we have begun to realise, so many devices we use all the time are reliant on microchips: burglar alarms, telephones & fax machines, credit cards, some kitchen machines, cars with in-board computers and so on. In shops the temperature-controlled cabinets and bar-code readers may fail, and transport will grind to a halt as traffic lights and rail signals fail. Bank safes will refuse to open; in the office there will be problems, at Government ministries, in the National Health Service, everywhere that keeps records or uses computers. Stock markets of the world may lose $10 billion in the following week through foreign exchange settlement failures. Will you trust the lifts in your tower block? Dare you fly the millennium skies when the bug might strike air traffic control? IBM has admitted that they are unable to change the software on the 40 specialist mainframe computers of the Federal Aviation Authority because they stopped making them a decade ago and have lost the expertise ….. Above all, what missiles might be zinging around out of control because of misread data? And what of the 65 nuclear plants in Russia and its former allies, whose situation is generally precarious but which may have major Y2K problems with control room displays and radiation monitoring ….. Meanwhile, elderly computer programmers were lured back from the scrap heap to refresh their use of Cobol, computer language of the 1960s, and try to make everything 'Millennium Compliant'. Another worry is the 'Dow Jones Bug', when the Index which is the gauge of the American Stock Exchange reaches 10,000 (as, surprise, surprise, the computers were only fed four numbers) and simply drops the last number causing dire results; and the 'Euro Bug', which has to do with the symbol for the new European currency being missing from computer keyboards. If we survive all that, in another 38 years there could be problems for the Internet; when it officially started on January 1st, 1970, all information was on Unix-based computer systems storing time in seconds in a 32-bit binary code, and by 2038 they will be full up. What is already full up is the famous 'equatorium', a calibrated metal wheel from 1600 which astronomers regard as the earliest machine to compute the position of the planets, which could only be used for four centuries.

If we are not completely skewed by the Millennium Bug, will it be a millennium of peace and international harmony? The nuclear umbrella may have shaded us globally since the end of the second world war; but nasty drips are coming through it like nuclear tests in India and Pakistan, and inadequate regulation of weapons and nuclear material in the old Soviet bloc, who are allegedly developing concrete submarines that can lurk deeper, and Shkval torpedoes that are three times faster than previous models. There is also the threat of terrorist activities from political or religious fundamentalists particularly from around the south and east of the Mediterranean, who will soon have the capability to threaten Europe with nuclear, ballistic, chemical or biological warfare. The West fights back by developing a laser curtain, or by developing radar-defying missiles; but above all through the so-called 'C3I'. That is, *Command, Control, Communications and Information*, such as electronic spying from unmanned planes or satellite, or by cyber-spying by hacking in to unfriendly countries' computers.

What transports of delight will we have in the future? Since 1896 when the first commercial car was made at Coventry, cars have become king. The new 'People's Rolls' continues its success, as does the Mercedes F200; in Longbridge, Birmingham, BMW/Rover bring out the successor to the Mini. Soon car radios, cigarette lighters and windscreen wipers will be solar-operated (cells on the roof), and with in-car navigation systems and ABS so sophisticated that the brake on each wheel will operate differently according to the conditions. Car numbers will be issued twice a year from March 1999, and by 2001 plates will identify the county of registration. The roads may be replaced by conveyor belts, or have 'smart' lines buried in them that send information up in to the car's in-board computer. The steering wheel will have been replaced by a joystick. By 2020 there should be self-driving cars and taxis. By 2034, it is estimated, 50% of people in the industrialised world will be driving clean electric vehicles, or gas-powered LPG (liquid petroleum gas) or cleaned-up diesel engines. Cars will be safer, with for instance 'smart' airbags that adjust to the size of the user. Safety cannot come too soon, as in the century that cars have been around, they have injured millions of people; indeed, three thousand people are actually killed in Britain every year. Will traffic jams have lessened? Or will London be gridlocked, as it already has been on one occasion for eight hours; and semi-permanent gridlock on what has been described as the deadliest stretch of motorway in Britain, the M.6 from Stafford to Birmingham? Or maybe we will all have to hang around a bit for longer for matter transfer .....

If you let the train take the strain, you will be in carriages owned by the privatised rail companies, who would at last be investing real money in them and the track. London Underground will also have improved their stock, maybe running their trains by 'Maglev', that is, magnetic levitation which floats the train a few centimetres above the track. That is the system reaching 340 k.p.h. in tests in Japan, and that being used for the 2000 Berlin/Hamburg railway. For long-distance rail travel, in twenty years you could go from London to America overland over the top of the world on a mainly-freight train by travelling east across the Russian tundra, under the Bering Straits in a fifty mile tunnel, and then through Alaska to Edmonton, Alberta, and east to New York, a journey of nearly five thousand miles. Air transport will be used more than ever, with even larger planes on intercontinental routes, all now fitted with TACAS (Traffic Alert and Collision Avoidance System); but in twenty years' time, according to the Science Museum, there will be a new breed of rockets to move around low space that we could all use regularly, taking us for instance to Sydney in two hours. Like cars, they will be designed in wind tunnels using virtual reality. There may be increased use of airships for sightseeing. One form of transport, united with home-making, would be if you had invested in buying a cabin in the huge residential ship known as the World of ResidenSea, to be launched in 2000. Larger than the QE2, it will follow the sun around the world and take you as though on a super luxury cruise for as long as you want.

One aspect of the Millennium thought is that as it is a religious jubilee, we should be cancelling debt in the developing countries. Sadly, the gap between rich and poor seems to be widening: where once the income of a comfortably-off person in the west exceeded that of a third world person by a factor of thirty, now it is 78:1. Bill Gates is worth as much as the GNP of Ecuador or Iraq; America has nearly 70,000 millionaires ..... but every year the Third World pays the West three times more in debt repayments than it receives in aid, and debt slavery faces every child born there. Asia has the greatest number of people at economic risk (UN estimate: 950 million), but out of the World Bank's list of forty countries most at risk, 33 are in Africa. It is a continent which is blighted by natural events like droughts and disease but also by corrupt

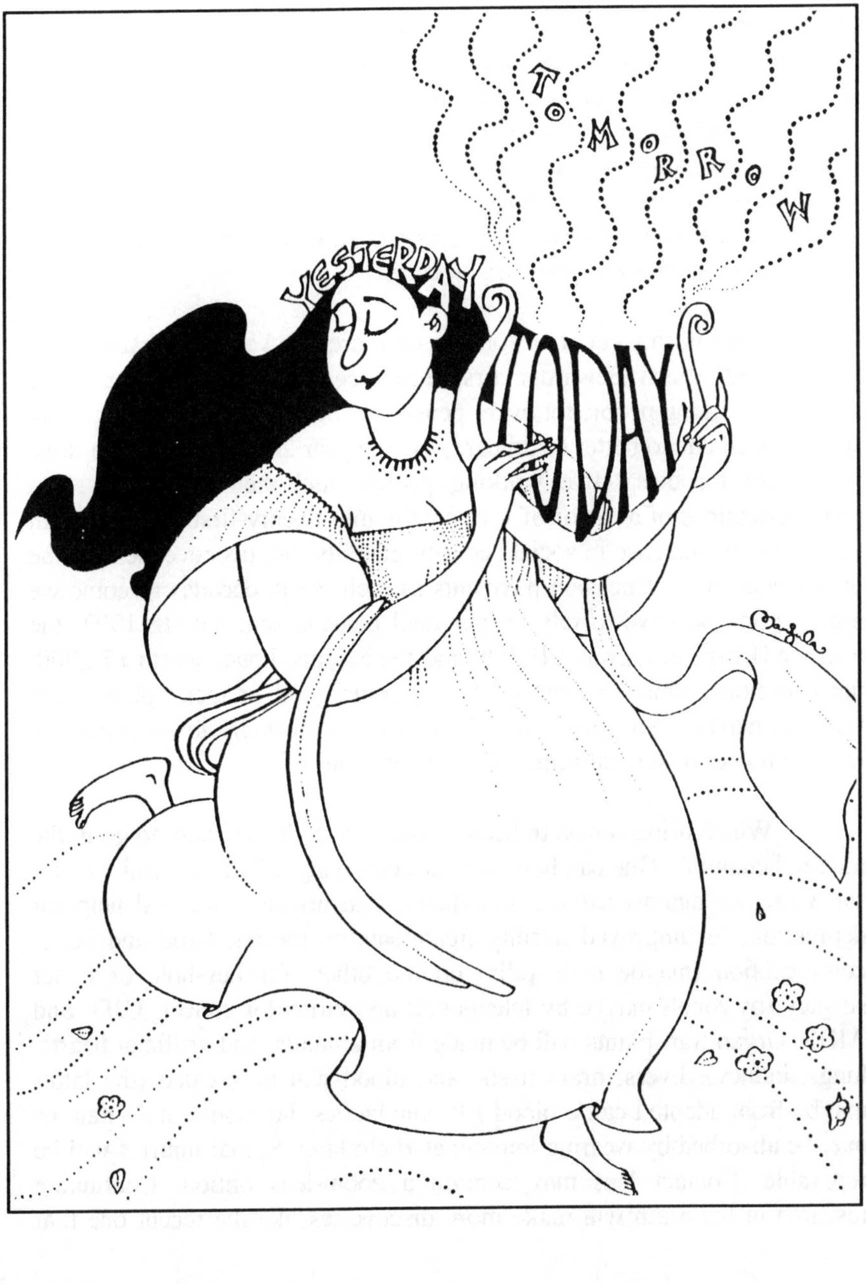
TOMORROW
YESTERDAY
TODAY

officialdom and the evils of internecine warfare. 83% of their Gross National Product (four times what they spend on healthcare) is required to service external debt. As the charity Jubilee 2000 says,

> *What better way could there be of celebrating the 2000th anniversary of the birth of a man who influenced the whole world with his teachings of love, self sacrifice and justice than to cancel the burdensome interest rates payable by the poorer nations on loans from the wealthier ones?*

Even in this country, some people are unaware of possible hard times ahead. When Beveridge first introduced the basic pension, there were five working people for every pensioner, but as a result of longer life spans (much due to better healthcare), by the year 2030 there will be three pensioners for every five working people, and there are even some prognostications of a factor of 1:1 by the mid-twenty-first century. With the enormous increase in social security benefits too, tax revenues will be insufficient to meet pension payments as well; so in decades to come we are all going to have to rely on personal pension schemes. In 1997, the average British wage was £19,000 and the average house worth £72,000, not enormous sums, so there has to be some good financial planning if you and maybe your spouse too are to live comfortably in an expensive nursing home for several years at the end of your life.

Which brings us on to health: where is medicine likely to go in the next millennium? One can hope for fat-destroying pills to control weight; for a vaccine against asthma and rheumatoid arthritis; for real help for depression; for improved fertility treatments on the one hand and better contraception (maybe male pills) on the other; for key-hole or cyber surgery (by robot, maybe by telephone); and cures for cancer, CJD and AIDS. Organ transplants will be made from animals, and artificial hearts, lungs, kidneys, livers, brain tissue and blood will be created (the latter maybe from adapted cattle blood.) Prophylactics, hormones and vitamins may be absorbed by wearing impregnated clothing. Spinal injuries will be reparable. Contact lens may contain a zoom-lens option. Continuing research in the brain will make more discoveries like the recent one that there is a gland at the base of the brain called the amygdala which chemically controls fear. Our health may well be monitored by computer examination of the iris (also to be used in 'iris recognition technology' as a security device.) Greater longevity is a major trend in health (in 2021 the life expectancy of men will be 77.6 for men, and 82.6 for women, a decade longer than six decades before; in Ancient Egypt it was only 36.) Elderly people who live alone may be monitored from a distance by alert alarms that would summon help in an emergency. It seems that the healthier you are overall, the shorter your period of dependency at the end of your life. Fashionable ways to shuffle off this mortal coil might be to have your ashes scattered in the Ganges, or be blasted off to infinity in a spacecraft.

Inoculation has been a great benefit to mankind. Maybe with prevention, polio and measles world-wide will go the way of smallpox; but it is not all good news. There is likely to be a great world-wide flu pandemic soon, echoing the terrible outbreak of Spanish flu after the First World War (which killed more people than died on the battlefields of the Great War), and two other serious outbreaks since then. Bubonic plague may reappear. Previous generations lived alongside large mammals like cows, which gave us a natural immunity to the great animal-originated diseases such as smallpox, measles and flu; but there is serious risk from Ebola, green monkey disease and other infections (as possibly with the AIDS virus) which may have come from jungles only comparatively recently disturbed by man. AIDS has already killed 12 million people world-wide, 2.3 million in 1997 alone, being especially prevalent in Africa which harbours 90% of the cases and may (according to the UN) soon 'rival' the ravages of the Black Death, which killed between a quarter and a third of Europe's population in the mid-fourteenth century. Tuberculosis unfortunately will not go away immediately; even malaria may be a real hazard if global warming continues. Some bacteria like the superbug *staphylococcus aureus* or *e. coli* resist penicillin, which has never been able to tackle viruses anyway. At the moment, each day brings the death in this country of the following number of people from the following causes: AIDS 1, drugs 3, car accidents 10, alcohol 100, smoking 300. How sad so little is being done against road rage, drunkenness and the dreaded weed; these are three great statistical causes of death are immune to inoculation.

Genetic engineering is about utilising knowledge about our 100,000 genes, found in the nucleus of cells wrapped in packages called chromosomes, of which we have 23 pairs (the great apes have 24). The science will benefit from the fact that by 2005 the whole human DNA sequence will have been mapped, and a decade later, the genetic links of all diseases will be identified, and our own individual genome will be on our medical card in the form of a barcode. DNA tracing will also help in solving crime and tracing missing people as it will enable forensic scientists to establish the suspect's race, eye colour, hair colour and even facial features. They can even note DNA from dried saliva on the back of envelopes or stamps. Gene research will also help in treating disease, like the three-year project by the Wellcome Trust to map the DNA of the mosquito and its link with malaria. Gene research will also lead to improved food crops, both by cloning and by genetic modification to transfer 'good' qualities like the ability to grow in acidic soil or resisting certain pests. The cloning of animals like Dolly the sheep will continue, but one hopes it will never be extended to humans (though Stephen Hawking has foreseen that it will happen in the next millennium.) Individual human fertility has been a worry for some time, as the male sperm count has dropped lower and lower. The overall global population will settle at a peak of about 10.6 billion (nearly double the present total of 5.8 billion) in 2080, and then decline; already, the average British family of three children in the 1960s has declined to an all-time low of 1.8, which is not replacement level (in Japan, it is 1.4 already.) When we are told that an average child costs £100,000 to rear, three times that if they go to independent school and university, it is a surprise that anyone can afford them! The current British population of 60 million is estimated to fall to below 50 million by 2097, then - surprisingly - down to 30 million in the following century.

The size of the world's population has, of course, important implications for the environment. Our fragile world, interlinked and mutually supportive, has been long been victim of rapine and pillage. She even has a price put on her; in an article in 'Nature', scientists calculated that the Earth contributes £20 trillion pounds a year to our economy, that is, twice the global gross national product. We have taken 30,000 tons of gold from her mines in the last 150 years. We have let the Brazilian rainforests go at the rate of 11,000 square miles a year. We have used and abused her wonderful resources for our own ends; we have slashed and burnt, carelessly mined and deforested her, and swathed her in pollution on land, sea and air. We have hunted some of her beautiful animals to death, from the Mauritian dodo onwards, and are still said to be losing three species every hour. Even if there are said to be 24,000 species of land vertebrates left, that total isn't going to last long unless mankind improves conservation.

Learned scientists warn of the malevolent human influence on the weather, mainly through burning fossil fuels and also by releasing greenhouse gases like carbon dioxide and fluorocarbons in to the atmosphere and using methyl bromide as a pesticide; but also by removing vegetation and building dams (thereby altering nature's balance). The ozone layer that protects us from rays from space is beginning noticeably to thin, and the alpine and polar ice-cap to melt in so-called global warming. Precise measurements are made through a range of instruments, including sending sound waves all the way round the Pacific; it is estimated that temperatures will rise 1.6° Centigrade in the next 50 years. That means seas must rise, and many low-lying areas will be inundated, including the millennially-special islands of the Pacific like Kiribati which might slip below the waves. Paradoxically, it might make the British Isles colder, as the melting arctic waters would push the warming Gulf Stream further south. Another paradox is that the raised world sea level may be followed by more activity in volcanoes, 90% of which are close to the sea, as water creeping in to the core makes steam build up, and explosions follow. The South Island of New Zealand, which has had earthquakes on average every 260 years, last had one was a quarter of a millennium ago. The El Niño climate crisis is also a great headache. Of course there have always been cycles of bad weather; but the El Niño, called after the Christ child because it is a huge swathe of warm water found off Peru at Christmas time every five or six years, is now acting very strangely, that starting in 1998 being the worst for a quarter of a century. This affects commodities essential to some third-world economies in South America and the Caribbean, and brings storms to the United States and drought to the western pacific and even southern Africa. The long-term forecast is not much fun, either; in two millennia we might be getting colder again, heading towards a serious ice age in about 50,000 years.

When the twentieth century began, one in eight people lived in cities; at the beginning of the twenty-first, it is one in two, by 2025 it will be two out of every three. Every week, the world's cities gain another million people, partly from births but also from migration from the countryside. They will not necessarily find that the streets are paved with gold; even in this country there are effectively a quarter of a million people without a secure home. Mike Mulstein of Chile (translated by Maria Teresa Raeched) wrote:

> *Para el 2045 nuestra ciudad será más grande, más moderna con más luz, musica y todo. Pero voltearan el rostro a ver quién esta y no verán a nadie.*
>
> *By 2045 the city will be larger, more modern, with more light, music and everything. But they will turn their faces to see who is there, and they will not see anybody.*

London loses a thousand people a week as they move out to greener pastures; and in America, many of the middle class are escaping the city and the suburbs for the so-called penturbia, where they may live safely in enclaves on the edge of rural beauty with access to the city's amenities, probably cyber-working from home.

It is heartening that many millennial projects, at least in this country (as we have seen in Chapter 7), are of an environmental nature. Apparently, more homes have to be built, mainly because of the increase in single-person households, and some of these will gobble up greenfield sites. Nevertheless, there is a real sense that houses should be more environmentally friendly by being built on a brownfield site if at all possible; and also with 'green' features like solar panels, recycling plants, water butts and so on. Shamefully, our homes have been the most wasteful in Europe, and we have a long way to go before we achieve energy self-sufficiency. It would be nice to think that we could face the coming years with some assurance that at last we are coming to appreciate our world - indeed common sense dictates that we must, or we are all doomed. It is her riches that provide all our basic needs, especially food and water. Children may choose to have their carrots chocolate-flavoured in the future, but we need the carrots to grow and the chocolate beans to ripen. Food will be brought to us as fresh as possible, maybe thanks to irradiation of fruits, and water will be purified by intense pulses of light. Algae will grow in the sea as a basis for various foods, and people may become more interested in 'functional food', that is food which has specific properties either within them naturally or in the form of additives, like orange juice with added Vitamin C, yoghurt enriched with fibre, or the so-called 'lady's loaf';

The rôle of the family, and the relations between generations, is a fertile field of study. We tend to look back on our own childhood as a 'Janet and John' world of chummy fun, japes and high jinks, the wireless our only regular entertainment, and walking to a school with structured lessons and caring teachers. At home, everyone had a father; mothers stayed home; no parents divorced; no man was unemployed; and everyone (for better or for worse) was Anglo-Saxon and sort-of Christian. Our parents - who had been through the trauma of at least one world war - were assiduous in protecting us from what was anyway probably a less-cruel world than before or since; but probably there was some terrible misery behind the lace curtains. There have been many changes since then, with twenty per cent of children growing up in single-parent households, and another ten in step-families, demonstrating fewer certainties in a confusing world. Dare one predict that the pendulum might start to swing back in the new Millennium? Could it be that, exhausted by the frustrations and insecurities engendered by the social changes of the last few decades, there might be a swing back to the secure family unit (as blessed by history before and since the Holy Family of two millennia ago)? Politicians at last seem to be realising that curious lop-sided legislation and irrational taxation has not just mopped up the sad casualties of family breakdown, but actively encouraged some to pursue their own thing shamelessly at the expense of their own children and their elderly neglected parents, and ultimately exploiting other taxpayers in society. Caring, whether for your children or your elderly relatives, should receive more credit and support. Thomas Huxley said *When you educate a man you educate an individual, when you educate a woman you educate a whole family;* but whatever the gender of the carer, they deserve all resources possible.

Education is the way that society hands on the baton of knowledge from generation to generation, so how will that change in the future? The school population is currently just over twenty million, and will rise until 2020 before decreasing at least over the following thirty years. Much of the 'education', in its widest sense, that a young member of society receives has always been in the pre-school years at home, or later after school itself by playing with friends. Now add to this the powerful twin tools of the screen: television, and the computer, in front of which your youngster will sit for hours absorbing information of all sorts (there are now V-chips, to stop children viewing harmful material, and computer programmes available for children called 'edutainment'.) These two also have their place in school, but nothing will ever replace an inspired human teacher, who should also be offering a measure of moral guidance too. Guided by published league tables of results, parents will continue to push for the best schools, and if they choose to pay for education, will demand good value for money. Similarly, society will demand that the national curriculum subjects be well taught, with emphasis in primary schools on literacy and numeracy (we only just scrape in to the world top ten in maths), and secondary school with the addition of good science. Thereafter, more people will go in to tertiary education, either in their late teens or later as mature students (maybe some of the 12% of youngsters who shamefully leave school without any qualifications at all.) The country will really tackle the 'skills gap' and give full grants to shortage subjects, be they academic mathematics or astro-physics, vocational plumbing or maintenance engineering.

From 2002, all 32,000 schools in Britain, plus all universities and colleges and libraries, will be connected to the National Grid of Learning, a collection of computer networks linked by the Internet. This will be used to deliver resources wherever needed, and to enable students to use their own e-mail tag, given them for life, to access useful information. It will encourage pupils to work together in teams, independently of their teachers who will be there for general support, and who in their turn may be working together team-teaching or concentrating on their specialisms. Libraries may also allow the borrower to take away an 'electronic book', looking and feeling similar to the tomes of old, which can be speedily and temporarily be 'printed' up with whatever text is requested.

What will certainly happen is that we will continue with learning for life, and learning throughout life. People will dip in and out of formal education, but keep going back for more. We will need transferable skills, to clutch with us as we go (as we probably will) from career to career.

The world of work will change. There will be the home offices, with dual career families in their his'n'hers offices networking through cyberspace (though many people, however they pretend to grumble at it, like the rough and tumble and gossip of office life, and feel the need to meet face-to-face.) Teleworkers will need a networked computer with 4 gigabytes of storage and a flat screen monitor, a roll-up screen to affix to a wall wherever you are, a fax/modem with voicemail, a printer that also scans and prints, a video-conferencing camera, on-line e-mail, and maybe voice-control dictation. Around the building you will use a cordless phone, but out of the office you are never uncontactable because of a state-of-the-art mobile phone (already a sixth of the world have them), which may become small enough to be worn as a pendant. If travelling, you may use the amazing British inventions of Trevor Bayliss, the wind-up radio or the clockwork torch (useful in those Millennium Bug electricity cuts.)

By 2020 it is estimated that one in five fathers will be a 'house husband', or partner, as people increasing live together rather than get married. Overall, there will no longer be jobs for life, with the extraordinary casualisation of the work force even for people in professional jobs. Where once a consultant meant only that he (less likely she) was a medical expert, now it means someone undertaking outsourced work for an organisation, in almost any field. Already one in seven British workers is self-employed, which is a trend that will accelerate (as will the trend for part-time work) The flexibility of this casualisation is good news in some ways, but requires people, used to more security-providing times of large paternalistic companies, to concentrate on the organisation of their own tax payments, portable pensions, life and health insurance. Of course it may involve periods of 'resting' between jobs. Over the last few decades many jobs have been lost; in middle management, not required in the 'post business-processed re-engineered organisation', in clerical jobs replaced by computers, and in manual jobs overtaken by automation and robotics. These jobs will never return as such - future jobs will be in the professions and service industries, where nothing replaces human contact, in the arts, education, tourism and retailing.

What of the world of fashion? In the 70s Zagger and Evans had a pop song called 'In the Year 2525', but what will it be like then in terms of lifestyle? We will live in homes increasingly run by robots and with digital technology. They will be properly insulated (at the moment, each house wastes at least £300 through the walls.) We will all have digital televisions, with flat screens hanging on the wall, maybe with signals coming through the net (how things have changed since Baird's initial transmission in October 1925). It might offer 430 channels as promised, but still nothing we want to watch ..... We will see our photos and video film that way too, taken on filmless cameras that download straight in to the computer. Our wrists will bear watch-size computers or videophones. We will either do a 'virtual shop' via the Internet on our credit cards and have goods delivered to safe bunkers on every front drive, or swish round the supermarket where every trolley is a smart cart which uses barcodes to add up your bill. You may occasionally go boutique shopping, or visit a mall just for the fun of it. Other recreation may be virtual tourism via the net and 'feelyvision'; or listening to hologram-decorated CD.

Our clothes will be pro-active; they may contain medicines, protect against ultra-violet light, be stretchable without cling, be self-deodorising and totally stain-resistant or of carbonised fibre fabric which can be electrically altered to the required warmth level. The patterns on them will have been created by computer-aided design, maybe with fibre optics woven in to them. They will be soft and flexible (DuPont have yarns 200 times finer than human hair) and 'wickable', letting moisture out but not in. We may be visually measured by computers in shops, so that clothes sizes can be instantly assessed. There may be spray-on shoes, and clothes change colour to reflect our mood.

The very *speed* of change will continue to accelerate. To reach fifty million users in America, it took radio 38 years, television 13, and the Internet only 4. Plumped as we are in the middle of the Information Revolution, the future will surely involve more technology and computerisation. There will be great strides in exploring the riches of land, sea and space, and in science; but maybe the most significant strides will actually be in exploring ourselves and our society, with the demographic, political and social changes to come. Miranda in 'The Tempest' cries out: *O Brave new world That has such people in't.* It is people who are ever-important. Indulging in futurology we tend to get dazzled by objects and forget the objective, that mankind can learn to live at peace with itself. The Design Council's interesting Project 2045 solicited ideas from all sections of society about the future, and buried in the prognostications for cyber this and virtual that, was the prediction from Liverpool John Moores University that there would be the Second Coming of Christ. You do not need to be a convinced millenarian to note that (likely or not) at least it takes note of man's spiritual longing. What if we gain the Moon but lose our soul?

And so our review of the millennium comes to an end. Of course, it is an artificial demarcation, it is only a date, and a pretty arbitrary and probably inaccurate one at that. However, it is truly an occasion that feels like everybody's birthday; and when we ourselves get to a round number, say our thirtieth or fortieth birthday, we take it as an opportunity to take stock of our lives a bit. It is as though we are all reaching a significant birthday at the same time. A time of rejoicing, a time of pondering, maybe even a time of prayer. May the Millennium be blessed for us all.

HOPE

Born in a shack in a Lagos slum;
Where the pi-dogs howled all night,
With water foul with a grey-green scum,
In the dark sounds the menacing beat of a drum.
For the baby new, what will Life become?
How long ere comes the light?

Does a star of Hope shine o'er this shack
(As the stinking drain o'erflows,
The moon is hid and the night is black,
And the dogs still howl in their flea-bit pack) ?
….. But from inside, through a gaping crack,
A guttering candle glows.

Bill Jarvis ©

THE FUTURE FOR CHILDREN

If a child lives with criticism
it learns to condemn.
If a child lives with hostility
it learns to fight.
If a child lives with ridicule
it learns to be shy.
If a child lives with shame
it learns to be guilty.
If a child lives with tolerance
it learns to be patient.
If a child lives with encouragement
it learns confidence.
If a child lives with praise
it learns to appreciate.
If a child lives with fairness
it learns justice.
If a child lives with security
it learns to have faith.
If a child lives with approval
it learns to like itself.
If a child lives with acceptance
and friendship
it learns to find love in the world.

Peace Pledge Union ©

259

260

from CHILDE HAROLD'S PILGRIMAGE

What is the worst of woes that wait on age?
What stamps the wrinkle on the brow?
To view each loved one blotted from life's page,
And be alone on earth, as I am now.

George Gordon, Lord Byron (1788-1824)

DEATH OF MY FAVOURITE UNCLE

You need a lot of bottle if you surf the Milky Way,
It isn't all that easy being dead;
It takes a lot of courage to go out beyond the earth,
It's not a path that you know how to tread.

My uncle died in stages, no, it wasn't with a bang,
A-crippled by the vice-grip of a stroke;
His masque-like face it twitched a bit, no more than that I fear,
'I'm smiling right inside of me' was all that he could joke.

He lingered on, he fought so hard, was brave to 'n'th degree,
He is still happy here, we all deduced:
As from the world of action, to the bedpan and the bell;
From independence, to the bed he was reduced.

He had his Christian faith, he had, right up until the end
Which really is a comfort to us now;
About his end-life journey he retained his certainty
And never questioned why, or when, or how.

You need a lot of bottle if you surf the Milky Way,
It isn't all that easy being dead;
It takes a lot of courage to go out beyond the earth,
But that's the path that he set out to tread.

from YOUTH

I remember my youth and the feeling that will never come back any more - the feeling that I could last for ever, outlast the sea, the earth, and all men; the deceitful feeling that lures us on to joys, to perils, to love, to vain effort - to death; the triumphant conviction of strength, the heat of life in the handful of dust, the glow in the heart that with every year grows dim, grows cold, grows small, and expires - before life itself.

Joseph Conrad (1857-1924). The phrase 'a handful of dust' was subsequently used both by T.S. Eliot and by Evelyn Waugh.

THE FUTURE

In the age of mechanical monsters,
When the world will be ruled by metal,
We will all bow down to robots.
Not a soul will be found at the park,
Or anywhere outside in the sunshine.
Family gatherings will be by the Internet;
Wherever you look, there will be
Square eyes staring at you.
Is this the future that you wish to have?

Ahran Arnold ©

MILLENNIUM

One thousand future thoughts I hold,
Of hope, of peace and more.
Will all our times be yet retold,
Or will there still be war?
Will Armageddon be our end,
Or will the world draw back?
United arm in arm with friend,
Back on a peaceful track.

Katie Fleming ©

THE HI-TECH FUTURE

Robots take over our lives and much more.
Life for humans is becoming a bore.
Computers rule the world.
Robots here and robots there.
Who do everything, from laundry to brushing our hair.
Computer screens are everywhere.
No more paper books, just floppy disks.
Colourful flowers exchanged for holograms,
Evening sunsets replaced with laser lights.
Food now comes in tablet form.
All this makes me so forlorn.
Is this the beginning of the end of human life?

James Butler ©

SPACE

No matter for the space that science speaks of -
I've enough trouble finding space for things around me!
The things pushed through the door - this so-called 'literature' -
If I should leave it where it falls I'd very soon
Become a prisoner within my home!

The Christmas gifts (so very kindly sent); the soap alone
Fills my large bath to over-flowing, never mind
The bubble-bath and talc, the liquid spray .....

Those little plastic pots, emptied long since, but so attractive;
This one, with the wreath below the rim, has quite a classic touch -
It might be Wedgwood, or even Minton;
Would it go inside this other one inside the cupboard?
Blast! The column topples! The whole lot scatters to the floor.

These you have loved? A mess of plastic!
Into the dustbin you! And leave me space within this fuddled brain
To worry o'er another molehill -

Perhaps a spaceman's outfit is the answer!
To shoot within a capsule far away
Where litter strews no pavements, cupboard shelves were never known
Where I may mindless, heedless, float through all eternity.

Time: The Present
Ninety-eighty four! Oh, nineteen eighty-four!
George Orwell has blundered, I'm perfectly sure!
With sexes now equal and women galore
It's Big Sister who's watching! Nineteen eighty four.

Freda Croft-Williams (born 1904)

from THE INFERNO

S'io credesse che mia riposta fosse
A persona che mai tonasse al mondo,
Questa fiamma staria senza piu scosse.
Ma perciocche giammai di questo fondo
Non torno vivo alcun, s'I'odo il vero,
Senza tema d'infamia ti tispondo.

If I believed that sure my answer was
To he who might never return to the world,
This flame no longer would be stirred.
But as no one has ever yet returned
Alive from this abyss, 'tis true,
Without fear of disgrace, I'll answer you.

Dante Alighieri (1265-1321)
translated by Aurora Llewellyn

from LOCKSLEY HALL

Locksley Hall, that in the distance overlooks the sandy tracts,
And the hollow ocean-ridges roaring into cataracts.

Here about the beach I wandered, nourishing a youth sublime
With the fairy tales of science, and the long result of Time;

When the centuries behind me like a fruitful land reposed;
When I clung to all the present for the promise that it closed:

When I dipt into the future far as human eye could see;
Saw the vision of the world, and all the wonder that would be -

Love took up the glass of Time, and turned it in his glowing hands;
Every moment, lightly shaken, ran itself in golden sands.

Alfred, Lord Tennyson (1809-1892

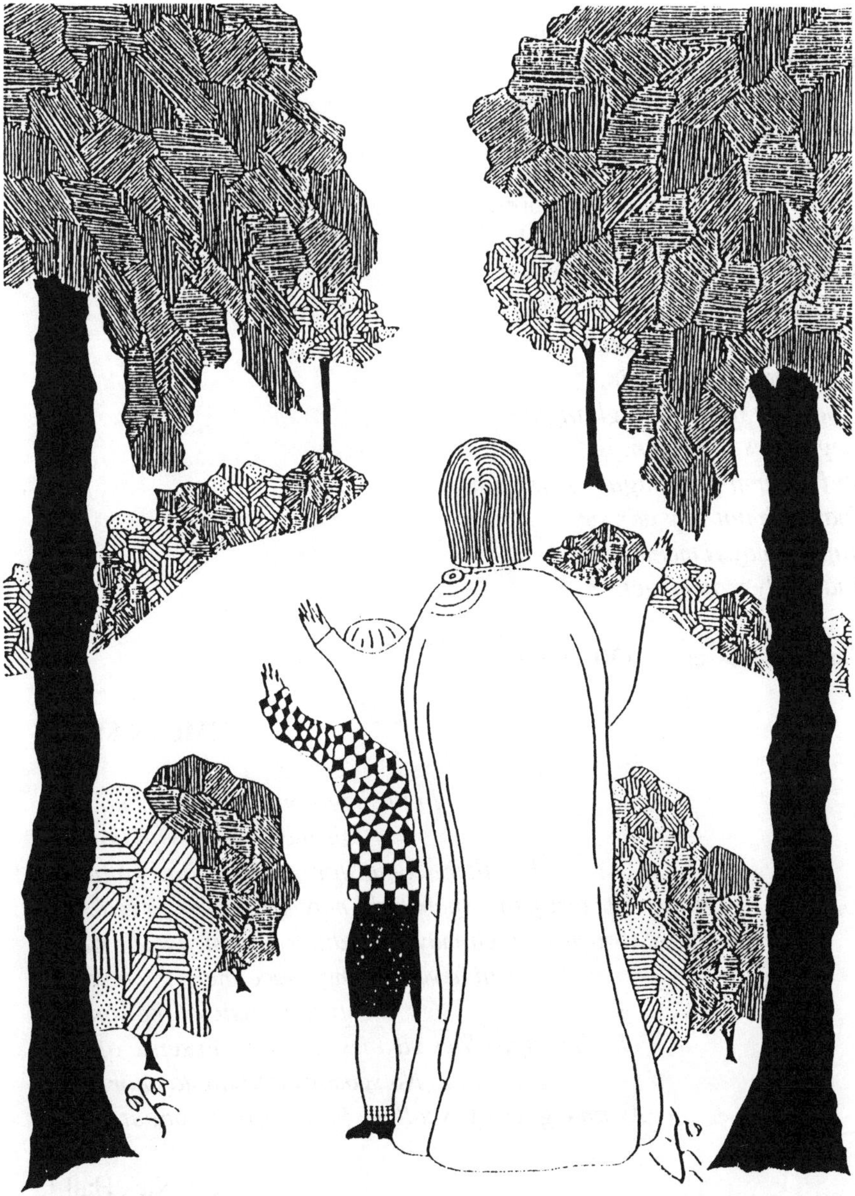

REQUIEMS

When I am dead, my dearest,
Sing no sad songs for me;
Plant thou no roses at my head,
Nor shady cypress tree:
Be the green grass above me
With showers and dewdrops wet;
And if thou wilt, remember,
And if thou wilt, forget.

I shall not see the shadows,
I shall not feel the rain;
I shall not hear the nightingale
Sing on, as if in pain;
And dreaming through the twilight
That doth not rise nor set,
Haply I may remember,
And haply may forget.

Christina Rossetti (1830-1894)

TIME IN SPACE

In the beginning there was nothing,
Timeless space with nothing.
Then there came stars, planets and galaxies :
Stars so far away that their light may take years to reach us,
Unexplored worlds which may have different time to our world.
In never ending space there is no sound,
Only the music of the spheres.
In the huge black vastness there is no sense of time,
No seasons and no day nor night.
As time goes by, shall we find out more about space?

Nick Hall ©

from **THE TEMPEST**

Our revels now are ended. These our actors,
As I foretold you, were all spirits and
Are melted into air, into thin air:
And, like the baseless fabric of this vision,
The cloud-capp'd towers, the gorgeous palaces,
The solemn temples, the great globe itself,
Yea, all which it inherit, shall dissolve
And, like this insubstantial pageant faded,
Leave not a rack behind. We are such stuff
As dreams are made on, and our little life
Is rounded with a sleep.

William Shakespeare (1564 – 1616)

LITERATURE ACKNOWLEDGEMENTS

Poems marked © in the text are by living writers, either specially commissioned or for which permission has been obtained. Efforts have been made to attribute all work where appropriate; any errors or omissions are regretted.

Anonymous: *C.17 Nuns* p.46, *Middle Age* p.52, *New Year Carol* p.93, *German Jabberwock* p.179, Matthew Arnold: *Dover Beach* p.135, *To Marguerite* p. 232, Ahran Arnold p.261, Jogeeta Banger p.155, David Barry-Jackson p. 60, Paul Beard p.133, James Berry p.172, , Romit Bhandari p.160, The Bible (Authorised Version): *Ecclesiastes* p.108, *Genesis* ps.23&153, *Isaiah* p.57, *James* p.238, *Letter of Peter* ps.57&158, *Proverbs* p.237, *Psalm 121* p.158, *Revelations* p.139, *St John* p.40, *Shulamite* p.63, *Solomon* p.158, Bible Society/Kater Luckett p.35, William Blake: *Garden* p.162, *Sunflower* p.70, *Tyger* p.148, Elizabeth Barrett Browning p.177, John Buchan (©The Lord Tweedsmuir, Jean, Lady Tweedsmuir & APWatt Ltd), p.111, John Bunyan, p.131, Ruth Burke p.175, John Burns p. 204,Robert Burns: *Auld Lang Syne* p.94, *Rose* p.188, James Butler p.262, Lord Byron p.260: *Childe Harold* p.260, *Growing Old* p.107, Thomas Campion p.134, Archbishop George Carey p.122, Ben Carne p.59, John Carter p.63, Catullus p.8, Chester Cathedral p.108, Hugh Cherril & colleagues, Ove Arup Partnership ps. 206 etc, John Clare p.192, Joseph Conrad p.261, William Cory p.93, Charles Cotton p.92, Freda Croft-Williams p.263, Peter Cronogue p.175, Cara Cummings p.91, Dante p.264, Kunal Desai p.147, Emily Dickinison, p.177, John Donne p.67, Elizabeth H. Drummond p.50, Albert Einstein p.237, Albert Einstein p.237, Ralph Waldo Emerson: *Days* p.114, *Quatrain* p.44, *Problem* p.188, Esperanto/Joan Dawson & Will Green p.32, Russell Forgham/ *Mail on Sunday* p.3, Thomas Flatman p.117, Katie Fleming p.261, Roz Gater p.16, Judy Gahahgan, p.153-4, George VI p.85, W.S. Gilbert p.182, Gilbertese prayer via Arthur Grimble p.231, Chris Godley p.228, Oliver Goldsmith p.51,Thomas Gray p.53, John Gummer p.205, Dorothy Gurney p.155, J.B.S. Haldane p.239, Nicholas Hall p.266, Sophie Hannah (© Caracanet Press) p.48, Thomas Hardy: *Afterwards* p. 194, *Century's Deathbed* p.82, *Time* p.110, Ted Harrison p.126, W.E.Henley p.215, Henry VIII p.65, Reinhild Hensle: *Haiku* p.193, *Zukunft* p.235, George Herbert p.42, Robert Herrick , *Book* p. 8, *Virgins* p.109, Maurice Hewlett (©Constable) p.10, Peter Higginson p.133, Arno Holz p.61, Thomas Hood p.140, Horace p.74, Father Neil Horan p.128, Susan Howatch p.45, Thomas Huxley p.254, I-ro-ha p.40, Jarvis: *Bagatelle* p.174, *Hope* p.258, Paul Jennings (©Random House) p.17-19, Jewish Meditation p.81, Dr. Johnson p.44, Jubilee 2000 p.248, Paul Kammerer p. 101, John Keats: *Grecian Urn* p.112, *Endymion* p.214, Joe Kerson p.224, Kew Seed Bank/Alison Mitchell p.142, Misba Khan p.80, Omar Khayyám: *Chess* p.176, *Muezzin* p.116, *Whence* p.11, A.J. Kilmer p.147, Sagar Kothari p.62, *LATimes*/Mike Faneuff p.225, Charles Lamb p.86, Jack Lattimer and friends p.104, Margareta Lee p.85, Leeds Tapestry/Kate Russell p. 186, Gael Lindenfield p.14, Peter Mandelson p.203,Tym Marsh p.144, Andrew Marvell: *Coy Mistress* p.115, *Garden* p.156, Tilly Maxwell p.162, Diana May: *Bush* p.147, *Creature of Legend* p.63, *Favourite Uncle* p.260, *Flight of Time* p.114, *Ghost Story* ps.89-90, *Hats Off* p.83&84, *Janus* p.90, *Millennium Xanadu* ps. 212-3, *Rondo a la Turquiose* p.47, *Millennium* p. 9, *Spirituality* p.139, *The Body* p.180, *Woodcut* p.159, *Words* p.43, Irfaan

Merali p.113, Meridian tree Line/Patrick Roper p.145 John Milton, p.112, Alex Morley p.66, Mike Mulstein p.252, Osman Mumtaz: *Future* p.151, *Timing* p.233, Satako Namino p.193, National Maritime Museum/ Dr Jonathan Betts p.102, National Memorial Arboretum/David Childs p. 145, National Trust/Hilary Moorcroft p.185&186, Pastor Niemöller, p.137, John Julius Norwich p. 2, Arthur O'Shaughnessy p.41, Terence O'Sullivan p.64, Wilfred Owen p.138, Sarah Packman p.230, Derek Palmer-Brown p.143, Chandy Patel p.230, Tejus Patel p.67, Peace Pledge Union (©PPU & Cath Tate cards) p. 258, Thomas Love Peacock p.169, Betty Peake p.12, Plato p.105, Jodie Omega Portugal p.70, Queen Elizabeth I, p.136, Sir Walter Raleigh p.14, Nick Raynsford p. 204, Gavin Reid, Bishop of Maidstone p.120, RNZAF p.233, Dr. Robertson p.138, Alan Rogan p. 186, Christina Rosetti p.266, George Sand p.2, Ivan Sanders: *If* p.210, *Prayer* p.134, *Song of Life* p.68, Linden Sanders p.173, Kate Saw p.150, Shakespeare: *As You Like It* p.96, *Hamlet* p.239,*Phoenix & Turtle* ps. 71&72, *Rose's Name* p.49, *Sonnet 12* p.154, *Sonnet 16* p.52, *Sonnet 18* p.160, *Sonnet 60* p.215, *Sonnet 64* p.110, *Sonnet 123* p.117, *Sonnet 124* p.154, *Sonnet 106* p.45, *Tempest* ps.257&267, P.B.Shelley: *Adonais* p.211, *Alastor* p.190, *Ozymandias* p.105, *West Wind* p.211, Shelter/Imogen Wilson p.132, Guy Shidlo p. 110, Brian Smith p.189, Godfrey Smith/*Sunday Times)* p. 79, Tobias Smollett p.204, Anik Sodha p.106, Edmund Spenser, p.208, Spinosa p.169, Mark Stent p.64, Hugh Stewart p.142, Sustrans/Sophy Cushing p.182, Dean Swift p.2, Alfred, Lord Tennyson: *In Memoriam* p.88, *Locksley Hall* p.264, William Thackeray p.59, Damian Thompson (© Sinclair-Stevenson) p. 126, Archbishop Tutu p.121 Voltaire p.98, Dr John Wall p.104, Paul Waller p.243, Michael Walsh p.226, Terry Warburton p.123, Alison Williams, p.151, Jennifer Williams p.79, William Wordsworth: *Nuns* p.47, *World* p.150.

In addition, I would like to acknowledge help in publishing, research and translating from: Ursula Aßmann, Carole Carter, James Cobban, Friederike Eggers, Gail Bray, Keith Durham, Michael Fanstone, Sue Gillingham, Mary Gostelow, Diana and Richard Holderness, Mariko Hosumi, Alexander Libby, Aurora Llewellyn, Andrew May, Susie Mitchell, Akiko Motoyoshi, Rej Pattinson, Brigitte von Peinen, Maria Teresa Raeched, Kay Robinson, Suzanne Trisk, Moira Wiltshire, Yaakov Wise.

ART ACKNOWLEDGEMENTS.

Gratefully acknowledged are pictures specially prepared for this book:

David Barry-Jackson, pages 11, 49, 60, 72, 116, 176, 232, and 267;
Frank Hinks, pages 13, 113, 157, 178, 209, 265;
Philine Kempf, pages 42, 106, 132, 149, 171, 191, 235;

Manjula Padmanabhan, pages 45, 54, 69, 87, 109, 163, 195, 236, 247
Juhie Sharma, 138,155
In addition, the following kindly prepared pictures: Tony Burne p. 152, Canon John Bowers p.130, Arthur Casey Jones p.136, Ted Harrison p.134, Judy Horacek (©Cath Tate) p.80, Keef (Keith Ratling) p.84, Hari Krishna ps. 65 & 259, Ken Messer p.140, Jan

Mitchell p.159, Akiko Motoyoshi p. 160, NMEC/Hayes Davidson/Chorley Handford p. 211, Natalie Raeched p. 40, Manjit Rai cover, Freda Williams ps. 161 & 189.

The author prepared artwork on the following pages: 9, 39, 62, 91, 95, 187, 213, 231, 262; I wish particularly to acknowledge design help from Stella Harvey, and from Caroline Thornton of Uxbridge College.

SHORT BIOGRAPHIES

James Berry is the doyen of Afro-Caribbean poets in this country. Born in Jamaica in 1924, he has also produced anthologies like *Bluefoot Traveller,* and the Brixton Festival Anthology

Sophie Hannah is a Fellow Commoner at Trinity College, Cambridge. Carcanet Press, who have published her two previous collections, will publish *Your Dad Did What?* In her third collection due out in 1999.

Satako Namino was born in 1960, and manages to combine writing *haiku* with raising her young family in Japan.

Ivan Sanders, born in Derbyshire, has practised law for many years in the Midlands, while writing poetry and running an annual poetry competition in honour of his parents.

David Barry-Jackson, after a successful military career, now lives in Steeple Bumpstead. He has illustrated all the verses of the *Rubáiyát of Omar Khayyám*.

Frank Hinks is a practising barrister, who also writes, illustrates and publishes delightful children's books.

Philine Kempf now lives in Karlsruhe, after some years in southern Chile. She crafts her art in many media, but is particularly famous for her distinctive modern jewellery.

Manjula Padmanabhan lives and works in New Delhi. Since winning the prestigious Alexander Onassis International Cultural Competition for her play *Harvest*, she is now concentrating on her drama-writing; which makes her pictures for *Miscellennium* even more special.

Thus ends the book - and the Millennium adventure begins!

On the following pages, you may choose to insert your own Millennium photographs, newspaper cuttings or drawings. Get your fellow revellers on December 31st to sign your copy; maybe use the blank pages at the end to pen your own 'Letter to the Future', a sort of written time capsule to look back on in years to come.